WHAT SLAVEHOLDERS THINK

WHAT SLAVEHOLDERS THINK

HOW CONTEMPORARY PERPETRATORS RATIONALIZE WHAT THEY DO

AUSTIN CHOI-FITZPATRICK

Columbia University Press
New York

Columbia University Press
Publishers Since 1893
New York   Chichester, West Sussex
cup.columbia.edu
Copyright © 2017 Columbia University Press
All rights reserved

Library of Congress Cataloging-in-Publication Data
Names: Choi-Fitzpatrick, Austin, author.
Title: What slaveholders think : how contemporary perpetrators
   rationalize what they do / Austin Choi-Fitzpatrick.
Description: New York : Columbia University Press, [2017] |
   Includes bibliographical references and index.
Identifiers: LCCN 2016028996 (print) | LCCN 2016041855 (ebook) |
   ISBN 9780231181822 (cloth : alk. paper) | ISBN 9780231543828 (e-book)
Subjects: LCSH: Slavery—History—21st century. | Human trafficking. |
   Forced labor.
Classification: LCC HT867 .C46 2017 (print) | LCC HT867 (ebook) |
   DDC 306.3/620905—dc23
LC record available at https://lccn.loc.gov/2016028996

Columbia University Press books are printed on permanent
and durable acid-free paper.
Printed in the United States of America

Cover design: Jason Heuer

For the children of Issachar

I am a master. I have employed people and done so much for them. I have fulfilled my duties toward my servant. They should realize this and fulfill their duties as a servant and they should maintain that master-servant distance. . . . If we don't supervise our servants then we'll be finished. So they should understand that there is a difference between master and the servant, and that the masters have a particular role and that the servants have a particular role.

—Radhesh (Interviewee 31)

If only it were all so simple! If only there were evil people somewhere insidiously committing evil deeds, and it were necessary only to separate them from the rest of us and destroy them. But the line dividing good and evil cuts through the heart of every human being. And who is willing to destroy a piece of his own heart?

—Aleksandr Solzhenitsyn, *The Gulag Archipelago*

CONTENTS

ACKNOWLEDGMENTS

A cknowledgments have long been my favorite part of a book. I've felt that between those thanks at the beginning—some fulsome, some begrudging—and the index at the end, one can get a feel for both the author and the work. It's a bit like a house, really; thanks to the institution that kept a roof over my head, thanks to the grants that kept food on the table, and thanks to the friends, family, and colleagues that served as the inspiration, comfort, and distraction for the whole affair. The walls, windows, and doors, of course, are the author's own responsibility. Don't blame others for the draft or the occasional leak.

As for the debts along the way, they are numerous. This book began its life while I was studying at Notre Dame. There I would like to thank Rory McVeigh and Kraig Beyerlein, as well as Daniel J. Myers (Marquette University) and Christian Davenport (University of Michigan). I owe the origin of this book to Rory McVeigh, who encouraged me to focus on perpetrators' responses rather than mobilization's origins. What a good idea!—and one that echoes something I remember learning from Jack Donnelly many years ago: Always turn dichotomies into a continuum. Many thanks go to Josh Dinsman, Lars Almquist, and Dana Chavarria, for their formatting, editorial, and design chops and to a host of folks for funding, including the Kellogg Institute and the Center for the Study of Social Movements and Social Change, both at Notre Dame, as well as the National Science Foundation.

A very special thanks goes out to colleagues in the United Kingdom and India: Dr. Bhanuja Sharan Lal, Dr. Sunit Singh, Kiran Kamal Prasad, Rajneesh Kumar, Vithika Yadav, Ginny Baumann, and Supriya Awasthi. Their creativity and patience made this research possible. Farheen Husain and I shared many long and dusty drives that always challenged me to dig deeper for answers and ask new questions. I owe a great deal to the following individuals who served as translators and transcriptionists at various points: Shinja Singh, Vinay Yadav, Kullyappa, Bonface Owiti, and Jon Rider. Heartfelt thanks go out to all of our friends who made our years in East Africa so enjoyable, and to Tinna, Francis, Lukas, Nuru, and Fred for keeping our household running smoothly while my wife worked hundred-hour weeks and I spent months alternating between India and a book-piled desk.

I owe a great debt to Wolfgang Reinicke, the founding dean of the School of Public Policy at Central European University, who encouraged me break the rules if necessary and challenge convention when possible. This project benefitted from the research assistance of Marija Stanovska Rupcic, from the close read provided by Pratik Phadule and Erjon Qirollari, and from the encouragement and support of my colleagues, especially Cristina Corduneanu-Huci, Michael Dorsch, Daniel Large, Simon Rippon, Bernhard Knoll, and Robert Templer. At the University of San Diego I would like to thank Patricia Marquez, for carving out the time for me to finish this book, and to Necla Tschirgi, for suggesting the book was written the wrong way round.

This project has developed and improved through reviews and conversations at various times with Doug McAdams, Sarah Soule, Joseph Luders, Jim Jasper, Jeff Goodwin, Ed Walker, Kirsten Foot, Brayden King, Rachel Einwohner, Kathryn Sikkink, Doug Johnson,

John Picarelli, Joel Quirk, Kevin Bales, Aidan McQuade, Ann Bunting, Michelle Clark, Brandon Vaidyanathan, Kiran Kamal Prasad, Tom Maher, Leon Oosterwijk, and Farheen Husain. Warm-hearted thanks go to Gina Neff and Phil Howard, for their generous mentorship and friendship.

I have also been fortunate to receive the smart support of Alison Brysk and the kind hospitality of Hank Johnston over the years. This project benefitted from feedback at annual meetings of the American Anthropological Association, American Society of Criminology, International Studies Association, and the American Sociological Association and from reviewers at the *Journal of Human Rights* and the *Journal of Human Trafficking*.

I would be remiss if I didn't thank the coffee shops where I hammered these ideas out over conversations or at my machine. In Mawnza: Tilapia and Ryan's Bay; in Budapest: Espresso Embassy, My Little Melbourne, and Coyote Café; in Marquette: Landmark, Ore Dock, and Black Rocks; in San Diego: Influx, Ballast Point, and Bird Rock. A thousand thanks for the double shots.

Slavery will not be ended by yet another book on the topic. It will be ended by people like Jenny Choi, my partner, who has committed her life to increasing opportunity and decreasing inequality the world over. She and our joyous furies—Eden Justice and Aila Pax—are the future and the hinge on which my life swings. Finally, to Joshua MacIvor-Andersen, for his companionship over all these years. I wouldn't have it any other way.

WHAT SLAVEHOLDERS THINK

1

IN ALL ITS FORMS
Slavery and Abolition, Movements and Targets

The worker is my cash machine, my fate.

—Aanan (Interviewee 39)

liked Aanan as soon as I met him.[1] My field notes read *What a nice guy, you can just see from his face. His favorite god is the god of truth.* Open-faced and conversational, he was enthusiastic about the explosive growth in his quarry operations and excited to show me around. Together we toured the open mines where his workers carve, day by day, into the earth. The process produces boulders, which are broken down into gravel by smaller laborers, often women and children. Together with his laborers, Aanan laughed at my efforts to repeat the process for myself, the sledge high over my head before arcing down, momentarily disappearing into shards and dust.

He showed me the crushing equipment that transformed gravel into silica powder, proudly explaining that the Indian multinational Tata was the exclusive buyer of his materials. I had met Aanan through a friend of his, a reference that considerably eased his concerns about speaking with an outsider regarding his operations.

I asked him how he managed challenges with laborers, something I knew contractors and farmers were having trouble with in every area I had visited as part of my research.

> You have to understand the mentality of laborers, and you should know how to make them work. You have to know why the laborer won't work, is it because of money? . . . To manage a group of laborers is like managing a group of primary-school children. They have to be provided with food or clothes, and they are taught how to behave and act in that environment. We have to apply the same tactic with laborers. . . . Sometimes they start drinking alcohol; sometimes they indulge in feasts. So we have to pay them with caution. We divide them into small groups because larger numbers of workers tend to form a union and sometimes engage in mass holidays or strikes.

For Aanan, the happiness of the worker is paramount. Understanding the obstacles to indebtedness and helping the worker stay in food and clothes, and out of drink, are each intended to serve as a protective cocoon around the laborer—and around Aanan's profitability. That this had the effect of insulating his operations against insurrection was not lost on him: "Since he is the source of income for me, it is my duty to look after him. The worker is my cash machine, my fate." In this one statement, Aanan has captured a central contradiction inherent in most human rights violations worldwide: rights violations often occur at the intersection of culture and capital, in the overlap between relationship and extraction, at the moment where care and exploitation intersect.

Though landlords complain about alcohol and other indulgences, these are also tactics for increasing debt-based dependencies. Taking advantage of this situation allows the landlord to maintain the upper hand both economically and ethically. The moral distance that alcohol puts between Aanan, as a Brahmin, and his untouchable laborers facilitates economic exploitation. It also shrouds the larger tactical terrain in a mist of paternalistic concern. When the workers "become defiant" and leave, Aanan says, he has little recourse.

There is no paperwork to reflect the nature of the arrangement to the police. For this reason it is important to predict and mitigate risk. He explains:

> We know that they will form a union. Like a shepherd who knows his herd like the back of his hand, we know the laborers. It's like understanding psychology. Anyone can become a contractor, but a good contractor knows the nuances of his job. He can gauge the mood of the workers and then make them work. . . . Thus, little by little, with caution, we claim back our money. It is the emotional pressure that works.

For Aanan, the employment of laborers in the quarry sector requires balancing the needs of the laborers with those of the owner. This equilibrium requires emotional pressure at the moment of economic vulnerability. It requires human-resourcing practices that increase worker satisfaction while minimizing the risk of mobilization.

While not every one of the slaveholders I spoke with in the course of this research was as frank as Aanan, his approach bears the hallmark traits of contemporary slaveholding: financial distress, emotional manipulation, illegality, and paternalism. At the end of our conversation, I inquired about Aanan with one of my research partners. Yes, they had heard of him. I updated my field notes: *Largest contractor in [town]. Current employer of numerous bonded laborers. Brahmin.*

When most people think of contemporary slavery, the popular imagination leaps to a desperate brothel, one pulled straight from the pages of a newspaper article or activist brochure. The scene is sordid; the victim, pure; and the perpetrator of this human rights violation, an animal of the worst sort. Reality is nowhere near this simple. Contemporary slaveholders, like contemporary slavery, come in many forms. Of course, these men have other terms for their socioeconomic roles and relationships, including "employer," "boss," "landlord," "farmer," "contractor," "master," and "landowner." The evil villain surely exists, but more frequently, contemporary slaveholders are respected members of their community, violating human rights but not social norms.[2]

This is exactly how I would describe most of the rights violators I met in the course of this study. Ahmed, a middle-class slaveholder in Uttar Pradesh, India, was eager to show me around the village where he was a member of the ruling elite. While I was grateful for the warm reception, I was visiting Ahmed's community because of the prevalence of gross human rights violations—bonded labor, child exploitation, and outbound human trafficking. Fathers pleaded for help in finding missing children, long gone, lured away by the promises of traffickers. Mothers who had recently and reluctantly formed a fragile women's group waited nervously to meet and discuss their progress in negotiating higher wages. Behind the weeping men and the expectant mothers sat the children lucky enough to remain in the community, hand-rolling local cigarettes.

These scenes are common throughout rural India and are repeated across the global South, where the intertwined pressures of poverty and hope have been more likely to terminate in rights violations than a better life. Individuals exploited in slavery deserve safer lives, smarter laws, and greater opportunities. There is a near-global consensus about victims' needs. But who are the perpetrators? Do Aanan and Ahmed not see the scene—debt bondage, child labor, trafficking—as I do? Conversations with contemporary slaveholders suggest that they do not.

The author Kevin Bales has argued that social movement activity over the past decade represents the most recent of several abolitionist movements to end human trafficking and slavery (Bales and Cornell 2008). Enthusiasm, activism, and funding have spilled over into those countries most affected, India included. The issue has found its way into the foreign policy portfolios of Western governments and into the budgets of major donors. Popular attention has focused on victims of contemporary slaveholding. Critical attention has been focused on the role of poverty in generating a supply of exploitable people. Activists' efforts have focused attention on the demand side of the equation—high expectations for low prices on sex and labor. Scholars have pointed out the important role played by globalization and macroeconomic forces. But somehow, amid all this attention, slaveholders themselves have come off as rather crudely drawn villains.

While this perception is rooted in the ongoing reality of violent exploitation, it does not help us better understand human rights violators as human beings going about their own lives. This is especially true in South Asia. Almost half of the world's enslaved people are thought to live in this region, where rigid social hierarchies are only lately facing serious challenges. Behavior now considered to be slaveholding had simply been part of the broader tapestry of social and economic relations and had enjoyed general support or, at least, gone unnoticed.

The small but growing body of scholarship on contemporary slavery has yet to analyze human rights violators in any depth. This is not surprising considering how recently the issue has come to public and scholarly attention. Yet this gap should give us pause when we consider the key differences in proposed approaches to eradicating slavery and trafficking, an effort to which the U.S. government has committed hundreds of millions of dollars. Indeed, the women's self-sufficiency group I met in Uttar Pradesh must deal with the slaveholder in one way or another if it is to gain the social and economic power it seeks. Likewise, movement organizations must approach wealthy and powerful perpetrators like Ahmed and Aanan with tactics matched to their real and perceived status. This lesson may be seen no more starkly than in the American South during Reconstruction, where plantation owners opted for a blend of sharecropping and social marginalization that produced durable inequality (Blackmon 2009, Tilly 1998). It is imperative to understand variation in exploiters and exploitation as well as the exploiters' own perspectives on how their lives are changing. Perhaps we will then better understand the difficulties involved in securing sustainable emancipation.

THE ARGUMENT

I am a sociologist working within an intellectual tradition focused on social movements. My academic colleagues and I ask how and why people mobilize together to demand change or to defend the status quo. Our go-to cases include the civil rights movement; three waves of struggle for women's rights; movements to change hearts, minds, and laws regarding marriage equality; and social inclusion for gays and lesbians. Our big debates revolve around the ways structure, agency, and culture shape collective action. Abolitionist movements provide an excellent opportunity to explore these issues, though it seems that the job of explaining earlier waves remains the job of historians.[3]

Scholars in this field should take note: collective action against slavery is the world's oldest vein of social movement activity. The London-based nonprofit group Anti-Slavery International (ASI) has been in operation since its foundation in 1823 as the Anti-Slavery Society, making it one of the world's first, oldest, and longest-running human rights organizations on record. ASI has served as an important and enduring institution across each stage of the world's four antislavery movements.[4] Its American counterpart, Free the Slaves, has adopted a social movement strategy for global abolition (Bales 2007). Antislavery work, historically and in its contemporary form, is fundamentally global. Efforts to remedy public and private wrongs have both broken new ground in broadening definitions of who counts as human while also exposing old fault lines of sexism and bigotry.[5]

While I hope this volume is of interest to many, I have taken this opportunity to point out several opportunities for expanding social-movement scholarship. These more theoretical observations are concentrated in chapter 2. Those wishing to get directly on to the story can skip forward to chapter 3. The book's primary theoretical contribution is as follows: First, at its core, this book is about how slaveholders, as human rights violators and as social movement targets, describe exploitation and emancipation. Defined in greater detail in chapter 2, "movement targets" are those individuals (or institutions and ideas) that social movements target for change. I am convinced that much can be learned from their frustration with broader changes and a sense of betrayal following local emancipation efforts. This book's second contribution is to use these perspectives to develop a tentative theory of *how* slaveholders respond to social movement challenges. I argue that although movement targets may respond with direct repression or oblique countermobilization, they may instead respond by persisting in the old activity (if they are able), continuing with a version of the targeted behavior, or quitting their oppressive activities altogether. The book's third contribution is to use slaveholders' perspectives to advance tentative hypotheses about *why* slaveholders may respond in this way. I argue that a combination of willingness and ability to respond to social movement attention shapes targets' response. This is complicated, as not all who would like to respond are able to do so. Some wishing to persist or repress may fail in an attempt to do so, particularly if the nature of their power has changed. That nature may change, for example, as a result of larger shifts in their worlds, especially those that challenge their dignity and livelihoods. Social-movement scholars may note that I adapt Doug McAdam's ([1982] 1999) political-process theory to demonstrate that macro change processes, interpretive processes, the attribution of threat and opportunity, resources, tactics, and strategic interactions affect both social movement challengers *and* their targets. This adaptation requires learning and reappraisal on the part of targets. The result is a more interactive explanation for how structural realities impose themselves on movement actors.

A caveat is in order. In framing antislavery efforts as *social movements for human rights*, I invoke two complementary but distinct approaches for explaining this case: social movements and human rights. As a scholar with some experience in both fields, I am motivated to see more work that clearly links scholarship on ends (human rights) and means (collective action). While not all social movements pursue human rights ends, and not all human rights ends are pursued via social movement tactics, many scholars are hard at work in the areas where they overlap. While I have anchored my more micro analysis in social movement theory, it is increasingly possible to conduct large-scale studies on these same puzzles.[6]

THE DATA AND THE STUDY

Around half of the world's slaves are held in debt bondage in India, Pakistan, and Bangladesh, where contemporary interventions against slavery usually take two forms (Bales 2012). The first general form involves radical breaks with the past, especially raids and rebellions. The second form involves more gradual transitions, such as community organizing, rights education, and voter mobilization. Radical breaks are often punctuated by conflict and disruptive challenges; more gradualist strategies prioritize a balance between social harmony and social change. In either case, interventions are critical turning points with obvious effects on the attitudes and behaviors of former slaveholders.

To assess these effects I have conducted 150 interviews with four groups of respondents in rural India: employers (current and former slaveholders), laborers (currently and formerly enslaved individuals), community leaders (village heads and others), and key informants from social movement organizations. These interviews were semistructured and lasted an average of eighty minutes per person, with eight to ten respondents per site. I conducted focus groups with an additional 150 people who had been rescued from severely exploitative conditions and whose slaveholders had absconded, were in jail, or were otherwise unavailable. The number of participants in each focus group ranged from a dozen to more than thirty. Each focus-group discussion lasted around two hours.[7]

In total, I spoke with individuals from sixteen intervention sites. By triangulating responses from a range of community members I am able to sketch a portrait of the life and times of small slaveholders in northern and southern India. Interviewees were identified in collaboration with research partners operating in three Indian cities: Allahabad and Varanasi in the northern state of Uttar Pradesh and Bangalore in the southern state of Karnataka. While research partners brokered initial contacts, I identified subsequent interviewees after conducting successful interviews with this original round of former slaveholders. This leapfrog approach to interviewing elites helped secure interviews with a broader range of interviewees than an approach brokered solely by my research partners.[8] This process also helped assuage the fears of reluctant interviewees.

Several of the more powerful or abusive employers refused to sign the study's consent form until we were done speaking. Paradoxically, those were the longest and most fruitful conversations, frequently lasting longer than two hours and in one case lasting more than three. While candor may seem unlikely, it is sometimes the product of a successful intervention. Collective-action interventions generate new social and political actors and spaces. Women's groups, through which communities maintain social contact, are one such example. Early in this study I asked a women's group, "Where is the person who was exploiting you through bonded labor?" The answer surprised me; the vocal leader of the women's group pointed to an unassuming man, sitting at the group's edge, who acknowledged the fact with a wave and an apologetic smile. In the final analysis, only two prospective interviewees, one a former laborer and the other the leader of the local government (*panchayet*), declined an interview request. It is important to note that all current and former slaveholders interviewed for this study had been targeted by a strategy of gradual transition.

In many places contemporary slavery occurs outside the law and beyond the public's eye. Slaveholders are social outcasts and criminals who operate in the shadows of underregulated sections of the economy. The conditions of contemporary slavery are different in South Asia: bonded labor does not take place in hidden pockets of the market. Rather, it happens on a regular basis as a broadly accepted (if misunderstood) form of employment. This study does not capture all forms of contemporary slavery that are practiced in India. Nor does it capture the most exploitative or violent perpetrators. Rather, I interviewed everyday oppressors, those whose relationship with bonded laborers has been culturally sanctioned for as long as anyone can remember. The lessons that emerge tell us more about changes to social norms than about criminal justice, and they represent a first step toward understanding a population that has generally been overlooked in studies on modern slavery and human trafficking.

IS IT REALLY SLAVERY?

The Bellagio-Harvard Guidelines on the Legal Parameters of Slavery extend the 1926 Slavery Convention's determination that "slavery is the status or condition of a person over whom any or all of the powers attaching to the right of ownership are exercised," including debt bondage in those cases where there is control over a person tantamount to possession.[9] This is in line with the 1956 Supplementary Convention on the Abolition of Slavery, the Slave Trade, and Institutions and Practices Similar to Slavery and the 1999 Rome Statute of the International Criminal Court. The International Criminal Tribunal for Yugoslavia includes in their definition "the control of someone's movement, control of physical environment, psychological control, measures taken to prevent or deter escape, force, threat of force or coercion, duration, assertion of exclusivity, subjection to cruel treatment and abuse, control of sexuality and forced labor."[10]

More sociological approaches also consider bonded labor to be a form of slavery, as seen in one of the more widely used definitions, provided by Bales (2012, 20): "people are enslaved by violence and held against their wills for purposes of exploitation." Focusing on its economic dimensions, Siddharth Kara (2012) suggests slavery "is the condition of any person whose liberty is unlawfully restricted while the person is coerced through any means to render labor or services, regardless of compensation, including those who enter the condition because of the absence of a reasonable alternative."

The approach adopted here follows a general trend away from the previously central role of ownership in arguing that the abuse of a position of vulnerability (Gallagher 2012) and the absence of any reasonable alternative (Kara 2012) combine in such a way to undermine voluntary choice dramatically, effectively establishing the bonded-labor agreement as the entry point into contemporary slavery.[11] This combination of high vulnerability and lack of alternatives is particularly salient in contemporary India (Tucker 1997).

Scholars of comparative historical approaches argue for the emergence of a new consensus that "classical slavery has ceased to be a singular, exceptional category, but has instead come to be regarded as one of many forms of contemporary slavery" (Quirk 2011, 10). Thus, while contemporary forms of slavery—debt bondage, domestic servitude, forced prostitution, forced labor, and human trafficking—differ in significant ways from more traditional forms of slavery, a number of core factors remain. Current scholarship in the West affirms bonded labor as an old but persistent form of enslavement.[12]

OVERVIEW OF THE BOOK

In the next chapter I present my theoretical argument, which will help frame my findings for social movement scholars (readers interested only in the story are welcome to move directly to chapter 3). In chapter 2 I argue that the political-process approach used to describe the emergence of contentious politics may be adapted to explain the ways in which the powerful respond. Empirical data from fieldwork in India shed light on how movement targets feel about broad changes as well as local challenges. These observations are used to sketch a broader range of target responses than currently considered.

These observations also allow some exploratory explanations of why targets respond the way they do. In the final analysis, I advance a two-stage process model to explain the onset and cessation of target activity. The opportunities and resources available to them, I argue, largely shape incumbent behavior. Attitudes are important, but resources and opportunities are critical.

Chapters 3, 4, and 5 draw on interviews with current and former slaveholders. Chapter 3 introduces the social movement targets and their description of ideal social relations between themselves and those in their charge. Perpetrators of bonded labor are not pathological rights violators. It is more likely that this abuse is engrained in the legitimizing myth of paternalism that serves to insulate perpetrators from the economic and ethical reality of abuse while bolstering a sense of civic and religious duty. Within India, caste serves as the overarching framework for these social relations: it provides an infrastructure, however subconscious, for the establishment and maintenance of interpersonal and intergroup inequality.[13] In this chapter we hear slaveholders' own description of the tactics they use to secure laborers. These tactics have been discussed in the literature on slavery and trafficking, but this chapter provides first-person accounts from perpetrators themselves.

Chapter 4 introduces slaveholders' accounts of the ways broader political and economic change interacts with social movement efforts. Current and former oppressors find themselves in the midst of radically new circumstances. An earlier consensus had formed around the notion that bonded labor was in the best interest of the laborer. This arrangement is called into question when social-movement activity—new opportunities to take advantage of new resources that help frame certain activities as unjust—combines with broader political and economic shifts. Although elites in rural India had previously sourced their legitimacy in age-old notions of caste hierarchy and this understanding had apparently received broad support, they must now contend with new interpretations of this relationship. Contemporary slaveholders often appear to have been blinded by their own rationalization of these relationships, having convinced themselves that they were helping the laborers in some way.

Chapter 5 provides an overview of slaveholders' responses to social movement activity. Here interview data are employed to suggest that while some movement targets respond with repression or countermobilization, they may also respond by simply continuing rights-violating behavior. Furthermore, targets may modify their activities in order to avoid further action, or they may quit altogether. Slaveholders lacking the resources to persist in the face of structural factors and movement tactics must shift course. Yet their responses are conditioned on the real and perceived ability to extend their power. Some former slaveholders in India would like to persist or repress but lack the opportunities, resources, or power to do so. Frustrated, they adapt, settling for less exploitative labor relations, or they quit exploitative efforts altogether.

Chapter 6 introduces the ways in which contemporary slavery in India is connected to larger cultural systems, especially caste. This approach builds off recent work by specialists in the region and allows me to theorize slavery as a culturally embedded social fact (Kara 2012, Ray and Qayum 2009). Thinking about culturally embedded rights violation invites the reader to extend the theoretical observations to other instances in which oppressors violate human rights but not local norms, a theme picked up in the concluding chapter.

Chapter 7 puts this particular case into perspective, arguing that current antislavery efforts are the fourth wave of the world's oldest social movement for human rights. This broader perspective requires taking seriously questions of contemporary slaveholding and emancipation. Sustainable emancipation is only possible with a broader view of perpetrators and a more comprehensive assessment of the relevant actors, the problem, and the solution.

In the concluding chapter I reassess the book's contribution to social movement theory. I highlight the extent to which the lived experiences of movement targets underscore factors critical to social movement scholarship: grievances and interpretations (chapter 3), threats and opportunities (chapter 4), and resources (chapter 5). I build off of these observations to argue for an iterative, relational, and process-oriented explanation of the way target-specific factors shape the emergence, evolution, and end of contestation. I conclude with a nod to unanswered questions and highlight the study's broader implications for all of us in our own lives.

BELIEVING HUMAN RIGHTS VIOLATORS

Before continuing, it would be wise to recognize that my decision to interview rights violators is likely to trigger skepticism or revulsion. How can we trust the word of those who have violated a widely accepted human right? There is no easy answer to this question, nor is there a simple salve for the general unease that lies behind it. At a methodological level, this book triangulates responses from former slaveholders with the accounts of others—bystanders, formerly enslaved survivors, and social movement actors. There is certainly a desire among those challenged by movement actors to stylize the reality of their situation. This may have led to the overemphasis on the importance of family-style relations and paternalism so clear in chapter 6. It most certainly limited confessions of force, fraud, threats, or coercion. Interviewees were confident that only their more exploitative neighbors were involved in such things. They themselves were rarely guilty. Though a handful admitted to such actions, more direct and transparent accounts of this behavior came from former bonded laborers and from movement organizers. Having multiple sources allowed me to make critical determinations regarding wealthy landlords like Aanan, whom we met at the chapter's start.

At another level, however, I am convinced that slaveholders, in rural India especially, are in the midst of several significant transformations—in the economic terrain, in their levels of confidence with their political representation, and in the exchange value of a previously valuable commodity: their caste. It is altogether possible that some are in the midst of rethinking their own identities just as others are reconsidering their livelihoods. It is at this very moment of liminality, between the exploitation of bonded labor and whatever comes next, that slaveholders' perspectives of their own actions—old acts in a new light—are worthy of consideration. We might not always get the truth, but we should certainly try. Even rationalizations are revealing.

2

BEST-LAID PLANS

A Partial Theory of
Social Movement Targets

The strong do what they will, the weak suffer what they must.

—Thucydides

Men make their own history, but they do not make it as they please.

—Karl Marx

There is a relatively broad consensus that the emergence
and success of a social movement are conditioned by a
combination of resources, opportunities, and perceptions.[1] Attention to these factors is rooted in a series of progressive movements that have emerged since the 1960s. Poor people's
movements in the United States, liberation movements in former
colonies, and more recent identity movements in the United States
and Europe have fundamentally transformed our understanding of
why people mobilize.

A trailblazing generation of social movement scholars cut their
teeth representing the voice and experience of protestors. A wave
of post-1968 scholarship on the civil rights movement provided
an important counterbalance to the more pluralist assessments of

society, protest, and change. Social movement studies came into its own in America and Europe at a point when observers were intent on demonstrating the very good reasons why the disenfranchised would engage in collective action against the status quo. This trend emphasized rational actors over emotional factors, progressive movements over conservative movements, and movement actors over their targets.

The result of this corrective is that the last time collective-action scholarship focused on movements from the adversary's perspective was, roughly speaking, in the era between LeBon's *Study of the Popular Mind* in 1895 and Gurr's efforts to explain *Why Men Rebel* in 1970. This era was perhaps best defined by theorists who assumed that society was a well-ordered machine and thus saw protests as flaws in an otherwise just and coherent system.[2] Scholars gazed down from their ivory towers and wondered why, in the midst of opportunity for all, a few would protest. The answers seemed clear: a few bad apples, or a general madness—protestors had taken leave of their senses and were generally misguided in their critique of liberal democracies. Student protests in the 1960s, however, shed new light on this story.

Young people with direct experience in protests and movements entered universities where they confronted scholarship that fundamentally misrepresented their emancipatory efforts. These students went on to be the founding fathers and mothers of contemporary movement scholarship.[3] Their work has discarded assessments of mobilization that relied on theories of relative deprivation and collective behavior, focusing instead on the legitimacy of protestors' claims. Along the way, elite perspectives on movements have been replaced by a view from those actually involved in social-change efforts. The critique was clear: Why would we focus our attention on those communities by and for whom history has always been written?

Within social movement scholarship, the impact has been significant: interviews with movement targets are few and far between. social movement scholars were certainly not alone in this effort to redirect attention to subjugated people and knowledges (Foucault 1980, 81). The social historian E. P. Thompson was representative of this trend: "I am seeking to rescue the poor stockinger, the Luddite cropper, the 'obsolete' hand-loom weaver, the 'utopian' artisan, and even the deluded follower of Joanna Southcott, from the enormous condescension of posterity" (Thompson 1991, 12). This approach, so evident across the social sciences, has increased our understanding of a previously silenced majority of downtrodden and oppressed people. But it has also narrowed our view of their oppressors.[4]

Viewing collective action from the perspective of its target provides valuable information about the ways core social movement factors like grievances, resources, political opportunities, and framing explain the emergence and impact of insurgent groups. Movement targets are dynamic social actors who are almost always more powerful—individually or collectively—than their challengers. That concentration of power is often the very reason social movement groups target them. It hardly needs stating that individual and institutional targets—the primary focus in this study— are often in possession of relatively more material resources and in more powerful institutional roles than are challengers. These resources are not only economic but political and cultural as well. Incumbent targets are often in active or passive control of the dominant conceptualizations of ideal social relations, i.e., the ideas that form the raw cultural material for counterframing efforts. As guardians of the status quo they often have better access to the media and may be significantly more motivated to retain existing privilege than the movement is motivated to obtain new benefits. Movement targets are also likely to have more opportunities— whether cultural, political, or economic—with which to respond to movement efforts. Finally, powerful incumbents create and reinforce broader status quo values and norms. Put another way, the values and norms held by powerful incumbents are very often the ideals that are considered more broadly to be normatively good (Fligstein and McAdam 2012).

A WORKING DEFINITION:
WHAT ARE WE TALKING ABOUT?

Important definitions provided by William Gamson (1975), Dieter Rucht (2004), and Neil Fligstein and Doug McAdam (2012) have laid the groundwork for this study.[5] As used in the following pages, the term *social movement target* refers to an *individual, collective, or cultural target of collective challenges for resources, recognition, or change.*[6] Put very simply, movements target individuals, institutions, and ideas. By *individual*, I mean embodied persons, such as presidents, voters, executives, union organizers, heads of ministries, and so forth. This is a single actor against whom claims may be made and issues may be framed. By *collective*, I simply mean a unit that is "united into one body." This may be a government or regime, board of directors, union, other movement group, and so forth.[7] The term *collective* describes a single collective actor that serves as the reference point for movement claims and issue frames. By *cultural*, I mean any non-physical target that lies in the cultural sphere, including identities, definitions, manners of speech, styles of dress, and so forth.

Movements target ideas, opinions, and practices. This definition of targets generally follows the approach taken by David Snow and Sarah Soule, in their definition of social movements as "collectivities acting with some degree of organization and continuity, partly outside institutional or organizational channels, for the purpose of challenging extant systems of authority, or resisting change in such systems, in the organization, society, culture, or world system in which they are embedded." This approach emphasizes the importance of existing structures and systems of authority, whether they are found in organizations and society or are rooted in cultural practices and worldviews. In a crucial nod to the role of culture, Soule and Snow emphasize that authority is often "based on underlying sets of interconnected values, beliefs, and interpretive frameworks that rationalize the distribution and exercise of the authority and provide vocabularies of motive that can be used not only to justify adherence to the regulations or procedures but also to challenge their perceived violations" (Snow and Soule 2000).[8]

The term *target* is not accidental. It refers in common English to *something you are trying to hit*. That something need not be a person. The terms *opponent*, *adversary*, and *elite* all suggest a person, group, or institution with authority and power. Ideas have tremendous power and are infused with authority. Popular norms about human dignity or value are often the subject of a movement's framing efforts. Any definition of the object of a movement's efforts must include the possibility that movements focus on objects *and* objectives, both things *and* ideas.

Targets are an oft-acknowledged conceptual category but an ill-defined, rarely consulted, and seldom understood social actor. To make matters even worse, many targets are incredibly difficult to access. The result is a general absence of accounts of mobilization from the target's perspective and a truncated assessment of the possible responses to mobilization. New work by Brayden King, Sarah Soule, Tim Bartley, Joseph Luders, and their collaborators have broadened our understanding of the larger factors that shape the responses of corporations, but we hardly ever hear directly from targets themselves.

Rucht's definition of targets—external groups that movements perceive as opponents or adversaries—appeared in the prominent *Blackwell Companion to Social Movements*, and it has been cited multiple times, but it is not utilized in any investigation of movement targets. Likewise, Gamson (1975, 29) argued that incumbents targeted by movements may attempt to co-opt, preempt, or threaten those movements. However, a review of the volume's citation arc suggests subsequent scholarship has tended to focus more on the movement's outcomes than on a target's behavior. An assessment of the entire population of articles published in the social movement journal *Mobilization* suggests a similar lacuna. With a handful of exceptions, mainstream movement literature has focused on countermobilization, policing, and repression dynamics from the movement's perspective.[9] While the state is the most discussed movement target, data from those bureaucrats and politicians who comprise the state are rare.

Current studies of target behavior are characterized by two key attributes: they are predominantly quantitative, and they tend to favor institutional targets (Walker, Martin, and McCarthy 2008). These factors are self-reinforcing, as analysts have focused on institutional targets about which data is available. This work has advanced a sophisticated understanding of a number of related issues, the foremost of which is threat, introduced by Charles Tilly (1978) and later resuscitated in his collaboration with Jack Goldstone (2001).[10] New developments within organizational sociology and on corporate behavior have extended the concept of threat to include the role of reputational threat, risk perception by managers, and decreased profitability in the form of stock prices and sales, all of which raise the cost of persistence.[11]

Corporate sensitivities to anything that threatens public opinion and profits are important to understand, but they do not explain how specific individuals within corporations feel, nor do they tell us anything about noncorporate targets. Yet the attitudes and behavior of individuals matter, and many social-movement efforts affect other institutions, create new institutions, or aim beyond institutions altogether, hoping instead to change cultural practices and relations.[12] Qualitative approaches are necessary in order to better understand the responses of non-institutional targets. Yet only three studies known to this author have attempted to trace target activity by actually speaking with targets themselves.[13]

Matthias Wahlstrom (2007) conducted interviews with twenty Swedish police officers in an attempt to understand better their decision making around alter-globalization protests. His interviews and ethnographic data provide a rare window into the complicated interplay between prior police knowledge of activists, their attempts to engage "counterpart perspectives," and the difficulty of implementing new policies. What he finds is police joking about how hard it is to appear personable and community oriented when wearing mountains of protective gear. He also notes the ways police use stereotypes of protestors in order to maintain their own constructions of reality. While we are in possession of very good work on the policing of protests,[14] it is rare that we hear from police themselves on the matter. Wahlstrom's most important observation lies in the way the worldviews of police officers shape their perceptions of movement challengers.

In a similar fashion, Rachel Einwohner's (2002) work involved interviews with the hunters and scientists targeted by animal rights activism, demonstrating the extent to which activists and opponents engage one another in the same strategic action field. Hunters' and scientists' claims that activists are sentimental and irrational fed into the movement's framing tactics. Activists responded with an effort to present themselves as "logical" and "rational" in future interactions with opponents. In this way, the adversary's actions shaped not only the movement's actions but also its identity. The qualitative data drawn from time spent with targets themselves provide a more sophisticated picture of how movement efforts are understood.

James Jasper and Jane Poulsen (1993) focus directly on the importance of target tactics. Targets, like movements and all other social actors, must work iteratively to get their response right. Initial missteps—blunders—and unique individual or corporate attributes—unpopular activities, internal factions—explain variation in the targets' abilities to resist movement efforts. Jasper and Poulsen's conclusion is that successful movements have the effect of solidifying the target's resolve and triggering more strategic responses, including countermobilization. While this finding is framed in terms of the *movement's* ability to succeed, it anticipates one of the key findings from my fieldwork: target actions are dynamic and iterative rather than static and fixed. First-order responses are never the last word. Targets err, adapt, and evolve.

THE IMPORTANCE OF FRAMING TARGETS

Social movement targets are culturally produced variables, not structurally embedded constants. Contentious action between incumbents and challengers is often the result of external shocks or changes that trigger a series of consolidations and reconfigurations. Cultural, economic, and political changes—in divisions of labor, in terms of norms and values, and in perceptions of structural factors— are the sources of movement demands. While a very narrow read of a very small piece of history may suggest movements tend to be about human rights, a more catholic assessment of collective action suggests movements are as likely to be motivated by conservative ideas and in favor of limiting rights and curbing debates, both in the past and the present (McVeigh 2009, Bob 2012, Parker and Barreto 2013, McAdam and Kloos 2014).

Cultural, economic, and political changes produce claimants, claims, and targets. Thus, targets are no more a fixed historical category than is any particular rights claim. Social movement targets must be created. This study sets out to explore not the broad universe of human rights violators and perpetrators but instead a particular subset: those violators and perpetrators who have been identified—*framed*—as targets by social movement actors.[15] This creative work is performed by norm entrepreneurs as they construct and popularize injustice frames around previously acceptable behavior or understandings (Brysk 2013; Bob 2005; Keck and Sikkink 1998; Risse, Ropp, Sikkink 2013). This is seldom easy.

My first and primary objective in this book is to provide a descriptive overview of how some targets view both exploitative actions and subsequent emancipation struggles. Data from targets themselves suggest that they are exposed to and experience a similar set of causal factors as movements. For scholars interested in explaining collective action, targets matter not only because they shape movement efforts but also because they act (Walker, Martin, and McCarthy 2008). Targets have their own repertoires, self-perceptions, resources, capital, and sources of legitimacy. They overreach, misunderstand, stumble, lash out, and wait patiently— they are tactically engaged social actors.[16]

A PARTIAL THEORY OF TARGET TACTICS AND OUTCOMES

In what follows I advance a target-centric account of the emergence of contentious action and hypothesize the individual target responses that help shape new settlements.[17] Does a shift in attention from the powerless to the powerful require new theories? I think not. Social movement targets may be accommodated through the adaptation of existing theory. The first stage of this process is a lightly modified version of the political-process approach introduced by Charles Tilly and refined by Doug McAdam and his fellow travelers (McAdam [1982] 1999; McAdam, Tarrow, and Tilly 2001; McAdam and Boudet 2012; Fligstein and McAdam 2012) and familiar to many sociologists and political scientists (figure 2.1).[18] While earlier scholars sourced social movements to piecemeal accounts of structural strain or specific factors, a wave of political sociologists has specified the way that politics, economics, and culture interact to shape the emergence of contentious politics. Perhaps the most important yet overlooked component of the political-process

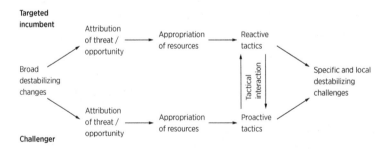

FIGURE 2.1   Phase One: Onset of Episode of Contention

approach lies in its recognition that targets are exposed to the same range of factors as their challengers.

This study's first and most basic contribution is an emphasis on targeted incumbents. The political-process approach has included movement targets in theoretical models for several decades (McAdam [1982] 1999). While the earliest explanations followed Charles Tilly's (1978) emphasis on the state, subsequent efforts broadened to include elites before finally settling on the more flexible category of incumbents. *Incumbent* is a very broad appellation that recognizes the fact that movement targets are often (but certainly not always) "those actors who wield disproportionate influence within a field and whose interests and views tend to be heavily reflected" in broader public opinion (Fligstein and McAdam 2011). Incumbents, then, may be found anywhere—in small teams, in large corporations, and in political systems, to name but a few examples. Incumbency is a position that gives rise to certain sets of affordances and assumptions.

The second advantage of a process-oriented explanation of targets lies in its emphasis on broad and destabilizing changes within the political, social, and economic sphere. While sudden moral shocks may also trigger mobilization (Jasper 1997), destabilizing changes are likely to produce deeper and broader responses, since their influences are more broadly distributed socially, economically, and politically. Significant changes affect incumbents and challengers differently, as their structural positions shade their individual assessments of the type and severity of the impact and whether current events represent an opportunity. These are not structures of political opportunity but deeply contextual processes in which practical meaning making and resource assessment are paramount. Material and conceptual conditions matter, but there is significant variation in individual perceptions of what these conditions mean and what responses are appropriate or desirable. Large-scale change processes call the status quo into question for both the challenger and the incumbent.

The third component of this approach is an emphasis on the importance of threat and opportunity. Scholarship has tended to focus on *opportunities for movements*, as if they are objective items that can be grasped (Meyer and Staggenborg 1996). Two observations must be made before we continue. First, broader assessments include threats, often operationalized as repression (Davenport 2015). Second, targeted incumbents perceive large-scale and destabilizing change processes as opportunities or threats. Joseph Luders has recently breathed new life into McAdam's original observation that challengers desire "the ability to disrupt their opponent's interests to such an extent that the cessation of the offending tactic becomes a sufficient inducement to grant concessions" (McAdam [1982] 1999, qtd. in Luders 2010, 2).

Movements, Luders argues, may impose two types of cost: disruption and concession.[19] Disruption costs stem directly or indirectly from movement efforts, with examples including the effect of protests on public opinion or issue salience—in simple terms, protests are costly (Luders 2010, 3). Concession costs are those real or perceived costs associated with capitulation to the movement's demands—surrender is also costly. Targets facing a combination of high disruption and concession costs will vacillate with an "unstable mixture of minor concessions, protracted negotiation, and support for movement repression," and they may eventually quit the targeted behavior altogether. This approach may lead a target to select a reactive tactic. Perhaps they adapt, repress, countermobilize, or quit.

At the other end of the spectrum are targets facing a combination of low disruption and concession costs—their actual and anticipated losses are minor, so they can afford to do nothing or to "resist or accept movement demands in keeping with dominant local norms" (Luders 2010, 5). Luders calls this category of targets *conformers*: they take their cue from social norms rather than the movement but are not necessarily motivated to repress, since little may be protected or gained from doing so. The next two sets of responses are more straightforward, lying at the intersection of high- and low-cost configurations. Targets facing low disruption costs but high concession costs—where it costs little to protect a lot—will "offer durable opposition to the movement" in an attempt to avoid the painful sacrifices involved in concession (ibid.). These resisters, as Luders calls them, respond with repression, countermobilization, or by simply persisting in the targeted activity. Finally, where disruption costs are high but concession costs are low—where it costs nothing to avoid a significant penalty—targets will accommodate the movement and quit the targeted behavior (ibid.).

This cogent assessment of initial tactical responses sheds important light on the way threats and costs work and lays the groundwork for additional assessments of opportunities and benefits. Luders clearly specifies the cost analysis underpinning threat, yet an emphasis on perception and attribution suggests that mistakes may be made in the diagnosis of a situation and that situations may be perceived to be opportunities rather than threats.[20] Powerful movements certainly threaten targets, but they may also provide opportunities. A multinational corporation targeted because of a negative environmental record may decide substantial negative publicity is an opportunity to pivot to a new green initiative that allows it to raise prices and match the movement's demands in one fell swoop.[21]

The fourth advantage of a target-centric political-process explanation lies in an inventory of the incumbent's resources. Movement-centric explanations conceptualize resources as the economic and institutional tools and capacity available to a social movement organization (McCarthy and Zald 1977) or, more recently, as the broader ability to secure important support through "social appropriation" (Fligstein and McAdam 2012). Incumbents, however, are often vested in well-established political, economic, or social interests and thus have at hand a different suite of resources than do their challengers. These resources are often broadly held across a number of areas. Some resources are culturally embedded and subject to broad changes that the target might not have recognized given the nature of incumbency. They may be social—connected to robust status hierarchies that reinforce inequality and exploitation. Other resources may be institutional, allowing incumbents to draw strength from the state, market, local associations, and international institutions. Political resources matter as well, brokering access to decision-making mechanisms and enforcement processes. The vulnerability of economic targets— Luders's primary focus—is critical, since economic capacity shapes an incumbent's access to the financial resources necessary to co-opt, repress, or ignore challengers. The fifth component—reactive tactics—emerges from the broad interpretive process that gives rise to attributions of opportunity and threat and assessments of which resources are available for appropriation. Interpretive processes are simply the *continuous process of sense making and collective attribution* in which all social actors engage (Davenport 2015). Practical sense making plays into both attribution of threat and opportunity as well as the appropriation of resources. The reason for this lies in the nature of incumbency. Thinking in terms of incumbency helps explain how material, ideological, and institutional processes mislead individuals and cause misperceptions about what broad changes mean and about which responses are sustainable. It may be too much to say that incumbency is a kind of false consciousness, but this analogy bears mentioning. Incumbency may produce misperceptions about the best way to respond to challengers. These interpretive processes may be rooted in any number of cultural, economic, or political assumptions about the previous status quo and about the broad destabilizing changes that are currently at play.

Initial assessments lead to reactive tactics. Reactive tactics are the knee-jerk responses that can run the gamut described by Luders. Contestation, however, is iterative rather than one-off. Once-acceptable repression may no longer be tolerated. As mentioned above, Gamson (1975, 1980) rightly argued that incumbents may choose to co-opt, preempt, or threaten movements. Luders (2010, 5) shows how costs shape whether targets conform to, accommodate, resist, or vacillate on movement demands. But first responses are not final. Tactics are not strategies. In other words, there is a round of play *after* the initial threat assessment. This possibility is acknowledged by Luders (2010, 51): "although a movement might be in a stronger or weaker bargaining position at the outset, outcomes nearly always depend upon the selection of appropriate strategies, the modulation of movement demands, and the relative efficacy of countermovement opponents." Resources, allies, abilities, and resources might need to be reassessed.[22]

The sixth and final component of the political-process theory is an escalation of uncertainty that results from the tactical interaction of the targeted incumbent and the challenger. Most models end here, since the independent variable—emergence of an episode of contention—has been explained. Yet if we want to take the story forward to explain outcomes, then we must recognize that contentious interactions generate new sets of realities and recognitions for both parties. Specific tactics create destabilizing changes that occur more locally than did the much broader change processes that may have triggered contention in the first place. This more local and specific tactical interaction triggers new processes that must be explained in their own right.

If first rounds are not final rounds, what does this say about movement outcomes and the target's role in that process? With suitable modification, the existing model may be extended to include a subsequent iteration, as incumbents work to resolve and address the specific and local destabilizing changes that have resulted from contentious interaction (itself the effect of events set into motion by broad, destabilizing changes). I propose a complementary and subsequent model that takes incumbent responses seriously. A two-stage approach recognizes that target decisions about how to respond to perceived uncertainty matter at the onset of contention as well as in the emergence of new settlements. Such an incumbent-focused and process-oriented explanation of outcomes suggests that tactical interactions create specific and local destabilizing changes that require a reattribution of threat and opportunity as well as a reassessment of resources. This reappraisal leads to a more proactive and sustainable strategic response, which lays the groundwork for the new status quo (figure 2.2).[23]

Adding a second phase to the traditional model allows us to link more clearly these factors to movement outcomes. The first factor—the specific and local nature of destabilizing changes—recognizes

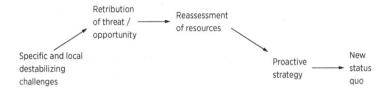

FIGURE 2.2   Phase Two: Incumbent Resolution of Episode of Contention

that contestation is an intimate affair. These struggles are rarely simple logistical considerations for participants on each side of the struggle. Strategic interactions are often emotional, risky, anxiety inducing, and surprising. By definition, they eschew the "business-as-usual" approach that defined the previous status quo. Sustained contention provides the incumbent with new and valuable experiences and information. Targets must now reevaluate a number of important variables, reappraising their assumptions in light of new information.

Recent work by Christian Davenport (2015, 43–45) points to the importance of *reappraisal*, as actors "identify what is taking place around them, putting the experience into the appropriate category, which then serves as the basis for subsequent action." Davenport (2015, 44) borrows this idea from the field of psychology to show that movements with an "appropriate reading of the environment" are better able to withstand state repression. Expectations matter, but they may also be reexamined and revised. This is exactly the opportunity local destabilizing changes make available to incumbents. For example, powerful targets may ask themselves whether the state is still supportive of a particular set of economic practices and social relations, or whether foreign and domestic markets are able to bear previously widespread economic practices that have fallen out of favor, or whether a boycott by environmental activists is a chance to apologize and raise prices.

This brings us to the second and third factors, a *reattribution* of threats, opportunities, and resources. Old activities must be reappraised in light of new information about the tradeoffs involved in maintaining the targeted behavior and thereby supporting the old status quo. One's reappraisal may conclude that broad, disruptive change represents an opportunity rather than a threat. Resource portfolios may be reassessed and new permutations of economic, social, and political power may emerge. The result of this sequence is our fourth factor: the original reactive and tactical actions are replaced by a more proactive, considered, and strategic response. Jim Jasper and Jane Poulsen (1993) show that, over time, targets learn from their mistakes and are less likely to retain early vulnerabilities and repeat previous blunders. The result is a settlement representing the new status quo. The notion of a settlement, borrowed from field theorists, suggests that movements do not produce fixed outcomes but instead help produce new interim agreements that might themselves be the sites of future contestation (Fligstein and McAdam 2012).

The most important impact of this line of argument for movement scholars is that movements may push incumbents to take action based on a wide range of considerations, with the movement but one of these factors. How they ultimately respond may have less to do with the threat posed by the movement than with broader forces and factors.[24] In sum, sustained contention creates new sets of opportunities and threats for both challengers and incumbents. With new information, targeted incumbents are better able to assess the situation as it really is, rather than as it originally appeared. With the implications of broader changes in clearer view, and with the movement's capacity and determination on better display, it is only at this point that the incumbents, whose power may by now be reduced significantly, can assess their options and act proactively and strategically.

TARGET RESPONSES

Laurie Pritchett, the police chief of Albany, Georgia, was successful in stifling movement efforts through the use of arrests rather than actions that would precipitate violence (Barkan 1984). With advanced planning, he cleared enough space in jails within Albany and the surrounding area such that the crowding of prisoners did not become a second mobilization point for the civil rights movement. Evidently, Pritchett had read "of King's admiration of Gandhi's method of filling the jails, and determined that this would not happen in Albany." This tactic earned Pritchett a congratulatory telegram from Robert Kennedy, then U.S. attorney general (Barkan 1984, 557, 558).

Things turned out quite differently for T. Eugene "Bull" Connor, the law enforcement official whose infamous choice of violent tactics during civil rights efforts in Birmingham, Alabama, drove up arrests, produced shocking imagery, and invited unwanted attention from the federal government (Nunnelley 1991, Raines 1977). Pritchett and Connor doubtless chose different strategies as a result of perceived threats or opportunities, existing resources and repertoires, personality type, prior experience, and perhaps an emotional decision arrived at in the heat of the moment, what might now be called a snap decision or hot cognition. The work of Steven Barkan is particularly illustrative here: segregationists would have lost less ground had they drawn from the civil rights movement's tactical repertoire and responded with nonviolence and legal challenges or invested in alternative institutions (Barkan 1984, Andrews 2002).

This book's secondary objective is to draw on data from targets themselves, to suggest how they perceive and respond to movement challenges. Like most actors, targets choose from culturally available action repertoires, a fact clearly demonstrated by Pritchett's innovative use of Gandhian means to thwart Gandhian ends. With two important exceptions, this range of motion is rarely described in the literature on target tactics. The first exception is again the work of William Gamson (1975), who proposed that movement outcomes could be explained by a combination of new acceptance and new advantages. Success was possible, but movements might also be preempted, co-opted, or threatened by targeted incumbents.

Since movement outcomes were the unit of analysis, however, target decision making was not explained. Gamson did not specify whether this list was exhaustive, nor did he hypothesize how targets chose or implemented these efforts.

The second exception lies in Joseph Luders's (2010, 5) proposal that targets respond with accommodation, resistance, vacillation, or conformity. However, his approach leaves little room for reappraisal and does not account for the possibilities of benefits and opportunities existing in addition to costs and threats. Taking reappraisal seriously affects Luders's typology, since *vacillation* ("concession, negotiation, repression, quitting") covers both process and outcome. This overlap is not problematic if we intend to explain an initial tactical response but becomes harder to work with if the unit of analysis is a new settlement. Drawing on the work of Gamson and Luders, I propose that five responses obtain in at least one of each phase of contention. These responses are admittedly not as tight as the two-by-two comparisons offered by Gamson and by Luders. They nevertheless retain some parsimony, especially considering that they cover three distinct phases in the mobilization cycle: before mobilization, during mobilization, and after mobilization. The full implication of these phases can be found in the concluding chapter.

PREEMPTION

Preemption is the act of reducing or eliminating contestable issues and is a byproduct of the conscious and unconscious exercise of power by the powerful.[25] In his seminal thesis on power Steven Lukes argues that power works in a number of ways (Gaventa 1982, Lukes [1974] 2005). At the most obvious level power may be used to overcome and overwhelm others. Less obviously, it may be used to structure the range of opinions available at any point in time. At its most sophisticated and insidious level, power is used to shape and structure desire. People get what they want, but what they want is something other than what they need. This thesis has proven difficult to verify empirically but goes some way toward explaining how it is that the powerful remain in control despite democratic institutions capable of channeling the interests of the powerful. The complex reality of this approach is emphasized in the following chapter.

COUNTERMOBILIZATION AND CO-OPTATION

If preemption is the act of preventing the emergence of issues, then countermobilization and co-optation are tactics used proactively to reduce the effects of collective action. A countermovement is a "movement that makes contrary claims simultaneously to those of the original movement" (Meyer and Staggenborg 1996, 1630). By co-optation, I simply mean those times when a movement gains acceptance but no new advantages.[26] Thus, co-optation, countermobilization, and repression occur in response to the threat of a movement gain, when the goals of a population are threatened and when political allies are available to support mobilization (Meyer and Staggenborg 1996). Recent work by Kenneth Andrews has convincingly demonstrated that it was the credible threat of desegregation, combined with resources held by both blacks and by whites, which led to the establishment of alternative schools for the education of Mississippi whites.[27] Countermobilization is filtered through civil society's forms of organization and action. It may be that this energy emerges authentically and from the grassroots. It is also often the case that the support for such "popular responses" is championed by or interlinked with the state. Politicians, bureaucrats, or political allies may provide sub rosa support for countermovements. Indeed, it is also facilitated by institutions, as described by Jim Jasper and Jane Poulsen: New York University had already been targeted for animal testing, and it used this prior experience to go on the offensive and defensive quickly. Similarly, Southern lawmakers who relied on an all-white electorate both instigated and supported resistance to the civil rights movement.[28] Slaveholder efforts to countermobilize and co-opt are found in the fourth chapter.

REPRESSION

A large and growing body of literature has focused on state-sponsored repression and on the mobilization-repression nexus (Davenport 2010, 2015; Lichbach 1987; Linden and Klandermans 2006; Rasler 1996). Repression is arguably the most highly visible of the options available to the state, and indeed scholarship tends to focus on state responses to collective action (Earl 2003, 2011). However, repression is rarely an option for many universities or churches and is not possible for some corporations and individuals targeted by social movement efforts in the global North. In fact, Charles Tilly's (1978, 100) quite broad definition of repression—"any action by another group which raises the contender's cost of collective action"—does not prescribe the presence of a state. Jennifer Earl's (2003, 46, 49) typology of repression likewise includes private agents as potentially coercive actors alongside agents of the state. The reality of private actors involved in repression is stark. Corporate involvement in repression extends from violent union busting to systemic physical coercion. Extractive industries are regularly involved in illicit agreements with militias, juntas, semiregular military personnel, and other non–state security actors (Mouawad 2009).

Incumbents may respond with repression when they feel threatened, and there is no reason to believe that the strength of this finding disappears when sources of authority other than the state are threatened, so long as this use of violence has legitimacy in the cultural and political context (Davenport 2007). Likewise, soft repression from nonstate actors may take the form of ridicule, stigma, and silencing; these are actions intended to exclude movements and movement actors from the cultural and political spaces where they are advocates or claimants.[29]

RESIGNATION

From the perspective of the social movement, the cessation of the target's behavior represents a victory, and victory may be easily contrasted with failure. Things are not so simple from the target's perspective. Movement adversaries may assess the broader context and resign themselves to the situation, simply deciding to quit. Alternately, targeted incumbents may attempt to repress, persist, countermobilize, or adapt. Quitting, by which I mean abandoning the behavior for which one has been targeted, is a complex process and rarely the first choice. It is composed, like each of these options, of a particular set of individual decisions (whether to repress or countermobilize) and abilities (whether one has the resources and position to persist). From the outside, this may look like movement success, and this is not altogether untrue. However, there is a difference between a movement rightly claiming victory and a target owning up to defeat.

PERSISTENCE

Persistence is the continuation, in identical or nearly identical form, of the originally targeted behavior. Repression, countermobilization, and co-optation are active responses to the original mobilization. Persistence is hardly a response at all—rather, it is the simple continuation of the status quo, albeit with minor modifications. Persistence may involve modifying exploitation into a nearly identical form. Most (or all) benefits enjoyed prior to mobilization thus continue under slightly different conditions (Blackmon 2009). In other words, the target undermines the movement's ability to exercise power, levy sanctions, and raise costs. Where repression aims to silence, crush, or arrest a movement's activities, and where countermobilization is meant to cancel out movement gains, persistence and adaptation are focused on pursuing the status quo while avoiding conflict (Jackman 1994). A business, for example, might offer to self-police for labor rights violations in order to avoid the deeper reforms demanded by the movement. Attempts to continue near-similar work under new conditions—to pursue old goals in new ways and not get caught—is nonconfrontational and certainly less risky than countermobilization or repression. This approach may also be pursued by targets that lack the capacity or propensity to shift out of the targeted sector of the economy or by a particular type of business practice that lacks the resources to quit altogether (see McAdam 1996, 27). Those lacking alternative forms of income or those with deep levels of commitment to social dominance may choose to persist as well.[30] Persistence may be a reflexive reaction underwritten by a default commitment to an earlier set of norms and ideals. Alternately, it may be the proactive product of a longer-term and considered commitment to the cultural or economic benefits provided by the behavior in question. Here we enter the realm of motives, where I am reluctant to speculate.

TARGET RESPONSES ARE SHAPED BY FAMILIAR FACTORS

And now we come to the book's third key objective: advancing a tentative hypothesis about why targets in this study respond as they do. I suggest that variation in response is fundamentally premised on a reassessment of the situation. Specifically, incumbents ask themselves whether the tactical interaction represents a threat or an opportunity and whether there are sufficient resources available to act on this interpretation of the situation. Strategic interactions may change interpretations, attributions, resources, or tactics, since such interactions are not one-off but take place iteratively, over time. These interactions produce emergent phenomena—new social realities that are greater than the sum of their parts. A target's ultimate response is primarily dependent on a more accurate assessment of their own resources and whether these changes are better thought of as opportunities or threats. In emphasizing resources, I do not mean to slight ideas, attitudes, values, or norms.[31] There is every reason to believe that some targets are more willing to persist than others.[32] But on the main, targeted incumbents prefer the status quo and will try to do whatever it takes to hold on to the power and privilege of the past. In doing so, incumbents are constrained by repertoires—those responses that they know and that have obtained legitimacy in their world.[33]

SUMMARY

In the final analysis, while movement scholars have spent the last few decades exploring poor peoples' movements, far less is known about how those at the top experience being targeted by such movements.[34] Oppressive attitudes and behavior are intimately connected to broader cultural systems of legitimizing myths—widespread ideas that reinforce the legitimacy of inequality (Gaventa 1982, Sewell 1992). Everyday oppressors are targeted on a regular basis. Certainly, challenges to inequality—whether through broader cultural changes or specific political transformations—affect movement challengers *and* rights-violating movement targets.

While human rights violators and movement targets indeed repress and countermobilize, this is often a reactionary first-order response. In the longer term, targets must choose whether to persist, adapt, or simply quit. This process-oriented and interactive explanation sheds new light on our understanding of how some patterns of human rights violations wither and fade while others persist.

As the next three chapters show, the capacity of oppressors to resist intervention depends on their position in broader cultural, economic, and political contexts. Employers linked to thriving sectors of the economy have clear incentives to continue behavior that is working for them. After all, they have the resources and political cover to deflect challenges—most of the time. These resources may also allow them to adapt, shifting into new positions that do not carry the stigma introduced by movement efforts. Well-resourced movement targets may be contrasted with those in declining sectors of the economy. Upper-caste but rural farmers in India, for example, are decreasingly able to maintain the status quo and often lack the ability to deflect intervention attempts. This is because they are experiencing multiple, simultaneous, and costly challenges to their economic, political, or cultural power. Cultural threats come in the form of lost respect from a previously docile labor force, often as the result of a successful reframing of the status quo. Economic challenges come in the form of competition with new sites of employment. Political stagnation comes in the form of acute disillusionment with political and policy processes. Social movements often target incumbents whom the movements suspect may be vulnerable—employers in thriving or declining economic sectors of the economy differ in their capabilities to resist a worker insurgency.[35] These contexts and decisions are not isolated and discrete but instead interact with one another in complicated ways.

3

JUST LIKE FAMILY
Slaveholders on Slavery

Like a shepherd who knows his herd . . . we know the laborers.

—Aanan (Interviewee 39)

WHO WILL HELP THE LABORER?

Aadi is a self-made man.[1] He speaks of coming to Karnataka with
nothing and building himself up from scratch. I believe him because
of the way he clambers up a coconut tree to recover the fruit for
us to enjoy before our conversation begins. No multigeneration
landholder from a "respectable" caste would do such a thing. That
is, after all, what laborers are for. As he climbs I turn to his fields,
ready for planting. Mulberry bushes. Acres of them. It has taken
some time to pin him down, and here he is, in the coconut canopy,
securing refreshments for our interview. I'm relieved as he slides
down the trunk, notches the fruit, and settles into our conversation. It is near sundown, but we are finally here, drinking coconut
water and watching a summer storm overtake the sunset and rush
over his fields.

The fields are laden with plantation crops—coconut and betel—but the lion's share of the land is dedicated to the mulberry bushes that feed the voracious silkworms that have brought him such success. Silkworms mature in just over one week, and they spend the entirety of their short lives devouring mulberry leaves by the bushel. The worms—which grow from a speck the size of a hair to a taut, wiggling mass the girth of your pinkie finger—eat around the clock. Around-the-clock hunger requires around-the-clock supervision, and these are exactly the working hours of a bonded laborer. The tour of Aadi's property finishes just as the rains set in for the evening. He describes his operation:

> I have two laborers, I paid 73,000 [1,300 USD] for one family and 42,000 [770 USD] for the other one, and those are the laborers who are working for me now. One is named Kadamb, with his family, and Pruthivi is only himself. The Kadamb family has two wives and five children. The first wife's kids are married, and the second wife's kids are lazy. When it comes time to harvest the cocoons, which is easy work, [the children] will come and work. Their contract is for one year. They're working for the cocoon.
>
> The daily labor people come today, but they drink; there is no guarantee whether or not they come back tomorrow. But these people [i.e., bonded laborers], since I have already paid them, if I make one call they will come anytime. And they stay here on the property, here in a family house. Yes, yes. To keep them happy I give them mutton, and some drinks. It's a kind of attraction, when you do something nice for them they are attracted. Daily laborers come at 10am and leave at 5pm, but [bonded laborers] will stretch the time a bit to work later.
>
> If they're doing well, then I don't want them to go, so I may go to them and offer them a larger advance to stay here, and then keep them like that. Usually they need money for a daughter's wedding. . . . I feel that I have to do it, because if they don't come, then I won't even be able to speak to you now, as I'd have to go and tend to things myself.

When I ask who needs the other more, he answers:

> The same! I have these acres of land, so I need them to help do this
> work. In the same way they may have made a plan. That they need to
> go to market and get some food and these items, and they need some
> help for that, so it's kind of equal.
>
> Bonded labor isn't used much around here. I only use it because of
> this sericulture, and I need workers to be here nights. But normally
> folks don't need this kind of work. If you're paying a daily-wage per-
> son, you have to pay for beedis, and all these other things.

While saving money on local cigarettes (beedis), he admits that
having bonded laborers involves a certain amount of risk. When I
mention the threat of runaway workers, he replies:

> Something like this is happening here too! It's like, "let the [debt]
> amount go, but the person should stay, since I've had that person
> working for such a long time, and know he's a very good [worker]
> so I'll give any amount to keep him." This happened to me. . . . Even I
> faced this.
>
> When that person left I went to the panchayet [local government
> body], but I couldn't go to the police station because we're not sup-
> posed to keep people in these conditions. But later I heard more
> about the worker who ran away, and he's in even worse condition.
> His parents can't earn money. He's not earning money. So I thought,
> "what can be done now?" So I just left the money. This is the problem
> I mentioned earlier, who will help the laborer?

The laborer he was describing was Tarun,[2] whom I had interviewed a
few days prior. Tarun's story is hardly unusual—as a teenager he had
taken a loan at his brother's behest. Educated to the second standard, he was a kindly and earnest young man, clearly guided by his
older and better-educated brother. He found the debt compound-
ing and remained in this cycle for the next five years. His indebtedness came to an end only when his brother—perhaps identifying

the 20,000 rupees in rehabilitation funds from the government as an opportunity to gain another advance from his younger, pliable brother—pressured Tarun to self-identify as a victim of bonded labor. Tarun agreed, approaching one of the groups in this study at his brother's prodding.

Tarun reported to me that Aadi had kept a record of his debts in a notebook, but he was unable to recall ever seeing what was inside or indeed ever seeing the notebook itself. When I asked, he indicated that he did not feel forced to take the debt, but he made it clear that he felt unable to leave sericulture work. It required his constant attention.[3] When I asked Tarun if he would ever employ anyone under the same conditions he shook his head, explaining he could not, "because I also went through it; I also know the pain. . . . Being in a very poor family, not having enough food to eat, and no clothes to wear—and we have to go out and ask for a huge amount of money."

This chapter, and the two that follow, are the empirical heart of the book. Here we are introduced to the way slaveholders feel about slavery, setting the stage for the following chapter, which presents data on how they feel about the freedom of their bonded laborers. International law on contemporary slavery is clear that the abuse of a position of vulnerability, whether it is poverty or culturally mediated dependency, is one of several means by which individuals enter exploitation (Gallagher 2012). Sympathetic economists have also weighed in, arguing that broader cultural contexts and decisions made by elites close off access to reasonable alternatives to indebtedness and thereby negate what appears to be the voluntary entrance into unfree labor agreements (Kara 2012). The absence of any reasonable alternative combines with the abuse of a position of vulnerability, effectively guaranteeing that the bonded-labor agreement is the entry point into contemporary slavery.

Understanding vulnerability is important to explaining how laborers enter debt bondage, but it also explains the way a year-to-year contract telescopes into five. Aadi suggests that workers always have needs and that a key mechanism in securing their ongoing labor is to identify the next opportunity to loan them money.

Laborers repeatedly mentioned, as Tarun does here, the need for a lump sum of cash, often to pay the dowry and marriage costs for a sister or daughter. Landlords, like Aadi, are constantly on the lookout for vulnerabilities in potential new laborers as well as emerging vulnerabilities among existing bonded laborers.

By all accounts, such strategies are important, since some employers' ability to coerce laborers through outright violence may be on the decline. One quarry contractor explained that people in his line of work are increasingly afraid to beat workers because of the fear that workers will leave the work, debts and all. Perhaps this explains Aadi's and others' insistence that they treat workers well despite their bonded status. While it is safest to assume these claims are made for my benefit, and interviews with bonded laborers often contradict these statements, persistent concerns of labor mobility suggests there might be some truth to these claims. Sericulture is difficult to mechanize, so the cheapest possible manual labor—i.e., bonded labor—is preferred. Brick kilns may be mechanized, but only at a significant cost.

In the next chapter, I use cases like Tarun's to refute the argument that debt bondage has been replaced by year-to-year contracts that secure an advance against a year's worth of work. This approach overlooks duty and obligation and thus assumes that a year's obligation ends with the year's end. There is plenty of evidence to suggest that there is no such "reset." Rather, the lack of realistic alternatives, a lack of credit, and the need to pay for schooling and marriages effectively guarantee that there is no single contractual debt between the landlord and laborer but rather a string of connected loans. These loans have the effect of increasing economic dependency as well as increasing a sense of obligation and gratitude. The result is that a year of work, rather than being a discrete event, is better thought of as a single link in a larger chain of debt and duty that keeps laborers bound to the creditor-landlord for the foreseeable future. Attempts to understand these patterns using only resources provided by economic theories will miss the deeper relational fabric used to stitch together this socioeconomic tapestry.

This point is emphasized by the director of one of the organizations involved in this study, who explains that employers may not intentionally seek out untouchable labor; rather, "Dalits themselves will go seeking relationships under bondage when they require money. The only way to mitigate the reality of their hardship is to approach the landlord, get the money, and agree to bonded conditions." His point is that the individual level of analysis is fundamentally rooted in broader and older caste dynamics, since "for ages Dalits have been rendering free service. They see it as the only alternative to mitigate their hardship. . . . Ultimately, this is how the system is maintained, by providing cheap and unquestioned labor."[4] In other words, the economics of vulnerability are stark, but economics alone is insufficient to describe the complex interplay of debt and duty at work in the relationship between Tarun and Aadi. Ideal social relations involve a fusing of debt and duty under the aegis of caste.

IDEAL SOCIAL RELATIONS

While Aadi was more gregarious and talkative than many of my interviewees, this conversation was by no means unique. Often, interviewees wanted to talk about, and we sometimes connected over, simple things—a desire for our children to do well in school, concerns about the rising cost of everything everywhere, frustration with our own employees. Their social conditions and status varied significantly—some were rich, some were poor. Some received loans from the Grameen Bank; others were secure as village leaders, industry representatives, and white-collar professionals. Some had family in Europe and America; others asked me if I could help them to emigrate to East Africa, where I was living during the course of this fieldwork and which has a large and powerful Indian community. Some were bitter; others were resigned. Some were nostalgic for the past; others were hopeful for the future. One thing they all shared, however, was an assessment of the ideal social relations between bonded laborers and their work and between bonded laborer and their landlord. Ideal social relations are rooted in the caste system's legitimizing myths, which give rise to a culture of servitude and paternalistic expectations.

I spoke to these men at the moment their caste-based social position and control is being challenged by low-intensity social movements and by tectonic shifts in India's economic landscape. For some of them, the loss is present and palpable; for others it is a burden they have been carrying for some time. Thus, their observations are just as likely to refer to the past as they are the present. Some of their reflections contrast the present with nostalgia for the better times of their forefathers. Others remember their own relationships with their laborers *before* the bonded relationship. Across the board, however, whether respondents were speaking of the past or the present, their animating vision for (and memory of) the ideal social relation between employer and employee is that of a family.

When I asked Goral,[5] an older man whose bonded laborer no longer worked for him, whether there had been any change in relationships between bonded laborers and masters, he replied: "there is no such change. We are like family." He explained that the bonded laborer who worked for him came to them as a boy in order to repay a debt assumed by the boy's father in a nearby village. Over time, Goral obtained the debt and the boy along with it. When I asked how their relationship began, he declared:

> There was debt—that is why we kept him as a bonded laborer! After repaying the debt also he worked as a bonded laborer for a few more years. His debt was 1,000 [rupees; around 20 USD], and he worked for four or five years. He remained with me because I had a shortage of labor, and the bonded laborer had some problems at home, so I requested that he continue for a few more years, and the bonded laborer continued as a bonded laborer.

Goral was proud of the extent to which he had been able to care for this boy as he grew into a young man. The legal fact that the boy worked for almost five years to pay off a twenty-dollar debt obscures the deeper social reality, which is that Goral cared for someone who "had problems at home." This win-win was, in Goral's retelling, an ideal form of mutual aid. It is what families do for one another. It is also perhaps this family-feeling—along with the lack of awareness of other options, no doubt—that motivates a worker to stay beyond the repayment of the debt. It may instead be some sense of obligation or some unnamed coercion. Whether it is family-feeling, obligation, or a form of coercion, the effects are the same: expectations for labor extend well beyond the original agreement, both in terms of time and emotion.

For Goral, the situation was ideal: "when bonded labor was high, society was strong and good. In the olden days, everything in society was strong—people were going to work and getting their work done. But now things are weaker; even our children won't listen to us!" This present state of affairs is a far cry from the past, when ideal social relations prevailed, requiring an employer to "clothe and give respect to bonded laborers. If you treat the bonded laborer like this, it is respectful. This is according to Hinduism. And whatever work is dictated by the master, it should be done by the bonded laborer without question or delay." Reciprocity is rooted in shared moral commitments, as both do their duty to one another, according to the precepts of Hinduism.

Goral is not alone in this perspective. As another landlord[6] explained to me: "The relationship between a daily-wage person and the landlord is simple: he comes to work in the morning, and he takes his money in the evening and he goes off. But in the case of a bonded laborer, he is like a son. We take care of him like a son itself. Daily laborers call me *Farmer*, but bonded laborers call me *My Farmer*, and *My Owner*." The familial model, of course, allows for the presence of a patriarch, a role that interviewees referenced consistently. I was told that, in better times, their fathers had ruled "with fear and respect."[7] In interview after interview, these paternalistic lines were easy to trace; respect was expected in exchange for care: "We served the people. If someone was lacking something, we would give it to them. It's like that; we helped them."[8] In the retelling, the laborer was always the net beneficiary. On only the rarest of occasions would a landlord suggest that it was they who needed the laborer. Strategies for control are thus framed as acts of compassion. How else may we explain Aadi's rhetorical sympathy: *who will help the laborer?* In this light, emancipation is the worst possible threat, a precipitous ledge suspended over the unknown.

Of course, respect was owed to a "master" for a whole host of reasons: culturally, because of caste status, but also interpersonally, because of the laborer's actual role as a beneficiary of the landlord's generosity in extending credit and allowing one to survive as a bonded laborer. These relational and economic dynamics weave together to form a set of expectations about worker's attitudes and behaviors. In the past, workers were motivated by a commitment to doing a good job, rather than by money.[9] "It was all about honesty," remembers one interviewee,[10] and "the relationship between the landlord and the bonded laborer . . . was full of respect for the elders," reflects another.[11] Laborers, in this nostalgic reckoning, were hard working, grateful, and honest. They held up their end of the cosmic bargain so central to caste.

Nowhere can we more clearly see the relevance of Raka Ray and Seemin Qayum's (2009, 25) argument that the rhetoric of love "functions as a discourse that encompasses employer claims of affection and familial relationships that bind servants and employers to each other." While Ray and Qayum's work is discussed at greater length in chapter 6, they emphasize the emotional work that comes alongside the staple provisioning of laborers within the household, noting it is part of a complex social relationship. As Bales has observed: "The right of the slave to fulfill basic human needs for food, clothing, and shelter are met though their bondage" (qtd. in Ray and Qayum 2009, 33). This approach allows the slaveholder to perceive the laborer as receiving the benefit and the landlord himself as providing for a vulnerable community member. A regular feature of my interviews with current and former slaveholders has been their insistence that they had been approached by landless laborers in dire need of money or food for survival. In one landlord's narrative, the bonded-labor arrangement was not intentional, and it certainly was not coerced. Rather, "I don't know, by mistake, or however, laborers approached our family for food and things, because they were in such a helpless condition. So we gave them food, clothes, shelter, even looked after them by giving them money here and there. And it went on in this way, and we haven't harassed our laborers too much."[12] The ideal relationship is that of a family, and talking about this requires a rhetoric of love that both masks and hides exploitation in a culture of servitude in which servants are often depicted as "part of the family." What slaveholders find hard to accept is the fact that the rhetoric of love is being replaced by what could be called the rhetoric of contract.

Ideal social relations are typified by obligation, duty, and respect, whose foundation stones were laid in a far earlier era and cemented by caste. In ideal social relations, the landlord provides protection to the bonded laborer, something he does not owe to daily laborers, as they have no such relationship. The bonded laborer, in turn, provides fealty to the landlord. This arrangement works so long as there is a collective commitment to the larger social order and to the caste relations in which these interpersonal relationships are embedded. Put simply, ideal social relations involve roles and responsibilities *in relationship*. The cultural practice of caste is the overarching, if unspoken, structure that holds this cluster of relational dynamics together. These relationships forestall mobilization. But mastery does not just exist organically; it must be managed and maintained. In the case of bonded labor, a particular set of preemptive tactics and strategies are used.

CO-OPTING IS PASSIVE, ACTIVE, AND RELATIONAL

This intentionality came through in my conversations with Aanan, the employer of seventy bonded laborers, who we met in the first chapter. He provided an excellent account of the relational strategies that are used to attract and secure bonded laborers and preempt collective action:

> You have to understand the mentality of laborers, and you should know how to make them work. You have to know why the laborer won't work, is it because of money? . . . To manage a group of laborers is like managing a group of primary-school children. They have to be provided with food or clothes, and they are taught how to behave and act in that environment. We have to apply the same tactic with laborers. . . . Sometimes they start drinking alcohol; sometimes they indulge in feasts. So we have to pay them with caution. We divide them into small groups because larger numbers of workers tend to form a union and sometimes engage in mass holidays or strikes.

This explanation makes clear that a number of strategies are required if one is to obtain and retain bonded labor. While the existence of these strategies has been documented by others, much might be learned from the ways perpetrators themselves articulate this important part of their activity. Aanan has managed workers through the use of particular cultural resources and engages direct and indirect tactics as needed. Indeed, his approach is not unique.

Perpetrators prey on marginalized populations. Knowing when a laborer is particularly vulnerable to debt bondage or is susceptible to the leveraging or increasing of debts requires some sort of relationship. The perpetrators I spoke with did not simply stumble across vulnerable laborers. Rather, they often have their eye on particular workers and know when the time is right to approach them for work, knowing what the laborers need and which tactics might be most effective. This is also true for recruiters who conscript laborers into national and international trafficking systems.

Another contractor described his approach as "an investment."[13] His tactic, he explained, is to "visit the area and identify those people who need money, who are preparing for weddings, or have some kind of illness or chronic disease. So, we invest in them and give them 10,000 or 20,000 rupees, and then bring them here to work for seven or eight months to repay the money. Then we send them back." Of course, the reality for many workers is that these seven to eight months are stretched out for years, as laborers work to repay new debts incurred either in the course of work, as a result of new financial pressures, or a combination of both factors. The contractor explained this as a simple process in which the laborers also take money for food and medicine, and that if they cannot repay that amount "they will return to continue repaying it again." When I asked who tends to need his services as a lender of last resort, he replied: "Poor people with needs, who often have too many children, and don't have any land, and therefore lack any sort of food security. Those are the ones who take loans, because everyone else knows it's not good to take loans and advances!"

Another direct preemptive tactic involves the fixing of wages. One landlord explained a coordinated approach to daily laborers: "What we normally do is to speak amongst ourselves in order to decide how much we have to pay the workers or laborers. Then, we give the same payment to all of them."[14] It stands to reason that employers interested in coordinating their approach to bonded laborers might also adopt this same coordinated approach. A final direct tactic is the use of the company store. This tactic involves providing laborers with exclusive access to basic resources—food, clothes, hygienic supplies, tools, and equipment—at exorbitant prices. This approach has the effect of either siphoning cash from workers' pockets or driving workers into debt. Both tactics are designed to increase vulnerability and ensure managerial control. As one former slaveholder explained: "Contractors don't want these people to earn more. If they earn 150 rupees in one day and their expenditure is 100 rupees, then they will just make them drink, invite them to feast together on expensive food in order to ensure that the workers spend each and every penny, so they have to return and continue working for these contractors."[15]

More indirect preemptive tactics may be seen in the use of relationships and emotional vulnerability, both nested in shared perceptions of reality. Landlords are clear in their conviction that the model for ideal social relations between landlord and laborer is the family. This fact creates additional tactical resources for addressing recalcitrant workers. One landlord told me that while daily laborers come and go, relationships with bonded laborers "should be like a friendship. If you treat him in a proper way, then he will do all of the work for us, and he will treat us properly. [It's] more like family."[16] He went on to explain that "misunderstanding comes if the farmer doesn't pay the money properly, or if the worker doesn't come to work very often." Those misunderstandings are resolved, he explains, by the community: "Ten people sit together in the village and say *If you don't want to work under him, that's okay, just pay [the farmer] back the money and you all can separate.*" Freedom is readily available to those ready and able to repay their debt in a lump sum. Another landlord detailed his strategy for the same problem, explaining:

> These [bonded laborers] are hereditary . . . even if a bonded laborer is absent for two days of work, we send a middleman to the bonded laborer and ask "Okay, why are you not coming to work? What's happened? What has the landlord not taken care of?" So in this way, with small discussions between people, we sort out our problems, and then they continue their work as it is.[17]

In both cases, the recalcitrant laborer's own community is drawn into the problem-solving exercise of applying relational and reputational norms. Countless bonded laborers over the years have asked me, rhetorically, *how can I refuse to repay a debt when I know it will ruin my name in my community?* This is all the more true when the landlord's rhetorical position is to ask *what have I not taken care of?* These tactics are widespread, effective, and, as seen above, quite intentional.

Another indirect tactic involves making up for lost labor by pressuring family members to work together with, or instead of, the bonded laborer. In an interview with one lower-caste farmer,[18] he responded to my question about laborers refusing to repay their debts in the following way: "This happens to everyone, and has happened to me also. I lend to them whenever they require money. But after that, I didn't force them to repay forcefully, because I understand their situation. So whenever these things happened, I made more of their family workers work in the field, so in that way I could get back their debt." Having never been faced with an explicit boycott, this landlord in particular has found ways to continue exploiting the laborer despite the explicit challenge of laborers refusing to work. Perhaps the muted nature of his response has more to do with his lower-caste status—he is a member of the same caste as most bonded laborers in his community—or perhaps it is a frank recognition of the limited range of motion for all farmers in his position. When I asked if bonded laborers were able to seek employment elsewhere, he expressed shock, declaring, "He can't sustain himself on his own! That's why he's linking himself to someone as a bonded laborer!"

The greatest preemptive tactic, as it turns out, is to not need any tactic at all because one simply knows what they need and when to help them.[19] This relational approach—rooted in individual need and operationalized through a particular set of cultural norms—need not be intentional and might not even be recognizable. While I am not in a position to parse motives, it is fair to assume that in at least some of these cases, such tactics may be rooted in something other than a pure profit motive. What I am calling "tactics" are perhaps more authentically described as *socially acceptable commitments*. Slaveholder tactics and ideal social relations are mutually constituted in a slave society. One former slaveholder observes that his recently deceased father was obeyed because of mutual respect. Until recently, his family did not have trouble with their bonded laborers. He notes:

> Before, people used to listen to us. They would listen to us when we would pressure them. We would pressure them and they would accept it. They accepted it because it was the right thing. [My father] was respected. He respected them and they respected him. Now they

have pride and think that they are bigger than us, that *we will do all of this work. But they keep going lower.* They always thought *Pandeyji is a big person, and he is right. He does justice and he is right.* No one could speak in front of him. They feared him or respected him. . . . He did whatever he wanted to do. He scolded people, and no one could speak against him. He did good. If he could he came to a compromise. He didn't fight, he stood up![20]

When I asked what would have happened had someone refused to repay their debt to his father, the compromiser, he replied, "they would have to repay. He gave them the money, so why wouldn't they give it back? He will ask why they are doing this, and then three or four people from the laborer's community will explain the situation to him and say, *Look, don't do this. . . . What will you eat?*"

With this statement, the power dynamics that underpin the paternalistic employer's worldview are laid bare. It is survival that lies beneath the obligation. Bonded laborers must work to repay debts because it is their duty; it is also their only path to survival. Once again, we see the tangle of cultural norms as employers' tactics play out in personal relations and expectations of duty, respect, and obligation. The employer may mobilize the laborer's own community against emancipatory efforts and urges.

PATERNALISM

Conversations about ideal social relations between employers and their employees served as important opportunities to discuss bonded labor, how it differs from informal daily labor, and what sorts of attitudes and behaviors are expected from respective parties. Conversations about what makes a good employer and how employees are expected to behave indicate a rhetoric of love and pervasive paternalism that elides altogether the exploitative nature of these relations. Five years paying off a paltry debt are seen in light of the shelter they provided rather than in terms of wages denied. An ideological commitment to caste hierarchy guaranteed that, across the board, employers who currently employed bonded laborers were clear in their conviction that landlords should treat those in their care as if they were family members and that laborers should reciprocate with humble service.

Even in conversations about daily laborers, it was clear that the gold standard for landlord-laborer relations holds for laborers under either status yet may only be reliably expected from bonded laborers. The landlord agrees to take care of everything for the laborer, and the laborer agrees to do anything for the master. While the next chapter addresses landlords' responses when this bond has been broken, it is important to emphasize the deep resonance this old standard has with each of the interviewees. But it is the expectation, not the reality.

All this talk of idealized paternalistic relations only takes employers so far. Conversations about tactics demonstrate that, at some point, this passive sense of obligation must be structured and enforced more deliberately. The identification of vulnerability, the process of price fixing, the exploitation of relational dynamics, and a heavy reliance on a culturally rooted sense of paternalistic caste obligation are passive strategies that slaveholders identified in our conversations. In the final analysis, these strategies and tactics are mutually constitutive of the broader social, caste, and class relations typified by paternalism.

Perpetrators of bonded labor are not pathological rights violators. It is instead more likely they have a socially constructed preference for inequality. The sociologist Mary Jackman (1994, 8) has argued that this preference is engrained in the legitimizing myth of paternalism:

> Because individuals in the dominant group do not feel personally accountable for the expropriated benefits of their existence, there is no impetus for them to contrive knowingly to manufacture such an ideology. Instead, out of the pressures created by their collective relationship with subordinates, there evolves naturally an interpretation

of social reality that is consistent with the dominant group's experience. That ideology is a collective property. It permeates the main institutions and communications networks of organized social life and is propagated with an easy vehemence that can come only from uncontrived sincerity. The individuals who comprise the dominant group are caught in the prevailing current: without any exercise of personal guile, they learn to defend their interests with aplomb.

A paternalistic worldview serves to insulate perpetrators from the economic and ethical reality of abuse while bolstering a sense of civic and religious duty. Within India, caste serves as the overarching framework for these social relations: it provides an infrastructure, however subconscious, for the establishment and maintenance of interpersonal and intergroup inequality. There is every reason to believe paternalism or similar frameworks perform this same function in other cultural contexts. Paternalism is but one manifestation of the incumbency described in the previous chapter.

The employer-employee relationship, therefore, is not simply one of economic supply and demand but is an important and constitutive part of the moral order. For this reason, the act of challenging an employer's control is a challenge to the moral order itself. When I asked one employer, Kshantu,[21] what sort of offense bonded labor represented, he replied: "Legally it is an offense, but culturally it's not. Culturally, so many thousands of people are doing this—taking money and working one year, and when the period is over, going back. Some people are working for twenty years in the same house, in the same place. They don't ever complain." Indeed, the relationship between social norms and Indian law is dynamic. For this reason, new laws, new political will in its enforcement, or new challenges and demands from laborers are seen as cracks in the moral universe, as the erosion of ethics and morality rather than as the expansion of individual rights. I am using the term "moral universe" to imply a highly spiritually laden moral order that reflects the belief that human society exists within a larger spiritual universe, and more specifically that human relations are infused with moral imperatives.[22] Paternalism, morality, family: what does all of this have to do with social movement theory?

INTERPRETIVE PROCESSES

The paternalistic expectations these rights violators have for social relations are manifested in the rhetoric of love introduced earlier. These expectations are perhaps best explained by social movement theory's attention to the way certain social actors perceive their world, movement claims, and the relationship and resonance between the two. Social expectations rooted in duty and obligation shape the way social movement targets interpret their own rights-violating behavior as well as subsequent challenges to their authority.

By interpretation, I mean to capture two important movement concepts: *perceived grievances* and *framing*. By perceived grievances I mean a sense of being wronged, and by framing I mean an assessment of why the grievance has occurred. Grievances are rooted in a perceived reality, and frames help provide a causal explanation of this reality. I have taken the liberty of dealing with both grievances and framing under a single broader rubric because both are rooted in culturally mediated interpretation. Incumbents' interpretations of reality are filtered through cognitive barriers that often limit—through the mechanisms of ignorance, anger, or privilege—their ability to perceive the broader range of options available to them at any point in time.

Of course, attribution issues abound. The qualitative data presented here provide solid empirical support for Neil Fligstein and Doug McAdam's (2012, 107) observation that "all actors have a certain stake in social order" and that while the current status quo might not be fixed—indeed Fligstein and McAdam call them "existing settlements," implying they are not fixed into perpetuity—it is perceived to be sufficiently real as to impose a "cognitive barrier to contentious action." It is widely recognized that this cognitive barrier, false consciousness according to some, is experienced by the powerless, i.e., the prospective challengers (Gaventa 1982). Less recognized, certainly since 1968, is the fact that the same phenomena, the same cognitive barriers to adaptation and innovation, affect incumbents. Cognitive barriers—along with precedents, emotions, and norms—shape the sort of tactics available to a movement's targets. Perceptions and emotions are very real, but they often eventually face the cold reality imposed by resource scarcity—the declining value of land or caste, for example. Some targets who want to respond with repression are simply unable to do so.

The construction of interpretive frames helps individuals recognize grievances and interpret them as worthy of collective action (Snow et al. 1986). At its broadest level, framing is the process of making sense of everyday life, and thus it relies on cultural schemata, namely, the "shared meanings created through sustained interaction" (Fitzgerald 2009). Shared meanings are best found in schemas that lie at what the sociologist Hank Johnston calls the "epistemological rock bottom" of any framing activity (Johnston 1995).

Framing, therefore, is a profoundly intimate cultural practice drawing on shared systems of norms and values. When effectively deployed, interpretive frames perform a range of functions: they help diagnose the problem (workers have forsaken their most fundamental obligations), they offer a prognosis of the problem (new laws and ideas are to blame for this change), and they influence whether people will take action (here, a sense that the paternalist past can never be restored, leading to resignation) (Snow et al. 1986).

Importantly, the oppressor's worldview is self-reinforcing. Dominant institutions, cultural patterns, and practices—through laws, jokes, language, educational systems, social norms, and so forth, the stuff of life—support and naturalize status quo dominance and normalize inequality. The more oppressed people are, the easier it is for an oppressor or a class of oppressors to sustain dominance. While the conditions of inequality may be constant, interpretations of these as grievances are not. Rather, they must be socially constructed. Cognitive liberation—the proper interpretation of grievances—is a critical component of mobilization and is the primary objective of most framing efforts (McAdam [1982] 1999, Snow et al. 1986).

Cognitive liberation is a broad notion of human emancipation that is often reduced to the more empirically verifiable concept of an injustice frame by which marginalized individuals properly consider their interests. It is the injustice frame that helps establish an interpretation of grievances, creating a legible wrong in the first place. Movement claims, like human rights, are socially constructed. Interpretations of problems and solutions need not be strategic and instrumental. They may be, and often are, emotional, spiritual, and deeply personal. Injustice frames are not just movement tactics; they are a way of seeing the world that is mapped onto deeper schemata—here, caste hierarchy is the epistemological bedrock. A sense of injustice is not limited to the victims of injustice.

Cultural frames are not the only sense-making devices or triggers for increased awareness. Scholarship on events that disrupt the everyday routines of social or communal life has emphasized the extent to which suddenly imposed grievances may trigger collective action (Jasper 1997). The causal importance of disruptive events, violations of community space, challenges to routines, and the disruption of social control in explaining the emergence of nonroutine collective action has prompted some to argue that grievances deserve renewed and sustained attention (Buechler 2007, Useem 1998, McVeigh 2009). For example, this renewed attention to grievances may be seen in a fresh reconceptualization of the Montgomery bus boycott in the United States, a signature moment in the civil rights movement. New scholarship suggests the boycott was rooted in localized grievances stemming from changes in the functioning of the public bus network: humiliation and a sense of abuse generated by a surplus of inaccessible seating was a significant causal factor in the boycott (Shultziner 2013). Furthermore, it may be that many of the structural threats and opportunities identified by movement scholars over the past two decades are causally similar to the structural strains and breakdowns of an earlier generation (Buechler 2007, 61–63).

Strains and breakdowns in systems of control (as seen from the point of view of those who favor order and control) may also be interpreted as opportunities for marginalized challengers (as seen from the perspective of those who favor such change).

The application of these lessons to targets is fairly straightforward. Movement targets have worldviews and must adapt to change. The social mechanism of cultural framing and personal grievances apply equally to targets. Disruption to the quotidian lives of everyday human rights violators, of the type emphasized in this study, trigger a sense of being wronged (Snow et al. 1998). Targets' assessments, whether emotional or tactical, and whether diagnostic or action oriented, are rooted in deep, shared, and cultural understandings of how the world should be. As we will see in the next chapter, slaveholders have injustice frames and develop plans of action from existing cultural repertoires.

SUMMARY

The notion of ideal social relations is rooted in broadly held notions of duty and obligation framed by the caste system. While the caste system has been greatly challenged over the past few decades and is a large and complex system that should not be reified, it remains *the* dominant factor by which individuals are differentiated in contemporary Indian society. The caste system represents a significant and broadly distributed set of advantages available to most landlords I spoke with. While individual upper-caste interviewees complained to me about the reservation system, whereby educational opportunities and jobs are reserved for underrepresented communities, in fact caste-based discrimination is pervasive in Indian society.

Opportunities remain open for the employer so long as the laborer shares this understanding of the intertwined nature of debt and duty. Opportunities are closed to the bonded laborer for the same reason—so long as the laborer also believes the legitimizing myths and buys into the dominant frames that make subordination possible. Movement challengers undermine this consensus view through the introduction of new ideas—individual rights, fair pay, children's education, access to benefits—but also through the experience, however small, of accessing or attempting to access those rights. These new challenges and new ideas may create new social, political, and economic opportunities, as well as new cognitive and collective perspectives for oppressed laborers, while creating new threats and obstacles for movement targets.

As will be seen in the next chapter, the mobilization of oppressed laborers sheds new light on these social relations, calling into question how ideal they really were and are. Previously, it was paternalism that had justified domination and exploitation on the grounds that they benefitted the laborers. Movement efforts threaten both individual livelihood as well as the collective moral order. How seriously movement adversaries take the threat often depends on how stable they are and how secure they feel about the other forms of power supporting them. Perceived threats in the form of newly disruptive ideas, attitudes, and behavior are taken not as specific challenges to particular sets of market-mediated interpersonal relations but as a fundamental and fatal challenge to what had been the reliable and abiding foundation of a good society.

4

AS IF WE ARE EQUAL

Slaveholders on Emancipation

Now they pay us no respect; they behave as if we are equals.

—Radhesh (Interviewee 31)

Forests once covered huge swaths of Uttar Pradesh. The last few decades, however, have seen the ground cleared to make room for quarry work in support of India's booming economy, industrial growth, and infrastructural expansion. This is true in Sonbarsa, where quarry work has long been practiced. Until very recently, quarry work and stonebreaking were done by hand—notably the hands of bonded laborers. These stonebreakers have been entrenched in debt bondage for generations, forced to work on land they do not own, secured through leases they do not control, in order to break rock they cannot sell. As members of the Kol caste, they are near the bottom of India's discriminatory hierarchy.

Several years before my first visit to Sonbarsa, community organizers began working with local laborers from the village, and together they set out to secure a lease for the workers. In so doing, they defied the local elites who had always monopolized the leasing system.

The villagers' efforts to meet with community organizers in order to strategize a response to this abuse led to more maltreatment, which only deepened the villagers' resolve. As one man put it, "on the basis of what they said and what we thought among ourselves, we started walking the path" (Bales 2012, 66). To everyone's surprise the community organizers' first meeting was packed. The reaction was immediate: *goondas* came with rifles, beating those in attendance. The workers responded, throwing broken rocks—the fruit of their labor—at the attackers. A member of the slaveholding class was killed in the melee that ensued. Eight villagers were jailed for the murder. The village was ransacked, then burned to the ground. At least one child died in the conflict.

The Sonbarsa uprising is the closest thing to a contemporary slave rebellion I have encountered in my work. This case, together with the historical record, suggests contemporary rebellions are short and violent confrontations that lead to either victory or repression. In Sonbarsa, community organizing and the uprising led to a victory—that is, local contractors and farmers released their claim to the laborers. Over the years, I have spoken with survivors of this confrontation as well as the community's slaveholding caste. Gaining this access was not easy, and I spent many hours building rapport and answering questions in order to secure interviews. I filled additional hours discussing rainfall and genetically modified seed costs, relatively innocuous topics that allowed the conversation to meander to the point where landlords were willing to explain what had happened. In the end, it was clear: the brother of the deceased explained, "laborers got united and they killed a contractor, because they were saying *we will now rule ourselves and won't let the* [debt bondage] *system continue . . . we will struggle and then be free from our old debts. . . .* Contractors lost five million rupees total [about 146,000 2012 USD]; that's between two and three hundred thousand rupees each."

Over the course of my conversations with farmers and contractors in this community, it was clear that there was a nearly uniform sense of resignation in the face of a landscape changed by new government policies and laborer intransigence. Sonbarsa's path out of bonded labor might be rare, but the dominant caste's ultimate response, and causal attribution, foreshadowed assessments that I heard again and again in my conversations with movement targets. Radhesh, the head of the family of the man who had been killed, explained to me:

> In 2000 this fight came, and the laborers refused to repay their advances, 10,000, 20,000, and 50,000 each. There is a Harijan [Untouchability] Act here in Uttar Pradesh that says you cannot abuse another person. The administration is supporting the workers, who lodge false complaints that higher-caste people are abusing them, and then the police come and take them to jail. So the higher-caste people simply quit asking for the repayment of the loan. Now the laborers are breaking and selling stones on their own. . . . Earlier they respected us. Those people had no options, so we would take care of them when they got sick. They treated us like gods. But now that MNREGA came in, and other facilities from the administration, now the workers have become less and less respectful—they are more independent now. . . . The farmers got cheated. We are now stuck, being held back, while the lower class moves forward because of the many things given to them by the administration. They used to have small mud houses, but now they have concrete homes. . . . The past will never return again. Workers will never come back and work under us.

These themes—government policies, worker disrespect, and a sense of resignation—prevailed among the slaveholding caste in Sonbarsa. The Mahatma Gandhi National Rural Employment Guarantee Act (MNREGA, a national employment program) had given "too much scope" and "space" to workers, who responded with lower-quality work. Yet, as Radhesh explained, "if I go to them and point out that they are not working hard they will get upset and leave me to work for some other farmer. And when they've done this they will say that they haven't taken any advances, and they will simply refuse to repay me."

Government programs, community-organizing efforts, and the uprising provide the conceptual space—cognitive liberation— necessary for workers to imagine walking away from a debt. The insult is not only economic; it is also personal and cultural. Radhesh says, "now they pay us no respect; they behave as if we are equals. Earlier, whenever I would arrive they would all stand and say *Master, please sit here*. But now they think *It's okay that we have fewer resources, and we work on your farms, but we are all human beings and we are equal*." He recalls that his bonded laborers left him after Sonbarsa: "since then they started behaving equally. The impact was very bad, because the administration has supported them, and provided them with security. So they've started feeling proud." Faced with this scenario, Radhesh has decided to "just give up my land for sharecropping, as I have no other options."[1]

From a combination of interviews and secondary data, it is possible to piece together a picture in which concepts familiar to movement scholars—injustice frames (in the previous chapter), opportunities (in this chapter), as well as resources (in the next chapter)—might be mobilized to describe the collective action from the target's perspective. The picture I paint is surely biased in favor of disempowered elites, that is, those perpetrators who are forced or willing to quit. And the stories disempowered elites tell are subject to bias rooted in misperception, deception, or a combination of the two. There are many responses to collective action, and in starting this chapter with a rebellion I hope to demonstrate that violent repression is real.

PERCEIVED GRIEVANCES AND INJUSTICE FRAMES

The slaveholding class in the previous chapter described the ideal social relations that are the benchmark against which subsequent social relations are judged. In every conversation with employers, bonded laborers were weighed on the scale and found wanting. Employers consistently reported being frustrated with worsening attitudes and declining behavior. These concerns are both sacred and profane. Employers are concerned with both the levels of commitment to a day's work (quantitatively) but also with the levels of commitment to the landlord's work as one's own (qualitatively). Declining levels of respect were interpreted not only as obstacles to getting work done but as loose strands in the fabric of society, early indicators of a form of equality that was considered to be both inopportune as well as immoral.

This sense of loss pervaded landlords' accounts of the ways landlord-laborer relations had changed in recent times:

> To be born in the higher caste has become a bane. Even when we do well, we are blamed and our rights are withheld. And the lower-caste people rise in their lives, even when they have no merits. The politicians are using this as a tool to remain in power. We are a minority, and they are a majority. Even when they are wrong, they have their way because they are in [the] majority. We are being ignored. It's a tactic to turn the landlords into workers. . . . The workers who bowed in front of us earlier now expect the same from us. Even when they do so now, they don't like it in their hearts.
>
> I will give you an example. A person worked for me for forty years and he was never denied anything. He was happy with me. We had a very warm relationship. He died here [in my house]. He had no children. He was a brother to me. We loved each other's family. He didn't leave my place for forty years. He didn't work anywhere but at my place.

The loss feels relational, not economic.[2] The sense of betrayal was palpable, as this man strained to understand and explain such disloyalty, especially as he remembered these forty years of service. The dominant metaphor of the family—*he was a brother to me*—produces a scenario in which violations of behavioral expectations—by forming a union, for example—are interpreted as unfaithfulness rather than as strategic alignments based on economic self-interest or self-preservation. This is echoed by another employer, who remembers:

In the olden days, they used to accept [payment] in kind, grains and all. But nowadays, they are not accepting grains; they are only demanding money! . . . In those days, people used to work with such commitment. They would even work beyond their time. Maybe they should work from ten until five, sometimes they would work until six or even seven. But now people aren't like that. If five is their time to go, they start looking at their watches. . . . In those days, it wasn't like that, not because they didn't have watches, but because they had in their hearts the commitment that if they work hard, and if their master really gets a good amount of grain, and that really helps their master, then even the laborer would benefit. . . . In the old days bonded laborers used to work as if it was their own work. By four-thirty in the morning they would already be up, cleaning everything. But nowadays they come by six in the morning, saying to their master, no, it's not time to start yet.[3]

The idea that in the past workers would perform their duties *as if it were their own work* came up repeatedly. Another employer complained that laborers

never feel *This work is ours, and we should do it . . . we should work hard, this is our own work, we are not working for the landlord, it is our work*, they will not think like this. They think that they need money, and that is all. In the old times they would work truly, they would think *this is our work*—they had that fixed in their minds. . . . The old mindset was one of honesty. Now it is one of laziness.[4]

For employers, then, the benchmark is not a certain amount of work but a certain relational disposition to the work. The phrases *this is our work, as if it was their own work*, and *they had in their hearts the commitment* point to the disappearance of the bonded laborer into the work of the master. It is not just a matter of a day's work well done but of a social posture vis-à-vis the landlord—"work from the heart for your real master, for god," as the biblical author Paul has it.[5] It may be tempting for an outsider to read these concerns as analogous to a simple decline in work ethic, the kind perhaps perceived by employers worldwide over the past few decades. Yet, the subtext here is of an ideal social relation that is embedded in the social norm of caste-based obligation, rather than an ideal economic relationship rooted in a particular economic outcome of profitability.

This may be seen in the same farmer's concern not for his own profitability, or for his own well-being, but in his professed concern for the laborer: "They cannot protect themselves on their own! When they are working, if someone beats [the laborer], it is as if we ourselves are being beaten. So they cannot protect themselves. We have to protect them." The abiding sense of paternalism within the caste mentality allows a bonded laborer's emancipation to be seen as a risk to the laborers themselves. And so we see the perceived double cost of emancipation: it threatens workers even as it erodes society.

Many landlords fondly remembered the care and support provided to bonded laborers: "they used to stay here, even their children and wives . . . even food, clothes, and everything."[6] This care and respect was part of the larger framework of social relations provided by caste. The erosion of laborers' dedication is thus a small betrayal, a failure to reciprocate or to recognize the landlord and his many perceived sacrifices. In those days, another landlord remembers:

> They were more respectful. They had some sort of respect, and fear, and they used to stay away from us as a form of respect. But now we have become equals, as if we are the same. . . . This is a bad thing for society, if money is with us, they respect us, but if money is not there, then they don't respect us. In the olden days, they used to respect according to the caste, but now, they respect according to money.[7]

This statement, and the oblique reference to untouchability—*they used to stay away from us*—underscore the salience of caste boundaries independent of wealth. Differences between people used to be clear, and respect was given in accordance with hierarchy rather than capital.

This is clearly contrasted with an undesirable present—*this is bad for society*—in which respect only follows money. It is important to emphasize the sort of respect that has been lost—it is not the pleasantries of day-to-day life that have been dropped; it is instead a social fear and distance that comes with untouchability (Davenport and Trivedi 2013). Dalit workers are compelled to maintain a certain social and spatial distance from upper-caste community members, whether or not they are employers or wealthy. What has been lost is not just respect between people but the bonded laborer's respect for the system as it has stood for generations.

Caste frequently serves as a backdrop for these conversations about the ideal past and the dissolute present. The requirements of caste ensured stability and a sense of unity, at least in the mind of the upper caste. "Earlier, the limits were fixed for every caste," another employer told me:

> They had certain places they could sit, and if everyone is sitting, certain castes would sit here and others would sit there. It's no longer practiced now that people have started having the feeling of caste differentiation. . . . It's not only because of caste, but it's because some people get more money and increase their position, then they start wondering, *why can't I do things like that big person?* So it creates distances within the community, and it makes groups of some people.[8]

For this respondent at least, earlier times were preferred for their order, stability, and a lack of greed and groupism. Society had a certain solidarity that encompassed the entire community; it is only with the self-assertion of the lower castes, and especially bonded laborers, that "casteism" and caste consciousness emerges. It is only with Dalit identity, therefore, that Brahmin identity is created—or so it is in the nostalgic memories of upper-caste landlords.

The old status quo is not only challenged but is being slowly replaced by a new status arrangement in which bonded laborers are independent social actors. For many farmers, especially, the laborer's lack of internal commitment to their duty is evidenced by the fact that they must now be monitored. Previously, this was not necessary, as a laborer's moral compass was, presumably, properly attuned to the master's needs. Earlier work was "done on trust, even if the contractor wasn't there, they would work. But now if the contractor goes away, they will stop working, and just sit and talk."[9] *Talk* is not in reference to pure laziness but may be read in light of the same landlord's concern that "every home has a leader now." The moral order has fragmented and narrowed to the point where it is not a caste or even a household that serves as the point of authority. It is instead a leader in every home, where individuals prioritize talk over duty—*earlier, the work was on trust*, he told me. The enforcement of old norms through appeals to ideal social relations is no longer possible. But the impact of idle talk is not limited to worker productivity; it also contains the threat of politics. A previously powerful employer,[10] bemoaning his community's decline, expressed that

> in the olden days, soon after taking part in small jobs and all that, laborers used to work in their fields, they used to think of their work. But nowadays, it is not happening. They come out, after taking a bath or freshening up, they come to a particular center, have coffee or tea, and somewhere here or there they sit and talk about unnecessary things that are not relevant to them and their field. . . . A kind of enmity, ego, and hatred has developed today. . . . Whenever a farmer doesn't have enough work, then they are deviating their minds to sit and talk about these things. But when they possess enough work in their fields, then this isn't a problem. . . . People never used to gather for unnecessary talk and all. They used to go early in the morning to their fields for their work, and stay until ten in the evening. They used to work so hard.

This statement is made about workers more generally, but the threat can presumably come from any free laborers, including former bonded laborers—the threat of a world unstructured by caste. The threat comes from conversations about unnecessary things that are not related to their work. It is unnecessary talk—democratic discourse, no doubt—that deviates the mind and creates enmity, ego, and hatred. The leisure afforded by advancement beyond sheer survival is interpreted as laziness, and past desperation is mistaken for commitment. In this light, open space for open conversations only invites trouble.

The German sociologist Jürgen Habermas (1991) famously argued that it was the open square and the public sphere that gave democracy its vitality. People gathered to meet, discuss, plan, and persuade. Critics have suggested the square was not as open as Habermas imagined, and this is exactly what the current study emphasizes: the powerful wonder how the powerless could have so much time to sit around the public square to talk about useless and potentially dangerous things. Presumably, there are many good reasons for laborers to sit around and drink chai together, passing the time. The problem is not that they are talking in public but instead that they have decided to associate in *any* form. The problem is that the appearance of leisure undermines the imperative of the performance of labor.

Leisure activities—talking, idling, drinking—appear as vices, tangible manifestations of social decline. Elites are not only concerned with bonded laborers leaving their financial and social obligations but are very aware of their lower-caste laborers entering into new social roles and civic spaces. Presumably there is an analogy here regarding race and space in the United States. The wealthy have significantly more private venues for pursuing leisure and consuming drugs and alcohol. There are fewer venues available for those without the money necessary to access private spaces, so leisure time and consumption are performed in public spaces. This identical behavior in the "wrong" space is then treated as a criminal activity.[11]

Landlords holding bonded laborers, whether in the past or present, are unanimous in expressing concern that the attitudes and behavior of their laborers have declined precipitously. Workers, they agreed, demanded more money, did less work, were less respectful, cared less for maintaining their traditional role and status, and were less appreciative and solicitous to their current and former masters. This drama was often explained—sometimes implicitly and sometimes explicitly—in terms of caste norms. Caste provides the raw material with which notions of ideal social relations are constructed, and a caste mentality is steeped in a paternalism that sees laborer challenges against injustice as attacks on cultural and moral norms. But why exactly were these things happening?

LABORER EMPOWERMENT AS INJUSTICE

The answer lies in new interpretations of the bonded-labor relationship—what movement scholars would consider to be the social construction of an injustice frame. As indicated in the previous chapter, an injustice frame is a "mode of interpretation that defines the actions of an authority system as unjust and simultaneously legitimates noncompliance" (Snow et al. 1986, 466). What emerges is an explanation that extends a step beyond general grievances and toward a particular causal attribution, as slaveholders try to sort out what is happening and how they feel about it and also try to understand *why* these things are happening and what may be done about it.

Landlords explained that workers had become "aware" and had subsequently refused to repay their debts.[12] The process of challenging indebtedness in a bonded-labor situation is, unsurprisingly, seen as a rupture in the ideal social relationship. In a fairly typical account, one landlord told me that laborers had changed: "Previously the workers would do whatever we told them to do, but nowadays, even if we tell the laborers to do something, they say they will only do it if we give them more money."[13] He explained why this was:

> The government is giving special priority to SCST people [Scheduled Castes and Scheduled Tribes, or lower-caste communities]. For small things farmers will scold SCST people, and then those workers will

go directly to the police station and lodge a complaint against the farmer. There are a few farmers, and even here I keep a few people on a yearly basis. I paid them 30,000 [rupees] every year and would keep them. But after only two or three months they never repaid me, they only lodged a complaint, saying that I had scolded [verbally abused] them, and that they had refused to repay me. This happened several times around here where the laborers are drunkards. That's why farmers take loans! Farmers lose their money because of the laborers and then go to the government to take a loan.

For this respondent, insubordination is rooted in a combination of laborer weakness and government policies. Laborers are greedy for both money (*only if we give them more money*) and alcohol (*this happens where the laborers are drunkards*). The first problem is the laborer's weakness, and the second issue is the government's prioritization of the needs of lower-caste people. These two themes—labor decline and the preferentialism of government policies—surfaced repeatedly. Seventy-seven percent of respondents attributed their labor problems to the laborers themselves, such as demands for wages and/or increased wages, increased awareness and education, and a decreased work ethic. Nearly as many—72 percent—said their problems were related to government policies and practices, including job programs, food-aid programs, police corruption, and favoritism toward the lower castes.

These two sets of challenges—from laborers and the government—are causally related in the minds of the study's respondents. In instance after instance, landlords, especially in the agricultural sector, made clear that at some level the government and its policies were responsible for the problems they experienced with laborers. These grievances are composed of three interconnected issues: (1) the passage or enforcement of pro-poor policies, (2) a decline in responsiveness from political parties and the police, and (3) broader issues related to education and migration. Taken together, these are interpreted as a threat to landlords, particularly those in the agricultural sector (Harriss, Jeyaranjan, and Nagaraj 2010).

DECLINING OPPORTUNITIES, INCREASING THREATS

The passage of new and enforcement of old pro-poor policies concerned landlords more than almost anything. These policies represent the most visible manifestation of their diminished status. Broad changes in public policies are interlaced with the perception that economic and cultural opportunities are disappearing as well. These programs work together in such a way that undermined farmers in particular. The first of these programs involves the sale of subsidized food in local shops through what is known as the Below Poverty Line Program (BPL). A central component of India's food policy involves providing low-cost staples to the country's poor, and these shops are a critical component of that policy. The program, which is more than half a century old, is plagued by corruption, which blocks funds from flowing to the laborers it is intended to benefit. Upper-caste community members are likely to control the establishments that sell subsidized food and are also likely to be related to those employing bonded laborers. Localized pressure from social movement groups has challenged these corrupt practices. In some cases, this pressure results in the transfer of the business to more ethical owners who are willing to provide food to laborers.

Social movement efforts to secure the actual implementation of the policy's benefits have the practical effect of freeing workers from having to *do anything* for food. Bonded laborers, employers, and scholars agree on the factors that push the poor into debt bondage, and this list almost always includes an inability to feed one's family. In-kind compensation in the form of grains is also critical in cases where an advance is needed subsidize a marriage or a sickness. A lump sum will be provided, but no subsequent money will be paid, only an allotment of grain as compensation for the laborer's total productive capacity. This has the effect of sustaining the laborer's family and increasing a sense of duty, obligation, and appreciation for the landlord. Therefore, the flow of subsidized grain from properly functioning BPL shops into a community undermines the landlord's role as the sole provider of the sustenance necessary for survival and reduces the laborer's dependency on the money-lending and labor-extracting landowner.

The second policy, and arguably the most critical, is MNREGA (the Mahatma Gandhi National Rural Employment Guarantee Act), passed in 2005. This nationwide program is designed to guarantee a minimum number of workdays and a guaranteed wage to those willing to do manual labor. The benefits are not insignificant. MNREGA should provide one hundred days of work per year for any individual who requests it. Compensation rates vary by state but tend to hover at between 120 to 140 rupees (two to three U.S. dollars) per day. The effects of this program are threefold. First, it creates employment competition with slaveholders. Second, it creates a nationwide expectation that a certain amount of money represents fair compensation for a day's work. India has a minimum-wage law on the books, but it is rarely requested, paid, or enforced. Third, the program's high profile ensures that it is relatively well known to laborers and employers alike. The program works alongside the provision of staple foods, so desperate laborers are no longer forced to turn to local elites for survival when an alternative employer has emerged to provide a fixed and public wage. Though the employment program is plagued with corruption, the mere possibility of a fixed daily wage has served as an important fulcrum for laborers as they challenge debt bondage. Historically, employers relied on laborers' need for grain and a lack of reasonable alternatives in order to secure unpaid labor. These policies have the combined effect of raising costs and effectively constricting employers' range of motion. In prior times, abusive landlords controlled both the rock and the hard place. Successful implementation of these programs erodes such mechanisms of social dominance.[14]

The third policy—the Scheduled Caste and Scheduled Tribe [Prevention of Atrocities] Act (SCST Act)—was passed in 1989 in order to abolish untouchability in all its forms, thereby facilitating the social inclusion of Dalits who have historically worked as manual scavengers, waste collectors, and bonded laborers. Corruption, a lack of political will, widespread denial about the nature and scope of the problem, and the centrality of caste to individual and group identity are all central to the SCST Act's ineffectiveness. These obstacles to implementation, however, may be overridden by motivated advocates or empowered laborers. Employers are understandably concerned by any effort to use the SCST Act to draw attention to the caste dynamics at play in bonded labor. As one group of farmers complained to me,[15] as if passage of MNREGA wasn't enough:

> Another law has been enacted. You can't coerce them! You can't say too much to them. If you do, the SCST Act will be charged against you. They are taking advantage of us. This is a political issue. [As for the police,] they understand, but they don't do anything; they have restrictions. . . . This is all about casteism. Laborers will never be found guilty, the fault will always be held against you. They are stealing, but they won't be accused of stealing; they will accuse you. . . . And there is one thing more: They receive compensation in the name of oppression. . . . They are paid in this way. . . . You are wealthy, you are eating and drinking. So when they trap you in the SCST Act you will also have to give them something.

As a result:

> If there is a need, sometimes they take a loan. But we don't get it back. Don't expect it. If you expect it and ask for it back, then you will be charged with the SCST Act. . . . If you go to the police, the police will say to us, "Did you ask me before giving the money to him?" That's the first question! Or, "Are you a moneylender? Do you have a license?" They will turn it back on you! That's why if the laborers refuse to repay, we don't go to them. If it's gone, it's gone. There is no hope.

The SCST Act, like the BPL program and MNREGA, is riddled with corruption and undermined by a lack of both political will and public support. If anything, caste-based discrimination and violence has increased, with little hope for large-scale transformations in public opinion nationally (Chidambaram 2010, Rai 2012). Yet the most significant issue is not whether these programs are properly implemented but instead whether they have created an opening, or latent opportunity, for laborers—indeed, the development scholars Anuradha Joshi and Mick Moore (2000) have similarly focused on the way that antipoverty programs may have an indirect effect through the creation of an enabling institutional environment for collective action.

The idea of, and access to, alternatives has created problems for employers who had relied on the fact that laborers lacked options or even the idea that other options existed. Now, one landlord in a focus group explained to me, "they are very lazy. Before, there weren't all of these government schemes. So, they worked harder to feed their families." Another landlord explained that MNREGA has affected workers such that "we are willing to pay the laborers whatever they want, but they don't work the way they used to. They have become lazy, and the quality of their work has gone down."[16] He recalled when "around four or six years ago some of my employees asked for money instead of rice." He explained that a government shop in the area had started providing staple BPL foodstuffs to his workers. No longer obligated to work for him for sustenance, they now demanded money.

And workers didn't place individual demands; they instead "used to have their meetings, and they demanded an increase in the wages. They threatened to stall the work for the whole area unless their demands were met. . . . They are getting educated. There is a growing awareness among them. They are becoming smart; they are not foolish anymore." The root of the problem is a combination of grassroots mobilization (movement-organized laborer's meetings and threats to strike) and public policy (MNREGA wages and grain disbursement in BPL shops). These two factors are self-reinforcing, as mobilization leads to greater awareness of existing benefits and attempts to gain these benefits leads to greater awareness of corruption, which itself encourages additional collective action.[17]

The importance of something as simple as grain is underscored by another interviewee, who emphasized that, in the olden days, people had to work to survive.[18] He clarified:

> Now they don't need to work to live, because the government is extending help in terms of providing rice, through fair-priced shops. . . . If the government hadn't done all of these things, the people would still be listening to us today. . . . When people used to listen to us, life was good. We were running our lives very well. But now, since they're not listening to us, even we hesitate to call them for work, and they hesitate to come to us for work. That's why things are going this way.

Fair-priced shops may be contrasted with the company-store model, designed both to make a profit and undermine laborers' financial independence.

The role of food in moderating desperation and reducing respect is detailed by another employer: "Earlier, they were paid with five kilos of grain, which is not much for the whole family to feed on. They thought it was too little, that it was insufficient, so they thought if they respect their masters they would get more grain. But now that the wages are fixed . . . they are automatically getting more, so it doesn't matter if they treat the masters with respect."[19] Another explained, "some workers get their food from the government shops. In the government shops, they get the food at a lower price. So that's why they say *I don't want to take your rice [as payment]*, *I would like to take the money*."[20] For these employers, access to government programs makes laborers more demanding and in the process spoils rather than frees. Many insisted that newfound wages are spent on drugs, alcohol, and beedis—local smokes—rather than on food. Past payments in rice guaranteed that employers knew what laborers procured and what they would do with it—and they could control its flow when necessary. These programs are not specifically intended for bonded laborers, but for social movement organizations policies such as MNREGA, the SCST Act, and the BPL program are the fulcra they use to pry power away from exploitative local employers (Gupta 2010). Laborers are now accessing these things on their own, without asking or begging, without genuflection or shame. They no longer need to accept the landlord's underwriting of weddings. This is seen as an affront, not an advancement.

INCREASING THREATS: POLITICS AND POLICE

Public policies are not the only problem employers face. In earlier times, they had, by their own accounts, relied on two relatively stable sources of support: political parties and local police. Yet, in conversation after conversation, interviewees expressed deep frustration and a sense of betrayal at the decline in responsiveness from these erstwhile allies.

Farmers had previously enjoyed considerable support from the party system, though a turn to identity-based party mobilization over the past two decades has undermined this arrangement. The rise of Hindu nationalism (*Hindutva*, championed by the Bharatiya Janata Party [BJP]) and the politicization of lower- and middle-caste identities[21] were central to this process. These organic-seeming sets of affiliations proved to be more powerful and compelling than were identities based on geography (the rural village) or occupation (farming and agriculture). Previously salient rural identities were undermined by these new configurations. Balamuralidhar Posani (2009) argues:

> The shared occupational identity as farmers might have brought rural India together in collective action for economic demands, but given India's heterogeneity, farmers have multiple social identities involving caste, religion, and region. . . . Occupational interests may well be overshadowed by considerations like caste, region or religion.

Over the course of a series of elections in the mid- and late 1990s, political entrepreneurs and identity-based parties splintered the

Indian party system. Congress' share of seats in the lower house, the Lok Sabha, decreased precipitously, and the sheer number of parties increased dramatically (Chhibber 2001). It is here that we begin to see the BJP's rise as a national force in favor of *Hindutva*—Hindu fundamentalism and cultural nationalism—and later, with the rise of the Bahujan Samaj Party (BSP), the election of Mayawati as chief minister of Uttar Pradesh, India's most populated state. Mayawati was the first member of the "untouchable" Dalit community to rise to chief minister, and the fact that she reached this post before she was forty, and did so representing a party that was only formed in the 1980s, is testimony to the rapid transformation of a previously stable political landscape.

Farmers and pro-farmer advocates were unable to mount a sufficient push for agriculturally supported parties, as more cultural and less occupational identities simply had more traction. Farmer's movements were weak because they tend to not represent the full range of concerns from members across the caste spectrum. For example, they promoted issues such as lower input costs and higher sales prices for their goods while overlooking others, including the enforcement of minimum-wage laws (Posani 2009, Varshney 1995). The removal of the left-leaning BSP from power in Uttar Pradesh, over the course of my fieldwork, was met with reserved optimism by the farmers I spoke with. They often did not seem so sure they trusted the newly installed Samajwadi Party (SP), which had held power prior to the BSP and had a reputation for more Machiavellian political techniques. Better the devil they know, it seems.

Motivation and enthusiasm for all political parties—whether Congress, BJP, BSP, or SP—have faded, as promises to represent voters like these farmers have been replaced by the reality of pro-poor policies at a national level by the Congress Party or backpedaling by the SP. Under Mayawati's thirteen-year tenure as chief minister, local and regional police faced increased pressure to follow through on caste-based rights violations, and local governing officials faced greater pressure to implement programs like MNREGA.

When respondents spoke of their community's Dalit population, their near-universal concern was that "the government is granting them a lot of favors. They are getting the good roads now. We are paying tax for the land. We pay for filling the land. We have to pay to plow the field. What can we save after paying all this? The [government's] attitude is partial toward them. There is partiality from the administration of the [Dalit] chief minister."[22] Government plans to reduce inequality were considered to be doing the opposite. Rather than empowering marginalized and untouchable laborers, government aid is considered by farmers to be a fundamentally unfair redistribution of wealth and resources from landholders to the landless.

This redistribution appeared to employers to be taking place at the same time as laborers had learned to take advantage of the system for their own gain: "The government gives grain to workers for nearly free. Just sitting around working in MNREGA for a day is 120 rupees. So they can get thirty-five kilos of grain for just sitting around." Furthermore, "their children study in government school. They get scholarships, studying for free. . . . They themselves are not handicapped at all, but they are getting a handicap pension. They are not elderly, but they are getting an old-age pension."[23] A farmer who had lost his laborers in the Sonbarsa insurrection was clear about this link when he described how MNREGA led to demands for more compensation and put workers in a "position to negotiate, otherwise they say *We won't come, go and do the work yourself!*"[24]

Employers are frustrated by national politics but also find challenges closer to home, as police, once a stable ally of upper-caste landholders, come under increased scrutiny. From the employers' perspective, political transitions, especially the election of the BSP in Uttar Pradesh, undermined the police's willingness to pursue justice in an unbiased manner. Police, in this account, had dealt honestly with conflicts between laborers and employers: "Earlier, there was no pressure from the administration on the police department, so they would honestly go around and ask everyone, and then find a fair compromise. But now they say they are forced to work like this, or else they will lose their jobs."[25]

Another employer describes how this connects to bonded labor: "Even if we give an advance, even a small one, like 500 [rupees], and we ask for help for two or three days, after a few days they get angry. If we scold them harshly, they will take us to the police station, saying, *he's scolded me in the name of caste, with bad words* and so forth. So, what we're doing is not giving large amounts, we only give small amounts." The backdrop for all of this, the same respondent explained, is the fact that government, "any government, whether it's Congress or another, provides the most benefits to the SCST community—houses, latrines, rooms, everything—and provides to them alone, and nothing to us."[26]

This combination of forces has the effect of increasing bonded laborers' avenues of recourse should something go wrong while also undermining laborers' vulnerability to indebtedness in the first place. As a result, they are far less likely to become indebted to local landlords and are perceived to have more ready access to legal solutions. Employers and landlords feel that laborer wage expectations are up, employer competition is up, and thus the price of labor is up, from nothing to something. For agricultural slaveholders, all of this is happening when the party system has stopped listening to them. No wonder they feel frustrated and threatened.

INCREASING THREATS: CITIES AND SCHOOLS

Name-brand government policies were not the only cause of labor problems. Economic development and urbanization were also blamed for the decline in laborers' attitudes and behaviors. To many landlords, education and awareness go hand in hand:

> The education is fast and the mode of information is fast; everything is fast. There's a reason why the generation has come ahead, and even the laborers: if I go to the laborers, laborers have a cell phone! And if I scold the laborer, he will make a call! So, he's that intelligent. He knows from television and other things what he has to do if something goes wrong.[27]

This is in stark contrast to the past: "In those days, there was no education, and now people are getting educated, and going to nearby cities. There are also government schemes. People are not respecting their elders because of these things."[28]

The effect of education is pronounced, though most farmers readily admit that education for laborers is a mixed bag. There is a general sense that, as one farmer told me, "education is a good thing, but those who become educated don't want to do agricultural work."[29] Farmers are not only losing agricultural workers to education; they are also losing bonded laborers to growing political awareness. Across these responses, it is clear that education is not thought of as formal schooling alone but is also related to political awareness and conscientization: "Pressuring them to complete their tasks won't work. They are aware."[30]

If education is awareness and not just schooling, then awareness comes not only from formal education but also from exposure to cities and new technologies. Cities change laborers' expectations—"people are going to the city. Now people don't want to work in agricultural land. They want to go sit in buildings and are getting more money there."[31] Perhaps rural employers would overlook this fact so long as laborers migrated to cities permanently.[32]

But those who move freely between India's rapidly expanding urban frontier and the country's withering countryside bring with them new technologies, new ideas, and new demands. Exposure to cities creates "bad attitudes and jealousy" because "when they come back, their attitudes change. It's normally seen to be this way. People always change. They go to the city, and come back changed. . . . Ninety percent of the people who go to the city come back with an attitude like *I'm from the city*."[33] Education and cities have also combined with new forms of communication technology in ways favorable to laborers and unfavorable to employers. From the fear that "scolded laborers" will "make a call on cell phones," it is reasonable to assume this same concern is braided in with awareness and cities.[34] In a focus-group discussion with a group of thirty workers who had recently escaped from a brick kiln, workers described their mounting concern when they discovered the body of a murdered worker in the ash of the previous season's kiln works. When I asked how they contacted the social movement group to initiate an intervention, the group's ad hoc leader pulled a battered Nokia from the folds of his traditional dhoti wrap. "I'd hidden this on the kiln site as soon as I realized something was wrong," he explained. Mobile phones and education, new and old policies, and indifferent politicians represent the most salient issues landlords perceive. In the words of one frank farmer: "If the government hadn't done all of this, the people would still be listening to us today."[35]

DIMINISHED RESOURCES

The removal of political and policy support and the increase in laborer demands come at the same time as interviewees at work in the agricultural sector face a number of broader economic threats. Socialist economic policies prevailed in India until 1991, when heavy borrowing and market fluctuations led to a balance-of-payments crisis. In that year, the fiscal deficit reached 9 percent, with farm subsidies contributing significantly to the crisis (Bhalla 2005, cited in Posani 2009, 35). The crisis was resolved through an International Monetary Fund and World Bank–brokered bailout, the World Bank's biggest at the time (World Bank 1991, 1). The required structural-adjustment program devalued the rupee, raised interest rates, cut subsidies and support to publicly held businesses, and liberalized India's trade policy (World Bank n.d.). The larger effect was India's transition from import substitution, in which the state supported local production of industrial goods and subsidized agriculture, to an export-oriented approach in which the state leverages its comparative advantage on the global market.

Farmers were especially affected, as the adjustment program cut subsidies they had relied on. Seventy percent of Indians live in rural areas, with the majority of India's labor force working in agriculture. With urbanization projected to grow at 3 percent annually, rural agriculture is likely to remain a critical social and economic sphere for the foreseeable future (Central Intelligence Agency 2013). Subsidy cuts, the rising price of raw materials—especially seeds, pesticides, and fertilizer—and the cost of fuel were all concerns expressed with consistency by employers involved in agriculture. While interviewees working in extractive industries were concerned about government programs and labor relations, they had benefited from strong and consistent growth in India's commercial sectors, as market liberalization spurred rapid growth in the service and industrial sectors—both of which increased demand for raw materials of the sort produced in kilns and quarries.

Farmers, however, faced increased input costs at the same time as they experienced a major slowdown in economic growth. The World Bank reports that crop yields in India lag significantly behind countries like China, Vietnam, and Indonesia, and the current slowdown in agricultural growth is linked to a lack of research and development, stagnant technology, overregulation, a lack of credit for the rural poor, poor infrastructure, and corruption (Posani 2009, Radhakrishna 2008, Subramaniam and Subramaniam 2009). The slowdown had the effect of reducing real incomes, as the cost of consumer goods outstrips the market price for agricultural products (Mishra 2007).

This situation represents a significant reversal of fortunes for the agricultural sector, which had enjoyed significant subsidies and institutional support from the state during the Green Revolution. The removal of subsidies and support after liberalization exposed previously lucrative cash-crop production to the vagaries of the market and increased "intellectual rents" for genetically modified high-yield seeds (Venu Menon 2006, Government of India 2006). The central government's support for farmers also declined after liberalization, and usurious middlemen willing to provide seeds at exorbitant rates of interest, with production put up as collateral and payment, filled this vacuum (Christian Aid 2005, Government of India 2007). In sum, the Green Revolution supported subsidies and closed markets that had the effect of encouraging cash-crop production. Market liberalization led to a reduction of subsidies and market restrictions, increasing price volatility and decreasing institutional and financial support. The loans required to smooth bumps in the market came at a significant cost, as the state ceded the lending environment to private, and often duplicitous, actors. These trends are reflected in conversations with both advocacy groups and farmers alike. The founder of one organization explained to me that while their focus is on bonded laborers working in agriculture, the reality is that

> the landlords, the farmers, have also been exploited! They are also an exploited group. Even before globalization, even after independence, in the modern economy, which is factory and industry centered. . . . The government invested heavily in the public sector: basic iron production, then big dams. And who benefitted? The industrialists! . . . Therefore, right from our Independence our economic policies have been favoring the industrialists, and the banking service sector. Not agriculture. The only exception was the Green Revolution, [which prioritized] production, fertilizer, and hybrids. That was promoting the capitalist farmer and not, by and large, the marginal and small farmers who should have been promoted.[36]

Radhesh, who lost a family member in the Sonbarsa uprising, suggests, "farmers are having more problems because not every farmer is so well off that he can afford mechanized equipment. Smaller farmers are suffering, and getting by as best they can. Big farmers have harvests from harrows and other equipment, but the smaller farmers are losing out," presumably because of their total reliance on manual labor. Other interviewees echo this sober assessment of the reality faced by small and medium-sized farmers. Questions about the future were often met with shrugs or silence. Many expressed a frustration similar to that of one farmer, who answered with a simple rhetorical question: "How can we dream?"[37] Another suggested he had a hard time conceptualizing reincarnation: "I don't know what's going on in this life—how can I say what will go on in the next?"[38] One landlord in the midst of a challenge from a movement group described:

There are no facilities; we have to pay double price for [fertilizer]. Even people who come for daily wages, we have to pay double for those people as well. And after the harvest, when we sell our produce, we don't get the proper value from the government either. We are in a very bad situation, where we are having to take loans, and are not even able to pay them off. There are lots of people around here in the same situation who could not cope with it, and committed suicide by eating poison. . . . Not only here, all the farmers are suffering. And on top of that, the rain is not coming, and we have to go get the seeds in order to grow cotton. And for this we again have to pay double! So this is the farmer's condition.[39]

Farmers perceive their current circumstances and future options in stark terms, with a growing body of literature focused on the solid and sustained uptick in farmer suicides in the past two decades. K. Nagaraj estimated that there were 166,304 suicides between 1997 and 2006, and subsequent analysis suggests this trend continued in an upward fashion thereafter (Nagaraj 2008, Sainath 2010). There is little doubt that these conditions threaten all but the largest agricultural operations, those who increasingly rely on machines rather than manual labor. While the service and industrial sectors experience explosive growth in India's new urban economies, conditions in villages and other rural environs have stagnated or declined, leading some to declare that the Indian village "is no longer a site where futures can be planned" (Gupta 2005, 752). New urban opportunities represent a draw to landless rural laborers who leave, thereby further restricting the labor market and placing an additional set of economic burdens on the farmer. Economic hardship is compounded as policies like MNREGA drive wages up. Changes in the broader cultural context, both as a result of direct movement activity as well as movements' indirect effects, have the effect of decreasing laborers' levels of commitment to caste-based deference.

In this way, exploitative employers in the agricultural and farming class are finding that the predominantly cultural form of power they had previously enjoyed now lacks political efficacy and currency, in that it is no longer useful outside of its intended context (Jodhka 2012). Caste's value in the village has also gone down, so to speak, as it is forced to compete with outside factors: a tighter labor market, more educational opportunities, increased physical mobility, pervasive technology and better information, and new employment opportunities in local programs and in distant cities (Harriss, Jeyaranjan, and Nagaraj 2010, 59). Thus, while the "catalytic significance of land" might have been visible in the India of 1969, it is no longer as evident, particularly because it is a type of power that cannot be easily transferred into another form—one cannot translate caste status alone into economic opportunities in the credit- and cash-based market economy (Aggarwal 2012, 126).

At least one farmer—Kshantu, whom we met in the preceding chapter and will meet again—recognizes this, as he explained that while his farm is not making money, he is holding out to sell his land to a developer. Money from Bangalore has extended further and further into Karnataka's interior, as the IT nouveau riche seek out the nostalgic village of yore. Once again, we find a nostalgia for another world, but, this time, held by globally connected urbanites working in India's Silicon Valley and desperate for a piece of "the real India." Yet it is very few who may launder power or trade in their old form of power for a new form. Most current and former slaveholders engaged in agriculture find themselves with diminished resources, no allies, and a set of difficult decisions.

ATTRIBUTIONS OF THREATS AND OPPORTUNITIES

Here again we can turn to social movement theory to help us make sense of the declining opportunities and increasing threats faced by most interviewees. A general sensitivity to the broader cultural, economic, and political context, especially during times of change, suggests that threats and opportunities play a significant role in shaping the way targets experience mobilization. Political-process theorists argued that movements take place in a larger firmament and thus directed scholarly attention to the importance of broader contexts as facilitating or inhibiting mobilization (Tilly 1978). While I emphasize threat here, the following chapter highlights the importance of opportunities in shaping target responses. What's more, the majority of the threats that incumbents reported did not come from the movement but were instead independent aspects of broad change processes. Movements are important, but they do not act alone.

This intellectual arc has been traced in past explanations of movement actions and outcomes. Targets appear as static fixtures in the structural firmament. This need not be the case. From this data, we may begin to sketch some early and reasonable assumptions about how these same factors affect targets. Targets usually have more opportunities and fewer threats. They are incumbents, after all. Whether a movement wants to strike a strong actor (producing a deterrence effect) or a weak one (producing an early victory) is a matter of tactical concern and considerable variation. Furthermore, ally splits and elite challenges create opportunities and crises for movements while likely generating threats for targets. Seasons of instability and crisis provide the chance to form new alliances, as the literatures on democratic transitions and social movements make abundantly clear (Linz and Stepan 1996, 165). In changing conditions, Fligstein and McAdam (2012, 105) argue that incumbents are inclined to "respond to any perceived threat conservatively, fighting tenaciously to preserve the settlement that is the political and cultural source of their advantage." They are likely to do so "even when it is apparent to most observers that the system is doomed." Such is the power of perception, whose fruits we will explore in the next chapter.

SUMMARY

For the social movement groups in this study, local emancipation processes are tied to perceptions of broader processes. For this reason movements choose tactics that create new institutions, like MNREGA, and then create struggles for access to those same institutions. This is no accident but is instead linked to a broader concern with the quality of democracy in India. As the founder of a partner organization explained:

> If our local governance units are not truly representative, if our democratic organizations are not functioning in a democratic manner, if marginalized communities continue to be excluded, it harms the growth of our democracy. And so that's why [we are] interested to bring all the marginalized communities into the mainstream development process. That's why [we are] interested to raise voice against the malfunctioning of the democratic institutions.

Of course, there is often a significant gap between this movement strategy and the adversary's experience. Movement efforts are seen as one of many threats, and their effects are often conflated with other phenomena. All of this turmoil and transformation requires some action—farmers especially have to do something, as the status quo is untenable. In this chapter, I have argued that slaveholders are experiencing the direct and indirect effects of movement efforts, but they are also experiencing a larger set of economic, political, and cultural processes that shape their assessments of their problems as well as their range of motion in response.

It is important to emphasize that this situation is not static. Mayawati, the Dalit chief minister of Uttar Pradesh, lost an election in the course of this fieldwork. The SP, which replaced her, is known to support the violent repression of Dalit claims. Some time later, the right-wing BJP decimated Congress in national elections. This same party then went on to rout all other parties to secure the prime ministership. The potential effects of these transitions was not lost on landlords. Before the election, they asked laborers *How much longer do you think Mayawati will rule?* Once the SP won the election, they taunted, *Who will protect you now?* These early and anecdotal observations serve as a reminder that movement gains having nothing to do with broader changes in social norms and public opinion may be reversed quite rapidly, and with little warning, so long as incumbents have sufficient resources.

Current and former oppressors find themselves in the midst of radically new circumstances. An earlier consensus had formed around the notion that bonded labor was in the best interest of the laborer. This arrangement is called into question when social-movement activity—new opportunities to take advantage of new resources that help frame certain activities as unjust—concatenates with broader political and economic shifts. Where elites had sourced their legitimacy in age-old notions of caste hierarchy, and this understanding had apparently received broad support, they must now contend with new interpretations of this relationship and with diminished resources to enforce this interpretation. Thus equipped, they must find some way to respond, as seen in the next chapter.

5

THE FARMER IN THE MIDDLE

Target Response to Threats

The laborers are below. The capitalists are above. The farmer is in the middle.

—Farmers Focus Group (Focus Group Discussion 45)

LEAVING FOR TOWN

I met Paratapa on his sprawling estate late in the evening.[1] It was everything I could do to arrange a meeting with him, as he balanced the management of his land holdings with a career in the city. When the topic of his laborers came up, he spoke in the past tense, as if a burden had been lifted: "In those days, we used to keep bonded laborers, and even if they required many things from my house, I would lend to them. . . . My costs have gone down because they have left our household." It was clear that he considered his own social position to be the reason these laborers turned to him. And who was he to reject community members who came with their problems? The burden of bonded laborers rested on his shoulders, in his mind at least, and these relationships were costly, both financially and legally:

> In those days, people used to stay here as family members. Even in our absence, they used to work, and they never used to feel apart from the house. But nowadays, there is no sort of relationship. They come as a daily wage, they go in the evening, and there is no sort of relationship. In my father and grandfather's time, there used to be ten bonded laborers here, but for the moment, no. They used to stay here itself, even their children and their wives and all. Even food, clothes, and everything, their expenditures and health and everything. Even marriages, we used to spend everything for the laborers. Nowadays, the relationship has changed. Now the cases are being filed, even against me. Two people filed a case against me. . . . People have filed old cases, from twenty years ago, but recent cases have also been filed. . . . In my situation in particular, they filed a case, but nothing drastic has resulted because I explained that it was because of their vulnerability they came to me, approaching me for something, and I accepted. I have not forced them to be my bonded laborers. So, everything went smoothly, and nothing more has happened to me.

Like other interviewees, Paratapa shifts back and forth easily between an earlier generation and the present. This slippage reflects a broader tendency to ascribe the worst violations of laborers' dignity to earlier generations while framing contemporary bonded labor as the costly but ethical response to the pleading of indigent community members.

He is also powerful enough to talk about his own case without fear of jeopardizing himself further. When insurgent bonded laborers—and doubtless a number of other factors—made agriculture too difficult, he responded by taking a position as the president of a cooperative agricultural bank. His confidence rests on the political and social influence that comes from such a presidency.[2] But it also rests on a conviction that the courts will recognize his benevolence, since "some of them refused to lodge a case against their master because they were treated well." The fact that his violation of the

Bonded Labor Act landed him in court is a minor detail; caring for the workers matters most. What bothers him more than the case, he says, is the lost family-feeling:

> We have a [sad] feeling about losing these workers. When they were here with us they had status as a family member, and we ourselves got a good profit and would share some of that with the laborers. . . . In those days, social bonds were strong, but now relationships are unstable. We cannot even lend money to these people anymore because there are these groups coming up, especially for the scheduled tribes and scheduled castes. Landlords are afraid of these groups because these people might go and complain.

His musings echo the sentiments found in the preceding chapters— paternalistic concern for laborers and a sense that emancipation erodes social bonds—but he continues with an explanation of what this means for employers, farmers especially, in this situation:

> Landlords themselves feel like quitting farming because of all these problems—power, labor, water—for all of these reasons, the landlords feel farming is a burden. . . . Sometimes I think I'll just leave agriculture for town. Even if we offer sharecropping, the workers are not ready to take up the work because there is no guarantee they will earn any money. . . . We're predicting conditions that will exist in the future, like a shortage of labor and all, and we're thinking it's better to go for plantation crops in the future, as they require less labor.

A puzzle lies at the heart of this chapter: if almost all perpetrators had similar expectations for ideal social relations, and if almost all felt similar pressures from their laborers, then differing responses may be rooted in something other than the social movement intervention, per se. Thus far, I have developed the argument that the range and mode of target responses are rooted in a particular political, economic, and cultural context, specifically in their expectations for ideal social relations, interpretation of events as unjust,

THE FARMER IN THE MIDDLE   95

and radical fluctuations in resources, threats, and opportunities. Here, we arrive at the book's second and third key contributions. These factors shape target responses in ways that trace political-process theory, as seen in the second chapter. In sum, these factors shape the way they desire to respond, the way targets think they can respond, and the way they are able to respond. Sometimes desire, intention, and ability align. Sometimes they do not.

The reality of interpretive processes is that repression and countermobilization may initially be adopted by a wider range of actors than can actually afford to keep them. Incumbency produces rather rigid expectations for reality, and when reality changes, something has to give. A longstanding and inflated assessment of one's cultural opportunities (such as confidence in paternalism) or sudden shocks (like a collective rebellion or an interpersonal confrontation) may trigger passionate, emotional, and even violent responses. Landlords may think repression is preferable to compromise. But if a landlord's power has diminished, this tactic may fail, and he may be forced to mount a subsequent response drawn from a shorter list of more realistic possibilities, such as adaptation or quitting. Presumably, the perpetrator eventually lands on the response he is able to afford, based on the resources and options available to him—as well as his willingness, I hasten to add. Poor farmers armed only with caste status quickly find they have fewer choices than they had previously imagined, as the gap between reality and perception closes.

Clearly, Paratapa feels in control of his life: confident that the courts will understand his benevolence, secure in his high status and his well-compensated position as a bank president, and able to decamp to the city at his leisure. In our conversation, he sketches the range of options facing farmers. Those without resources may sharecrop, though they will find it tough going. Those with resources may turn to politics or plantations, though these require social and economic capital. Choosing among these options is no small matter. Where caste was once an overriding determinant of one's prestige and possible success, the institution is now facing an onslaught from more urban and economically oriented sources of power and prestige. How well-positioned employers are to navigate this transition has a good deal to do with how well they manage social movement challenges and the perceived erosion of the moral order described thus far.

TARGET RESPONSES

Qualitative data suggest preemptive tactics are used to prevent insurrection (as seen in chapter 3). Maintaining power usually involves targeting the weak, dividing laborers into different groups, cycling pay, limiting repayment rates, requiring family labor as collateral, using emotional force and false sympathy, and sharing these strategies among themselves. A broader range of responses is needed if a full-scale insurrection emerges. These responses, I argue, are best thought of as occurring in two phases. In an initial round of contestation, incumbents will choose tactics that they believe will help them win. For powerful incumbents, this is likely to include attempts to countermobilize against or co-opt and repress the movement. In a second phase, targets will have collected valuable data about their own strength as well as that of the movement.

While perceptions of ideal social relations and the attendant collapse of the moral order are broadly distributed among upper-caste landholders, their reactions to these challenges are not. As Paratapa's case indicates, a range of short- and long-term responses exist, though these options are not uniformly available to employers. In deciding how to respond, targets draw from a familiar repertoire of strategic action as well as their own capacity and desire (Swidler 1986, McAdam 1996). For contemporary perpetrators, this repertoire of strategic action varies based on one's resources and opportunities. Targets may choose to continue, or they may decide to quit, depending on how existential of a threat they feel the movement represents. Target responses are constrained by their abilities,[3] and these abilities are both real and imagined. The strong do what they will, in a manner of speaking, along these major routes.[4]

REPRESSION

Yet the strong do not always get what they want. Or, rather, those who think they are strong may not actually be so. Perception matters—many individuals interviewed for this study thought they were strong. But cultural, political, and economic resources are needed to persist, repress, or countermobilize successfully. Those with other opportunities (or a change of heart) may opt out early, but persistence requires the right resources. Having the right resources is a function of how profitable a given sector is and how much money and power the individual has to persist—themselves functions of their broader power and position. Attempts do not appear to correlate with these broader factors, since perception of opportunities or threats matters more than their reality when it comes to a movement adversary's *initial* response (Goldstone and Tilly 2001, Kurzman 1996). I came across many instances in which incumbents mistook threats for opportunities. While landlords' caste authority had previously combined with a lack of laborer options in such a way that ensured a steady and dependable labor supply, the previous chapter suggests this authority is under considerable strain. A mentality of caste entitlement may persist, nevertheless.

Kshantu, an employer who earlier explained that bonded labor is a legal rather than a cultural offense, learned of this distinction the hard way.[5] After spending nearly a decade working in Kuwait, he returned to Karnataka to try his hand at farming. Along the way, he took a bonded laborer. When the worker rebelled, ran away without repaying his debt, and collaborated with an advocacy group to secure a release certificate from the government, Kshantu responded in kind by countersuing to reclaim the debt. He told me that he had looked everywhere but had been unable to locate the laborer.

While the case will probably remain in court for the foreseeable future, Kshantu's response is unique in its explicit deliberation. It is also notable for its hubris—he lodged a lawsuit to reclaim something established law clearly states was never his in the first place.

The Bonded Labor Act of 1976 explicitly forbids the kind of relationship Kshantu had with his charge. A small Brahmin landholder, Kshantu's efforts have come to naught. It may be that he could find the laborer if he had additional time or money to pursue the case further, but in our conversation, he expressed concern over paying the lease on his new tractor, shifting his children to a new school, getting the right price for his turmeric crop, and transitioning to organic farming. He was indignant that laborers no longer expressed thankfulness and embodied obligation. Kuwait, it seems, was free of such problems. "I want to sell and go back," he confided in me, "because I've lost confidence in this place."

In the short term, however, his efforts to threaten his former bonded laborer, Tanmay,[6] have continued apace. "Whenever I see him," Tanmay says, "he tells everyone within earshot, *I will go to court and I will teach him a lesson, and someday I will call people and break his legs*." Kshantu does not know that I have spoken with Tanmay, and so he tells me that he cannot find the boy—perhaps he is unwilling to admit the extent to which he has lost control of the situation. He is fundamentally unable to recognize and admit the failure of the traditional ideas and relationships.

In Tanmay's assessment, his former master's belligerence is rooted in the fact that, after so many years abroad, he returned and "didn't know anything . . . he cheated everyone and he could not afford to find people [because] nobody is going to work with him now. . . . I don't know what his mentality was like twenty years ago, but I feel like it was from the old tradition." The old tradition included maintaining caste boundaries that ensured caste cleanliness through untouchability, authority through the dispensation of commands, and status boundaries through an aloof approach to workers. Kshantu may not have the resources to succeed, but he certainly had enough of a moral shock, and sufficient righteous indignation, to fuel threats and a lawsuit for the foreseeable future.

In the next section, we will hear from farmers who have resigned themselves to these new realities, and in the longer term, Kshantu's frustration may lead him to give in, "sell this land, and go back to my work." In the meantime, however futile it may be, he is doing what he can to resist the bonded laborer's challenge. He is an excellent example of a perpetrator who would like to hold on to the older cultural practices but is unable to do so under new conditions. His appeals to paternalism sound hollow: they echo in a new social, political, and economic reality that he is ill-prepared to confront. In many instances, I heard accounts—most often from laborers or movement workers—of attempts to countermobilize, repress, and persist. All but a few of these attempts failed when a social movement group was able to leverage broader structural changes against employers.

Repression is used in an attempt to halt the exodus of workers. Here we must rely on the testimony of survivors, as I did not find a single employer willing to speak freely about the force, threats, and violence that are used to coerce laborers.[7] Repression comes in many forms, the most direct of which are death threats from employers or their emissaries. Workers may be threatened with being pushed off the landlord's land, or worse. When a group of kiln workers insisted that they had long since repaid their debt, the workers recall a representative of the kiln owner saying, "I will throw you into the kiln and kill you if you will not work for us."[8] Such threats are not uncommon in extractive industries, where higher levels of profitability increase the likelihood that local operations have strong support from powerful political and economic actors.

Perpetrators' other economic activities were a consistent theme in the focus-group discussions I had with rescued laborers. In addition to owning sites that practiced bonded labor, they were also involved in agriculture, owned transportation companies, managed retail shops, and worked as attorneys. These resources underpinned their ability to secure the compliance of police, though the police have turned out to be a fickle ally, as their allegiances are coopted by the demands of the local administrative officials in case of a raid, frequently initiated at the behest of a movement group.[9] Connections with the police, real or perceived, allow perpetrators to increase the salience of their threats. Eighteen survivors of twenty years of intergenerational bonded labor found the police to be little more than an extension of the kiln owner's security force:

> Whenever we made a plan to go to the police station, someone definitely knew where we were going. . . . Sometimes someone waits at the police station, and they call the policemen, [asking] "why are workers going to the police station?" [and] "Your father already took an advance, so go and work for them, what can we say?" They [the kiln owners] definitely have very good relations with the police. Some of the women in our group went together to the police station to talk to someone. Then they beat us because they think we are trying to oppose the kiln owner.[10]

Threats serve as an ideal form of repression, especially when they seem credible based on past behavior. The survivors speaking above were the children of three brothers who had been bonded by the current kiln owner's father. The fact that the kiln owner's managers had beaten one of these brothers to death lent credibility to verbal threats. In another case, an interviewee was threatened prior to the raid—"If you do not work for us, then I will kill you. Otherwise, I will throw you in a kiln" and "As a Musahar [untouchable caste] you want to become a *goonda* [thug]? If you want to become a *goonda*, then I will break your hand and leg and throw you in the kilns"—and also after the raid had been completed, when the kiln owner would widely proclaim, "Whenever I see him I will beat him!"[11] The force of such threats is raised if laborers have found evidence of past abuse.

Threats are frequently followed by action. In another case where I also interviewed members of the former slaveholding class, the founder of another group of escapees recalls that after laborers refused to let their children weave carpets to repay the family's debt, the moneylender came and "found the children who were not working, and there someone was boiling the water, just beside their huts, so he took the water and threw it onto the children. [They were burned] on the hands and legs."[12]

In another less violent incident referred to in the previous chapter, local elites responded to efforts to secure higher wages by destroying a local access road. The movement group worked to connect at-risk children with local schooling, only to discover that landlords had destroyed the road to the school as punishment for these mobilization efforts. "At the time," the same director explained,

> [workers] didn't realize that this is a human rights violation, that this is our right to get a road and nobody can harm us, even though they are upper caste or moneylenders and landlords. They took the initiative, went to the district magistrate, went to the assistant district magistrate, they started a case in the court, and, after twelve years, they got the road again.[13]

This approach started with an education campaign but ended in a victorious court case against elites' efforts to block their access to a public school. From the movement target's perspective, laborers' efforts to access the school were successfully blocked a decade prior, but the social movement group turned this old defeat for the community into a new focal point for a fresh round of mobilization.

COUNTERMOBILIZATION AND CO-OPTATION

Efforts at countermobilization may be seen in the case of the Sonbarsa rebellion discussed in the previous chapter. Interviews with laborers over the past four years have taken place at the edge of the community, in an unincorporated no-man's-land. The laborers' homes were destroyed at the time of the uprising and had not been reclaimed or rebuilt at the time of this writing. Countermobilization tactics have also been used in attempts to disintegrate self-help and savings groups supported by social movement efforts. In one instance, a self-help group was significantly weakened and nearly destroyed after quarry contractors sponsored two different group members to compete for the position of village leader (*pradhan*).

This had the effect of splitting the group. Elsewhere, a group of survivors obtained a lease for their own quarry work but were thwarted when an upper-caste employer from another village used the name of a Dalit worker of his own to obtain an overlapping claim to the land. This succeeded in creating a division within the Dalit community and blocking them from their own land. By all accounts, similar low-level repressive tactics are widely used.

While more comprehensive and representative data would be needed to make the case, qualitative data suggest that perpetrators in extractive industries are more likely to resort to heavy-handed threats and to back these threats with action. Why might this be the case? Potential answers lie in a combination of resources and opportunities—stronger connections with police, politicians, and other income sources—as well as particular individual motivations and attitudes that I cannot discern. The opportunity cost to replace workers with a machine is prohibitive. One kiln owner told me that he could replace his hundreds of workers with a single machine. But the machine costs nearly 9,000,000 rupees (200,000 USD), an amount neither he nor any but the most powerful can afford. Likewise, quarry work can be mechanized, but none of the contractors I spoke with had resources that could match the large crushing operation that operated nearby. So, along the path between exclusive reliance on bonded labor and full mechanization lies a maze of compromises arrived at based on the landlord's cultural and economic resources and commitments to the ideas underpinning bonded labor.

The stories of survivors of slavery are replete with instances of both repression and countermobilization at the moment when it became clear a community was on the verge of securing additional benefits that would undermine existing power dynamics. Rights-violating interviewees are understandably reluctant to discuss these issues. As a result, we are often left to fend with data from survivors and movement groups. What their experience demonstrates unequivocally is that when targeted, perpetrators long accustomed to power and control are likely to take action in order to protect their investment, their dignity, or both. Yet, are perpetrators armed only with culturally rooted forms of power, like caste, able to succeed in this effort, despite threats to their way of life and declines in resources? This section suggests an answer in the negative—initial outrage may trigger older, habituated responses, but these are not sustainable without control over key resources, especially from politicians, police, or profit.

RESIGNATION AND QUITTING

When faced with a social movement intervention, many respondents in this study resigned themselves to the situation and quit altogether. There is a near-consensus among laborers and landlords that after an intervention, less than 10 percent of employers in the region persist with the practice, though it is not clear if this estimate is correct. Those who quit the practice in the face of social-movement organizing do so for a number of reasons: as a tactic, because of a change of heart, or because they were simply unable to persist. The term "resignation" is meant to suggest both action and emotion—a cessation of activity, a decrease in willpower, or both.

Quitting in the face of movement mobilization and other obstacles appears to be a strategy for some perpetrators. This is my assessment of Paratapa's situation. He may have exaggerated his relief at no longer having to care for bonded laborers, but his assessment of being taken to court and losing his workers was situated within a larger set of considerations that included his career as a bank president and his ability to shift easily to nearby Bangalore. He had other opportunities. The same may be said for Tanish, a budding industrialist who voluntarily released two bonded laborers from his brick kiln, blamed their condition on a subordinate, and used this experience to demonstrate his commitment to the goals of a kiln owner–NGO collaboration formed to draft employment policies for the brick-kiln industry.[14] There is no way to divine his motives, but Tanish's strategy had the effect of putting him on the right side of history, so to speak.

For some, it may also be a sense that an era has passed, and as movement efforts draw attention to standing laws, some find they are not willing to continue behavior that now has a certain social and legal stigma, if only in their community. Perhaps a few have had an honest change of heart, as with Gurumanji, a former farmer and contractor who quit his businesses in order to follow his god and a preferred guru. Over shared betel nut, he explained his pursuit of truth: "There is nothing left for me to do as a businessman. I have done theft and looting; I have done everything. But I realized that when you are young you can do everything, but when it is the time of dying, then you remember god, and then god will ask, *You didn't remember me when you were doing those things, so why should I listen to you now?* So I left all of that."[15] Here too it is difficult to discern motive, but it seems plausible that as human rights interventions reframe bonded labor as a criminal practice rather than as an acceptable cultural norm, this fact may precipitate a break between those willing to continue despite the new stigma and those unwilling to do so for personal reasons. Whether this is the case deserves further attention.[16]

For the majority of interviewees, however, desperation—the recognition that they lacked the political opportunities and economic resources sufficient to bolster their cultural strength in the face of a movement challenge—explains why they had quit, or were in the process of quitting, their involvement in the bonded-labor system that had sustained their families for generations. It is here that the theme of ennui and world-weariness reemerges, after making brief appearances in the previous chapter. In Sonbarsa, because the original efforts to launch a countermobilization failed to suppress the laborer insurgency, farmers have resigned themselves to doing the work themselves. The head of the family of the murdered contactor explained that that the laborers are now afraid of his family and that, although the insurgency affected everyone in the community, it was farmers who got cheated and are being held back. This is of serious concern to him because the past "will never return again. Workers will never come back and work under us."[17] With these options closed, he confides that he is tired of farming and asks me how he can emigrate to Tanzania, where he knew I lived at the time. Resignation takes many forms. For some, it means doing the work oneself or giving up on farming altogether. It may involve settling lawsuits rather than engaging in extended courtroom struggles over bonded labor.[18] For others, the decline in status is too severe, so leaving the community may be a last chance to salvage one's dignity.[19] "Somehow," another landlord told me, "we just have to sustain."[20] Resignation often requires patching things up with laborers informally or in settling court cases with a more formal compromise.[21] It may also involve overlooking subsequent issues, since it could prove difficult to get a loan back if a worker refuses to repay or work it off. Rather, "we have to think first" and hire daily laborers, not bonded laborers, because "if you get bonded laborers, and they leave and don't repay the money, then nothing can be done. It's our mistake only."[22]

This realization is particularly salient for those lacking capital. Most smaller farmers do not secure bonded labor with cash that they have on hand. Rather, they will take a loan from other landowners,[23] "from a bank, or pawn gold and jewelry, or pawn their land papers."[24] For smaller farmers, the loss of a bonded laborer may mean bankruptcy. When I asked one farmer whether the bonded-labor arrangement would stop if the cost gets too high, he replied, "it's already happening! We wonder why we should take such a great risk, and give them the money, and then lose it. It's been the last two years. [Bonded labor] might even go away altogether; now farmers are thinking, *It's okay that workers aren't here, we will work in our farms ourselves.* It's happening in the whole state."[25]

While we have already seen how workers' attitudes and behaviors are in decline, those laborers who have some land of their own are thought to be even more derelict. While a worker may come to work on the farmer's land, they produce less, as they are also "saving their energies to work on their own lands." This is contrasted with the landless, who are more likely to "work properly." The net effect, for this farmer at least, is that "it's no use fighting them, all

I can do is watch. . . . If I pressure them, then they won't work for me. They will leave me. I am helpless. . . . Where will I go if I force them? Who will do my work? I cannot manage my land alone."[26]

Some former employers, especially in the agricultural sector, simply become resigned to conducting the work on their own. Others do not feel they can manage. Some say they are too old to farm; others confide that it is only the old and those without other employment options who are still farming.[27] Those determined to continue their work with day laborers find that they are competing with factories and other city jobs where there are higher wages and arguably better working conditions. Those who want to maintain the family business may find that the next generation is simply not interested. In the final analysis, many decide simply to give the land for sharecropping.[28]

Many of the farmers I spoke with have resigned themselves to their situation, lacking the resources, the wherewithal, or the desire to persist in this form of exploitation. This is not only a practical and economic decision. Resignation is also an emotional state that came through in our conversations. It often took the form of nostalgia for the past and a lack of enthusiasm for the future. This sense appears pervasive among landlords involved in agriculture. Often, they have nothing else, or they are going to take advantage of what little they do have, such as a relative in the city or a plot of land to sell. Their predicament obscures their motives. Perhaps they would prefer to maintain the old style of socioeconomic relationships and in so doing restore the moral order. One can only surmise.

We can state with confidence, however, that interventions affect the strong and the weak differently. I did not speak to a single powerful landlord whom I would consider resigned to their condition. They had doubled down on the bonded-labor relationship through repression and had found new ways to extract resources from laborers through adaptation. Subsequent mistreatment takes many forms. Exploitation identical to, or adapted from, bonded labor permeated my interviews with both bonded laborers and landlords. Sufficient resources allowed the powerful to persist or pivot, as they chose. The once powerful had far fewer options available to them.

This broader context is indicated by a partner group's leader, who explained that the real issue facing rural employers was the gap between urban and rural regions and between technology-rich and technology-poor sectors: "So it's not that there is a huge gap between landowners [and laborers]. The gap is between urban and rural."[29] In other words, the gap is between growing and shrinking sectors of the economy. This came through in countless interviews with targeted incumbents—larger and more powerful employers are able to innovate while smaller landlords, often farmers, are left behind. This fact is underscored by the rash of suicides among farmers over the past decade (Patel et al. 2012, Kennedy and King n.d., Mishra 2006).

PERSISTENCE AND ADAPTATION

Persistence is the continuation, in identical or nearly identical form, of the originally targeted behavior. We tend to know less than we should about movements that fail, and as a result, we know little about the persistence of targeted behavior. This gap exists in the literature on contemporary slavery as well. There do not appear to be reliable statistics on what percentage of movement targets are able to persist after being targeted for trafficking or bonded labor. The leader of an antitrafficking initiative suggests that in 20 percent of their cases, a movement target will persist in their efforts to exert control over bonded laborers.[30] Perpetrators with strong and stable cultural, economic, and political positions are able to choose whether to persist in exploitation by virtue of their financial resources, caste and social position, and political context.

Lest my argument be mistaken for a tautology—that weak targets cannot keep bonded laborers, where weakness is defined as an inability to keep one's bonded laborers—a counterexample is worth examining. When human rights advocates[31] helped Tarun[32] escape from the sericulture operation where he was bonded, the landlord—Aadi,[33] whom we first met in chapter 3—replaced him with two additional bonded laborers, who continued the work along with their wives and children. When I interviewed Aadi later in the year, he reported matter-of-factly on this continued use of bonded labor: "I only use it because of this sericulture, and I need workers to be here nights." Bonded laborers do not leave at the end of the day but instead "stretch the time a bit to work later." As indicated earlier, Tarun had come back to work, this time as a daily laborer doing the same work as he had before. Aadi struck me as less interested in holding on to the older cultural practices than in protecting an economically fruitful enterprise. It may be worthwhile to explore briefly why his experience lies outside the model presented here.

Why has Aadi not quit despite being targeted? As a relative newcomer to the state, he does not hail from an extended and embedded family in the region. As a member of an Other Backward Caste group, he is "middle caste" but by no means of sufficient status simply to power his way forward on caste alone. Likewise, he has a small truck and a bore well, making him generally independent of others for raw inputs, transportation, and the like. Part of his land is dedicated to plantation crops, and combined with his well, this presents a component of his enterprise that could be expanded and adapted to replace the sericulture production. In sum, he has adequate resources to transition to a new form of production but does not appear to have so many resources that he can behave with ambivalence in the face of a movement challenge. Nothing in my many hours of conversation with him suggested that he held on to bonded labor for any reason other than profit and convenience. The fact that Tarun returned to his plantation as a daily laborer is perhaps testimony to that fact.

There are several reasons why Aadi may have persisted despite these countervailing factors. The first is the possibility that sericulture is simply too profitable a cash crop to give up and is therefore worth risking an escalated response from human rights advocacy groups. The second, and more probable, reason is the fact that Tarun continues to work for Aadi in an effort to repay an additional 2,000-rupee loan. While receiving support from a human rights group and working on the meager plot of land he now shares with his brothers, Tarun now lives in freedom with far less certainty than he had in bondage. Emancipation has meant economic uncertainty where previously there had been the repetitious ritual of duty. Considering the options available to him, it may be the case that actually losing Tarun, losing a second round of laborers, or being targeted by a more invasive movement strategy would push Aadi to shift from sericulture to plantation crops. This outcome depends entirely on the movement's ability to respond to this new situation with a strategy that recognizes these factors, including the postintervention challenges faced by the former bonded laborer. This cannot be overemphasized.

Background interviews with other movement groups working on this issue suggest that profitability provides the resources necessary to persist. In one instance, a perpetrator's operation was raided and the perpetrator held before being released on bail. As that first case moved forward in the courts, it came to light that he had retrafficked laborers into the same operation. He was rearrested, and the second wave of laborers was released. Upon posting bond, he returned to his operations to retraffic a third wave of laborers. This story suggests anecdotal support for the argument that perpetrators will go to great lengths to protect highly profitable enterprises and also that highly profitable enterprises (and the political and economic clout that comes with them) provide perpetrators the means to continue their work despite the involvement of the police, courts, and human rights groups.[34]

Two techniques are used in the process of persistence in the cases under consideration here. The first is a shift away from formal paperwork. The second is a shift to a year-to-year contract system. Bonded laborers themselves consistently reported to me that there is no longer any need for their debt obligations and the terms of their labor to be captured in written form, since now everything is "done by trust." Trust is a euphemism for the fact that unscrupulous employers have eliminated hard evidence of the debt and its repayment history. It is unclear whether this is in response to increased concerns of being caught or in response to better-educated and more inquisitive laborers. I suspect it is the former. Though laborers insisted there was a log of their debts and repayments, many had never seen the putative book. Even if they had seen the book, not a single respondent had seen its contents.

The second technique to obscure the nature of the bonded-labor situation, despite its persistence, is the year-to-year contract system. This system appears to address laborers' need for cash and lack of credit by providing lump-sum payments in exchange for a single year of the laborer's total productive capacity. Yet, under these conditions, the laborer incurs running debts that ensure that at the end of the year they cannot leave unless they repay the new debt amount or find someone willing to pay the debt on their behalf. In the case of Karan, a middle-aged bonded laborer, his current employer paid his previous debt and in this way secured Karan's labor for the foreseeable future.[35] By his own account, Karan had been working as a bonded laborer for twenty-five years, ten years of which have been year-to-year contracts strung together in an otherwise unbroken decade of debt bondage.

There is a tendency in some academic circles to mistake these multiple consecutive year-long contracts as individual agreements that reset at the end of every year. The lack of realistic alternatives, demands for education and marriage fees, a lack of credit, and the duplicitous tactics adopted by employers guarantee that the annual advance is not the only economic interaction between the landlord and laborer. Rather, a host of new needs and old debts conspire to increase, rather than decrease, the laborer's economic exposure and obligation to the landlord. A year of work, in reality, is not a discrete event but rather one link in a larger chain that keeps laborers bound to the landlord-creditor until that point when—barring some unforeseen event—the debt is purchased by another, as happened when Karan came to work in his current condition.

Persistence is fundamentally attributable to profitability. A number of sectors kilns, quarries, and large scale agriculture are connected to an urban and globalizing economy rooted in the commodification of sand, stone, and cement. What these sectors share is a reliance on manual labor combined with high profitability from growing segments of the Indian economy—the country's national growth rate has been relatively high over the past decade, despite some ups and downs.

Agriculture, conversely, is on the ropes. The implication of this was clear to interviewees, who told me that bonded labor was only for large and powerful farmers.[36] Furthermore, those farmers with large amounts of land have a greater range of motion on a number of issues, not just labor. The sense from smaller farmers was that "we may be suffering, but the big landholders are not suffering anything. They are making money and have investments. The small farmers like us are suffering too much."[37] One landlord who lost control of his bonded laborers complained to me that "others, big and powerful farmers, they wouldn't let the workers go until they repaid their debt."[38] The implication is clear—when it comes to human rights violators targeted by social movements, Thucydides was on to something when he declared that the strong do what they can, and the weak suffer what they must.[39]

ADAPTATION: RECONFIGURING EXPLOITATION

While former perpetrators may attempt to reestablish control through repression or countermobilization, many realize they have insufficient capacity to maintain such tactics in the face of sustained pressure. Rights violators may instead, or subsequently, respond in a way that avoids bonded labor but has the net effect of reconfiguring patterns of inequality and exploitation. In this category are employers who work to survive in a way that maintains a semblance of the old system, including land attachment and sharecropping. This category also covers the shift into new sectors altogether, such as politics and extractive industries like mining. These tactics have the effect of adapting and reconfiguring systems of inequality despite social movement efforts. A recent assessment of bonded labor, sponsored by the Government of India Planning Commission (2012), did not find any instances in which perpetrators attempted to reexploit laborers. Interviews with bonded laborers and employers alike suggest a greater level of complexity at work, with many more opportunities for exploitation than simply a relapse into debt bondage. Sharecropping and land attachment are two survival strategies that draw on and perpetuate certain aspects of the old system of debt bondage.

ADAPTATION: SHARECROPPING

Many farmers, upon losing bonded laborers, are left with naught but their name, their land, and a set of recently reconfigured social relations. Efforts to recombine these resources in such a way that ensures survival often result in sharecropping. Sharecropping—in which the laborer works the farmer's land and the harvest is divided between them—may be continued with the same workers, on the same land, with very similar power dynamics. One farmer in a focus group explained that, if a farmer has a labor problem, he can give half the land to laborers, and in this way, the farmer's income remains constant. Presumably this tactic also has the effect of pacifying laborers, since "what you get, you get in peace."[40] Another tells me farming is no longer worthwhile.[41] Since his sons are employed as engineers in Gujarat and Madras and his daughters are married and living elsewhere, he turned his large farm over for sharecropping.

For laborers, sharecropping may be a step forward from debt bondage, and the former perpetrators may hold no ill will toward their former charges. However, I consider sharecropping to be a social and economic relationship that has the effect of maintaining dependency and inequality, regardless of the landlord's intent.

While the practice may lead to benefits for both groups, sharecropping laborers rarely have easy access to capital, rendering them vulnerable to usurious advances on everything from seeds and fertilizer to food and medicine. Sharecropping under these conditions is more likely to evolve into new forms of caste-based inequality.

This complexity may be seen in the system of sharecropping prevalent in the American South after the Civil War. While sharecropping was a suboptimal solution for both plantation owners who wanted slavery and for former slaves who wanted economic freedom in the form of land, it was preferred to the alternatives, which included chain gangs and landlessness (Royce 1985, 1993; Shlomowitz 1979; Woodman 1977). Its origins notwithstanding, the effect was that the new institution of sharecropping was laid overtop of the old institutional arrangements, roles, and relationships. It is not difficult to see a similar process at work among landlords and former laborers. The prominent social theorist Charles Tilly (1998) argued that inequality is durable for that exact reason—institutions can be replaced or overturned, but there is likely to be persistence in the material and cultural conditions that underpin inequality.[42]

There is some evidence, however, that while sharecropping may be preferred by landlords eager to work the land with another's hands, broader labor scarcities and laborers' reluctance may thwart this effort. As laborers are freed up, they are likely to try to migrate to urban opportunities or to search out jobs in growing sectors of the economy. A once powerful landlord explained to me, in the midst of his fallow land: "Sharecropping happens here too, but people are no longer willing to farm. Most of the laborers have gone to Bangalore, where it is easy to get work, so why should they be stuck on the land? There are many ways the laborers are being attracted to the factories and the metros."[43]

The postintervention puzzle in the agricultural sector is the task of properly matching remaining laborers and the land. Sharecropping brings erstwhile bonded laborers back to work under a new scheme in which benefits and risks are more evenly distributed. This approach predominates, since it is virtually always the case that laborers have no land of their own. In a handful of notable cases, however, bonded laborers may own small parcels of their own land that they simply cannot afford to cultivate. It is also possible that an emancipated bonded laborer will have received a small plot of land as compensation for their exploitation. In both cases, the newly emancipated laborer tends to lack capital and may thus be convinced to essentially sharecrop his or her own land. Under these conditions, a land-attachment arrangement may be proposed.

ADAPTATION: LAND ATTACHMENT

Land attachment is similar to sharecropping in that it draws on many of the same raw resources—labor and land—yet it is a solid step closer to extractive dependency in that it makes use of the *laborer's* own land but leaves the worker reliant on the landlord for raw materials. In these cases, the bonded laborer's former employer may agree to advance all of the material necessary to work their land in exchange for a portion of the harvest. Former bonded laborers pay a premium to till land they already own. While the former perpetrator was obligated to provide a measure of grain to the laborer, the laborer is now obligated to repay a significant percentage of the total harvest.

Social movement groups admit that postemancipation scenarios are complicated and that these situations are not necessarily forced on laborers. Indeed, a staff member at a partner organization makes it clear that "we have discussed this with the workers who are giving these lands to the landlord, and we said not to do it. But they are not ready to do this. They say, *What will I do being free? I cannot cultivate anything over here. So at least I will go and ask his help, something will come, a small amount.*"[44] The land-attachment system perpetuates dependency and reinforces inequality by ensuring that the landlord continues to be the lender of last resort and that the laborer is only able to access resources through credit obtained by the landlord against future crops. While land attachment and sharecropping maintain a semblance of the old system, former perpetrators may also shift into new sectors altogether, including politics, finance, and industries such as quarry and stonebreaking.

ADAPTATION: CONTRACTING

Contracting in the quarry industry is thought to be lucrative or, at least, more lucrative than farming. This potential for higher income has attracted farmers and farmers' sons. Mining may be pursued with only a modest capital investment, since only a lease, rather than outright ownership, is required. This is especially true in parts of Uttar Pradesh, where agriculture, brick kilns, and stone quarries are often situated within the same region. The second requirement, alongside the lease, is laborers. Laborers in extractive industries are more likely to be brought in from nearby states, though this varies by industry and by proximity to states with high unemployment. It is reasonable to assume that securing and managing laborers draws on management and personnel skills honed in the agricultural sector.

Farmers who can afford to may shift laterally into an exploitative and higher-yield industry. As one formerly powerful perpetrator explained to me, "some rich farmers sold their farms and went into quarry work."[45] Indeed, several of the contractors I spoke with had been farmers or were the sons of farmers. Like land attachment, contracting work may be benign, or it may reproduce bonded labor and even expand into human trafficking. Powerful farmers who face declining options and restive workers may shift their operations to more accommodating regions or to sectors of the economy where patronage and profits remain sufficiently high.[46]

ADAPTATION: POLITICS AND GOVERNMENT

Well-resourced incumbents may also choose to go into politics or government service. Policies like MNREGA have funneled an incredible amount of money, or control over money, to local governing bodies. According to one report, an estimated 70 percent of MNREGA funds are lost to overhead and corruption, suggesting that oversight of MNREGA in a particular locale may be a lucrative position (Rai 2012). Rukum, the son of a bonded labor–holding family, has helped manage his father's land.[47] However, he says he has moved on from farming. He is now responsible for implementing MNREGA benefits in the area. When I asked him about recent changes in his community, he was glowing in his assessment of how greater awareness of rights had led to greater respect and more demands for wages, and that technological advances had increased crop yields. While I cannot gainsay his enthusiasm, this assessment of the community's condition seemed more closely linked to his role as a government spokesperson than as a member of a recently challenged landholding caste. There is no evidence from my interviews in Rukum's community that he is currently engaged in fraudulent activity, but the shift from his father's profession into the management of a government-run aid program ensures he is in a position to continue distributing resources to the landless and to skim from the top if he so chooses.

Prabhav, a former perpetrator who made a move into politics as the village leader (*pradhan*) but who clearly had larger ambitions, was the only employer I interviewed who initiated a conversation about bonded and child labor.[48] When we first met, he launched into an animated explanation of how "these things" had been prevalent but that he had gotten involved in politics "for the people." His preference for the ruling Congress party, the party of Nehru, was rooted in their commitment to all people, unlike the Dalit chief minister Mayawati, whom he perceived to be biased in favor of the lower castes. When I asked who in the area persisted in maintaining bonded laborers, he answered that it was a small percentage—"1 or 2 percent"—who are able to continue because they have "500 bigha [roughly 165 acres] and the ear of politicians." From this perspective, it makes complete sense to go into politics, as it is a high-profile form of power and the source of new benefits and resources.

Politics is also a place where proxy struggles with social movement groups play out. Each of the organizations involved in this study pursues a strategy in which groups of emancipated laborers are encouraged to stand members for election. This gives laborers an opportunity to engage in collective action and to experience important successes or failures. These challenges also provide opportunities for landlords to create schisms—as indicated earlier by the quarry contractor's effort to split a self-help group by sponsoring competing members—while also providing an avenue to create new, or maintain old, forms of power. In some of these instances, local leadership—in the form of the village leader—becomes an important symbol of the continuance of past power. The head of an important family, who briefly lost an election after more than four decades of uninterrupted control over the position, seemed pleased to inform me that a laborer under his control had won a recent election, thereby restoring their position of influence in the community. Such incidences suggest that, while landlords may lose their bonded laborers, they go to great lengths to maintain overall control.

The net effect, one organization's founder argues, is that landlords are not only powerful in terms of bonded labor, but they are often also

> in control of all the old and new economic ventures. They keep control over them and pocket the benefits. Like now MNREGA—only workers should get it, there should not be machines. But [landlords] will employ the machines and employ ghost records [of laborers] and pocket the money. All sorts of things go on. They will be pocketing all the contracts of the government.[49]

These forms of adaptation—whether through sharecropping and land attachment or contracting and politics—point to the extent to which power evolves in ways that affect laborers and landlords alike. Efforts to respond to movement mobilization and laborer demands have the effect of tracing over existing cultural patterns and caste dynamics, thereby perpetuating inequality. The greatest impact of this process is on formerly enslaved individuals, a fact that highlights the complexity of developing sustainable emancipation strategies. Land ownership has been shown to be the most effective and durable form of postemancipation compensation. Leaving aside the fact that it is extremely rare for workers to obtain compensation in the form of land, an assessment of landlords' coping mechanisms suggests that this benefit runs the risk of being co-opted.

RESOURCES AND OPPORTUNITIES

Here we may finally return to this book's third and final puzzle: why do these particular targets respond as they do? Interview data presented here suggest that options and resources are *the* key causal mechanisms that explain the difference between who quits and who continues with bonded labor in rural India. This is especially true in the absence of broader shifts in cultural norms. Under ordinary conditions, the powerful are able to retain their position despite the threat that broad changes pose to existing settlements. Their survival is predicated on key resources, including social status and financial means. In the absence of these two sources of power, however, success is not guaranteed. Resources matter for movement mobilization and success, and they certainly matter for target repression or resignation. Targets are in a unique position, since they often possess resources associated with incumbency, and these resources are often rather diverse.

Outrage and entitlement carry the day only when they are backed by newer forms of coercive power, especially capital. Since the 1970s, social movement theory has recognized the critical role of resources. Movement mobilization was seen as a logistical and organizational puzzle—how is it that those isolated from political venues can bring their grievances to the attention of decision makers and the general public? The answer, the resource-mobilization theorists Mayer Zald and John McCarthy (1977) argued, lies in the increased mobilization capacity provided through the infusion of new resources.

In this light, mobilization is the process by which "a social unit gains relatively rapidly in control over resources it previously did not control" (Etzioni 1969, 243). It is this expansion of resources, not social alienation or social strain, that explains mobilization. Movements required an influx of management and money and also the role of institutional infrastructure, such as unions and churches, in helping movements solve collective-action problems. The unspoken assumption is that movement targets do not face significant problems mobilizing resources. By now, the reader may anticipate my critique: target resources and opportunities are not constant. We now know, for example, that actual resources and perceptions of market strength play a significant role in explaining how corporations will respond to collective action (King 2008).[50] In fact, we can invert Etzioni's (1969, 243) conceptualization to define demobilization, deflation, and resignation as those moments *when a social unit loses relatively rapidly their control over resources it previously controlled.* The sociologist Rory McVeigh (1999) shows one possible outcome from such power devaluations: right-wing mobilization. It would be reasonable to anticipate the emergence of conservative farmers' movements in rural India in response to the sorts of grievances articulated here.

SUMMARY

A brief look backward in history suggests these efforts to mask and continue exploitation are not new. Through the 1990s and 2000s, the carpet-weaving industry in Uttar Pradesh was at the center of anti-trafficking and child-labor advocacy. As a result of this unwanted attention from advocacy groups such as Mobilizing for Change and Rugmark, loom owners shifted their work into worker's homes and initiated a complex leasing scheme that kept costs low but protected the owners legally. The net effect was that laborers continued to work under similar conditions, elites maintained control, and costs were suppressed.

Slaveholders report facing similar challenges from laborers yet respond in a wide variety of ways. This chapter reviews major responses to movement activity and suggests that resources and opportunities shape the decisions made by targeted incumbents. These ultimate decisions often differ from initial responses, an observation we return to in the book's conclusion. Tactically, even in those cases where powerful perpetrators quit, their manner of quitting differs significantly from the less powerful. While those threatened with escalating costs had to content themselves with sharecropping, when they could get it, or tilling their own fields, if they could stand it, those with a more flexible form of power were able to take on more impressive opportunities, such as bank presidencies, brick kilns, management of village leadership, and other alternate forms of power.

This observation circles back to the fact that perpetrators feel that their world, certainly in agriculture, is in decline. A paternalistic caste mentality, imbricated in the everydayness of social and economic relationships, left many respondents with few options when movements singled them out. The prevailing sense of resignation is evidence of this fact. Perhaps paternalism works best with the wind at its back, the road lying before it, and the marginalized willing to follow the rules. Significant changes in the broader political economy undermine some targets' ability to mount a robust and sustained response to mobilization, despite initial attempts to do so. Over the past two decades, India has experienced tectonic social and economic transformation. Like all such transformations, it has created both winners and losers, and a certain class of employers senses this. As one interviewee explained: "The laborers are below. The capitalists are above. The farmer is in the middle."[51]

6

PRIVATE WRONGS

Slavery and Antislavery in Contemporary India

We are a minority, like the lions.

—Raakesh (Interviewee 68)

B angalore is the "New India." New roads, gleaming autos, and new glass buildings pushing themselves up from streets lined with Western brands and cosmopolitan shoppers. Billboards advertise a lifestyle of luxury goods—cars, homes, jewelry. At the Hard Rock Cafe, the metro class of emerging professionals drinks, smokes, and chats over the roar of Soundgarden, Nirvana, and other cultural artifacts shared by our generation and demographic. I'm sitting with new friends who started out in call centers but have moved on to more dynamic sectors of the economy. They're a cursing, smoking, partying lot—a guy tells me that he doesn't drink on Mondays and Wednesdays but that the rest of the week they're all out late. I'm invited to a ska show. I agree. Someone else leans in with an anecdote about the time they took a train across the state—they all laugh at his fear of being accosted by a eunuch in this apparently unique adventure *beyond Bangalore.*

It is difficult to sketch India without repeating the "two Indias" mantra that has typified Western efforts to understand the country's cacophonous blend of languages, practices, histories, religions, and castes. Yet a flight from Bangalore to Varanasi—always via Delhi, the country's administrative anchor—conjures the mantra all the same. The holy city of Varanasi is best approached by air. It is only from this vantage point that you can properly appreciate the geography of exploitation. In circles and squares a city that has been home to humans for more than three millennia inscribes itself into the earth and into the lives of the tens of thousands of bonded laborers who call this corner of Uttar Pradesh home. Dusty and vibrant, Varanasi is the living soul of India. It is pockmarked by poverty and punctuated with beauty, home to ancient Buddhist temples, the holy waters of the Ganges and its riverfront Ghats, and Islam's Gyanvapi Mosque. Varanasi itself is some 3,500 years old, "the world's oldest living city," many tell me, "the soul of India," claim others. From the air, you can see the city, ringed by farmland and brick kilns. The agricultural production is laid out in perfectly symmetrical right angles, squares, and rectangles. These small but tidy parcels are plotted out as far as the eye can see, unbroken except for the intersection of two roads where a small town has sprung up. I say "sprung up" as if this is a recent happening. In reality, most of the region is thousands of years old.

The second thing best seen from the air is the expansive tapestry of brick kilns. Their layout is always the same: at the center lies a smokestack five stories tall, surrounded by hundreds of tons of bricks, neatly stacked, and interlaced with footpaths trod by the hundreds of workers required to maintain the operation. The owner, more likely than not, lives in Varanasi. A middleman of some sort manages the kiln's day-to-day operations. Whether he is a contractor or a cousin hardly matters. More important is plausible deniability for the abuse required to keep so many workers working so hard for so little.

India has a rich cultural and political heritage, but it has also been straddled by caste, colonialism, poverty, and corruption. In contemporary terms, India's economic and political position is critical. India is many things—the world's largest democracy, the world's second-most-populated country, home to a unique political culture, and a social movement society in which hardly a day goes by without a major protest event closing down some major institution, industry, or thoroughfare (Ray 1999, Ray and Katzenstein 2005). These historic attributes are amplified by India's emerging economic and political power. India is transforming from largely rural and feudal into a more urban and outward-focused society.

This may be seen at the Hard Rock Cafe in Bangalore, more broadly in the loosening restrictions on multinational corporations and foreign direct investment, and in the spread of cell phones and Wi-Fi hotspots. These developments contribute to strong year-on-year economic growth that has pulled many out of poverty and is widely regarded to be "lifting all boats." India's dynamic political and economic scene is the backdrop for the story told here. Even further in the background is India's unique role in the contemporary global context as a country and its unique internal processes and contradictions as a society and economy. The challenge is to frame this tectonic activity properly—inarguably a process that touches the lives of virtually all of India's billion-plus citizens. Of course, India's particular attributes matter, but only insofar as they shape the micro socioeconomic relations and experiences of the individuals I interviewed. The focus is on their experience, rather than on the India visible through national balance sheets, public-opinion polls, or electoral politics. The emphasis is on particular cultural traits as interviewees see them, rather than on orientalist conceptions of India as exotic and wholly other.

This approach follows Amartya Sen's (2006, 31) sense that, rather than being cast in amber, India's traditions are constantly negotiated and that this negotiation happens across religious, class, caste, and gender boundaries. Such a perspective recognizes one of India's most obvious traits—heterodoxy—as a strength and a pivot point for debate and change, since "traditions have their own interactive influence, and it is necessary to avoid being imprisoned in formulaic interpretations [that] oversimplify India's past and present."

SLAVERY IN INDIA

By our best reckoning, South Asia is home to ten to twenty million people living in bonded labor (Bales 2012; Breman, Guerin, and Prakash 2009, 334; International Labour Organization 2012),[1] more than half of the world's inhabitants who live as slaves (Bales 2012). The magnitude of the problem outstrips estimates of those trafficked, held in commercial sexual exploitation, or held in any other single region on earth (Belser, de Cock, and Mehran 2005; ILO 2012). India itself has more people living in slavery than any other country on earth (Lerche 2009, 364). Bonded labor is widespread. It is also persistent, having deeper roots in feudal social relations than in the global political economy (Quirk 2011). It is these deep cultural roots, rather than present economic gains, which explain this prevalence, since other forms of slavery, especially human trafficking for sexual exploitation, appear to be far more profitable (Kara 2009).

If bonded labor is the least profitable form of slavery in India, debt bondage in the rural agricultural sector appears to be the least profitable form of bonded labor (Kara 2011). In other words, bonded labor in agriculture is the least profitable version of slavery's least profitable form. While other forms of contemporary slavery flourish in ungoverned pockets of the global economy, bonded labor thrives in feudal social practices. While other forms of slavery are driven by a desire for significant returns on investment, bonded labor, in agriculture especially, thrives on tradition.

Slavery has persisted in India throughout its recorded history, and current practices are rooted in ancient teachings regarding debt, obligation, and caste.[2] Slavery in India poses a stark challenge for the Western mind. While in Greek and Roman political philosophy slavery was the antithesis of freedom, in India slavery exists at the far end of a "continuum of various degrees of subservience" (Kara 2011, 17). The *Arthashastra*, for example, set forth nine ways one can enter slavery, including four that specify bonded labor: "One whose life is saved during famine in exchange for enslavement; One pledged to be a slave upon acceptance of money by a master; One who becomes a slave upon release from a heavy debt; and One who becomes a slave in order to receive basic maintenance" (Kara 2011, 18).

Slavery here rests on poverty and obligation rather than on ownership and lost freedom. The implication is that slavery is its own reward: one may become a slave in order to gain something. In Western philosophy, the language of duty and loss persists to this day in the way many of us conceptualize both slavery and freedom. But in India, it is rather the sense that the oppressor has done something *for* the oppressed that defines slavery's fundamental nature. The slave has exchanged something of comparably little value (freedom in poverty) for something of great value (enslavement in sustenance).

Historically, virtually all of those suffering from enslavement have been at the lowest end of India's steep caste ladder. The caste system is critical in both curtailing other options for vulnerable laborers and in corralling them into exploitative relationships with those of the higher caste. This is true whether or not the exploitative relationship is secured through debt bondage. If the historical pattern of enslavement in India has been one of culturally reinforced inequality, the colonial era saw little improvement.

When Britain outlawed the slave trade in 1807, the colonies were not included in this legislation. When the British banned chattel slavery with the passage of the Anti-Slavery Act in India in 1843, bonded labor was allowed to persist. Elites reorganized exploitative labor relations around bonded labor as a purely contractual relationship, which provided legal cover for the prioritization of the contract and the broad use of bonded labor as a substitute for slavery (Breman and Guerin 2009, Pouchepadass 2009). The reason for this was simple: bonded and forced labor was necessary to maintain British exports.

India's postcolonial efforts at emancipation are marked by similar contradictions. While the ILO's Forced Labor Convention was passed in 1930, it was not ratified by India for another twenty years. It wasn't until 1976—more than 130 years after the Anti-Slavery

Act—that the Bonded Labor System (Abolition) Act (BLA) addressed bonded labor. The act recognizes that rather than an aggregate of one-off instances of exploitation, bonded labor takes place within a "system of forced, or partially forced, labour under which a debtor enters . . . into an agreement with the creditor to the effect that"— whether through interest, "customary or social obligation," generational debt, or "by reason of his birth in any particular caste or community"—the laborer would sacrifice wages, labor mobility, physical mobility, or the right to sell property at market wages.[3] Lest there be any confusion on the matter, the BLA clearly states: "bondage is slavery."[4]

The approach advanced by the BLA is in line with international legal norms while also recognizing the unique nature of bonded labor in the context of the subcontinent. The recognition of both social obligation and caste brings the broader social context into focus (Srivastava 2009). Debt bondage in India is never a simple matter of financial exchange or legal contract, as some would have it. Stark economics are only one part of a broader mesh of social and interpersonal relations, especially in the village context, where hierarchy and dependency punctuate relationships (Quirk 2011, 196). Previous chapters have shown the extent to which contemporary bonded labor harkens back to classic feudalism characterized by a "reciprocal system in which obligations implied servitude to an individual with superior status . . . in return for protection" (Campbell 2005, qtd. in Quirk 2011, 196). Dominant castes recognize debt as testimony to fealty, familiarity, family, and trust, rather than evidence of exploitation and abuse. There is broad agreement that those officials tasked with enforcing the BLA are likely to identify the system as reciprocal rather than exploitative, with courts inclined to agree (Gupta 2003, Sankaran 2009).

The passage of the Bonded Labor Act attracted some early attention. While the number of identified cases reported by the Government of India Planning Commission in the late 1970s stood at 26,000, it leaped sixfold to 163,000 in the 1980s before tapering off in the 1990s (56,000) and 2000s (24,000).[5] Yet the total number of cases identified and the subset rehabilitated from the late 1970s through 2007 (267,000) pale in comparison to the estimated size of the problem.

The large gap between the estimated size of the problem and official numbers has long plagued scholarship on human trafficking (Gozdziak 2009, Laczko and Gozdziak 2005). Yet it appears that in India the disconnect between estimates and rehabilitation is attributable to general ambivalence and inaction—"official apathy and absence of any concerted effort," in the words of one report—rather than an inability actually to identify and prosecute cases (National Commission for Enterprises in the Unorganised Sector 2007, 105).[6] While the power to investigate and report on bonded-labor abuses falls to the Human Rights Commission, it does not have a mandate to enforce the law. This task falls to 640 district magistrates spread across the country. District magistrates are tasked to investigate abuse, but many are as likely to have connections to those employing bonded laborers as they are to have a commitment to the rule of law (Gupta 2003, Breman and Guerin 2009).

Furthermore, the actual condition of those "rehabilitated" during this period deserves scrutiny for two reasons. The first is that beliefs about caste-based discrimination, including untouchability, persist, especially in rural areas. The second is that most government-led rehabilitations have focused on the simple disbursement of benefits rather than on a broader strategy of equipping former bonded laborers to advocate for their rights economically, politically, and socially. Subsequent analysis suggests that benefits alone have a high failure rate when it comes to sustainable rehabilitation (Government of India Planning Commission 2012). The cultural notion of ritual pollution (i.e., untouchability) and the reality of caste hierarchy have created a social space where notions of dominance persist. Indian scholars note that in the early nineteenth century, "the pariahs were always looked upon as natural slaves, and became the property of any person who contributed to their marriage expenses"—a relational dynamic and cultural expectation that "was the usual practice at that time for initiating hereditary slavery" (Vidyasagar 1985, 130). The majority of bonded laborers are estimated to be from untouchable communities (Anti-Slavery International 2001). This is not to conflate untouchability with slavery but instead to emphasize the significant preexisting cultural conditions that contribute to dehumanization before, during, and after emancipation. Bluntly put, vulnerability persists despite technical emancipation.

While corruption and official apathy are significant aspects of slavery's prevalence in the subcontinent, the persistence of bonded labor is the product of durable inequality rooted in the caste system. Indeed, caste mitigates against the emergence of a collective concept of humanity and contributes to a dehumanization that facilitates human rights violations. It is true that the vigilance committees established by the Bonded Labor Act do not meet. They should meet. It is true that the district magistrates and subdistrict magistrates charged with bringing cases of bonded labor forward rarely do their job. They should do their job. It is true that virtually none of the individuals held in bonded labor have been identified. They should be identified. It is true that benefits do not reach beneficiaries. They should do so in such a way that survivors are able to rebuild lives of their own choosing. It is true that many cases advanced against perpetrators have resulted in acquittal. They should instead end in jail time and steep fines. But the root of the problem is not a lack of resources for vigilance committees, or a lack of time or knowledge from magistrates, or an inability to identify bonded laborers, or a shortage of benefits for survivors, or a shortage of lawyers to prosecute cases.

Bonded labor persists because too few of these actors—magistrates, lawyers, and community members—consider it to be a problem. This official indifference mirrors that of the general public—bonded labor is not considered to be a problem by Indian society at large. The committed work of social movement actors and nonprofit groups has resulted in piecemeal outcomes. There is strong evidence that the root of the problem is that India has yet to develop an indigenous commitment to "comparable humanity" for all of its citizens

(Kara 2011, 12). The most superficial evidence of this failure is the institution of untouchability (Davenport and Trivedi 2013).

SLAVEHOLDING IN INDIA

> I had imagined for years what I might say if I ever met a trafficker. Would I demand to know how he could knowingly profit by sending women and children to be tortured? Would I throttle him, turn him over to the police, demand a list of victims and destinations so the slaves could be freed? When I met Salim on a sunny, crisp day in the remotest reaches of Bihar, my mind went blank. He was so ordinary— just a man, wearing simple village clothes. His aspect was common, his mustache trimmed, his hair neatly combed. He spoke without emotion.
>
> —Siddharth Kara

Very little is known about slaveholders, despite the vast number of interventions intended to arrest their activities. Perpetrators are often seen in ideal-type terms: scowling villains willing to rape and enslave for profit. This framing helps galvanize public opinion and motivate policy makers, but it sheds more activist heat than scholarly light on slaveholders' attitudes and behaviors. It stands to reason that the prototypical trafficker or slaveholder in the literature and on the advocacy circuit does not describe the reality of most perpetrators. Recent studies seem to support this assessment. To my knowledge, only one other study has attempted to engage contemporary slaveholders in India. In a larger study on trafficking of women and children, Sankar Sen and P. M. Nair (2005) draw on data from twelve Indian states, as well as Delhi, Bangladesh, and Nepal. A number of important factors emerge from interviews with brothel owners and traffickers. Brothel owners were predominantly middle-aged, lower-caste, and illiterate Hindu women who had themselves been victims of commercial sexual exploitation prior to taking ownership of the brothel. The majority reported feeling that they had no choice but to enter management. A significant majority, nearly four-fifths of those interviewed, reported that when they retired they would leave the business to someone like themselves. Even in the commercial sex industry, the image of the leering and lecherous male brothel owner is undermined by data suggesting perpetrators are formerly exploited women doing what they can to survive. Indeed, the study found that the mean annual income for these owners and managers was about 4,000 dollars, or about $13 per day, making them lower middle class.[7] This is well above the poverty line but hardly wealthy.

The same study's findings on traffickers suggests that the average trafficker is married, illiterate, just as likely to be a woman as a man, middle aged, and predominantly Hindu. Their monthly incomes are below those of the brothel owners. A majority suggested that trafficking is a "social evil," but almost half did not think that the problem could be solved. Hardly any reported being afraid of the police, though traffickers, brothel owners, and managers alike reported police satisfaction as a key priority in their operations. While few were forthcoming with details, it was clear that both brothel keepers and traffickers used the devices within their means to pacify police. Many respondents were probably simultaneously perpetrators of gross violations of human rights, including rape, torture, and child sexual exploitation. But these data also present a rather prosaic image of slaveholders and traffickers as businesspeople and entrepreneurs.

Studies outside of India support these findings. Interviews with incarcerated individuals accused of trafficking in Cambodia showed that the vast majority of interviewees were "poor uneducated women" who lacked other forms of livelihood and who earned very little for their troubles (Keo et al. 2014). An earlier study, conducted in Cambodia, found that many female traffickers had themselves been trafficked at an earlier point in time (Brown 2007), and a study conducted in Israel found that 10 percent of perpetrators of trafficking were women (Levenkron 2007). A study overseen by my colleague Ami Carpenter (2015) drew on interviews with jailed gang members in the United States and determined that while many were involved in some aspect of "domestic human trafficking," very little of this resembled organized crime. Erin Denton analyzed seventy-two trafficking cases in the United States and found that most perpetrators were of the same ethnicity as their victims (Denton 2016). Likewise, Anqi Shen conducted interviews with women who had been involved in the sale and trafficking of children in China (Shen 2016). Although the sample size was small, her research suggests that these women were often poor and socially isolated. As a result, they were rarely able to negotiate their compensation with the slightly stronger or better-networked individuals who managed more sophisticated elements of the exploitation process.[8]

CASTE AND CULTURE EXPLAIN PERSISTENCE MORE BROADLY

If particular combinations of resources explain persistence *after* a challenge, what explains why India is home to half the world's slaves in the first place? Why does this radical exploitation and inequality persist into the present? An important part of the answer lies in the caste system, which gives rise to a culture of servitude that affects landlords and bonded laborers alike. This worldview is punctuated by paternalism, which frames exploitative labor relations in familial terms, with the landlord as the caring parent and the laborer as the dutiful child.[9] Caste, cultures of servitude, and paternalism are all specific and local examples of the legitimizing myths that persist in all cultural spaces.[10]

In their work on domestic servants in West Bengal, the sociologists Raka Ray and Seemin Qayum (2009, 3) suggest this labor arrangement has given rise to a culture of servitude in which "social relations of domination/subordination, dependency, and inequality are normalized and permeate both the domestic and public spheres." The use of *culture* in this approach "treats the total social process of experience and consciousness in terms of power," while *servitude* captures "the persistence of forms of dependency and submission." Though Ray and Qayum are writing about domestic servitude among urban elites, the same may be argued for their rural counterparts. Servitude is normalized and "legitimized ideologically such that domination, dependency, and inequality are not only tolerated but accepted . . . and . . . are reproduced through everyday social interaction and practice." In such a cultural space it becomes "virtually impossible to imagine life without it, and practices, and thoughts and feelings about practices, are patterned on it."

Since this culture of servitude is also bound up in "collective patterns of subjectivity," it leads to relationships that carry "meanings and values as they are actively lived and felt," in the words of the critic Raymond Williams (1977, 132). These meanings and values include a sense of familial duty and obligation not just from the laborer to landlord but also from the benefactor to the supplicant. Contemporary efforts to end slavery in India face a unique challenge. They must address exploitation in the absence of popular outrage or popular notions of illegality—as well as exploitation in the presence of genuine emotional bonds. The complexity of this challenge may be seen in a practical comparison of the dominant notion of slaveholders with the reality of slaveholding in India.

The author Kevin Bales (2004, 25) has argued that perpetrators of contemporary slavery, especially in South Asia, are often "businesspeople (usually men) who tend to be family men . . . pillars of the local community . . . well integrated socially, well connected legally and politically." This theme has deep roots. Slaveholders in the American South claimed they were responsible for slaves' well-being (Davis 1999, Fox-Genovese and Genovese 2005). Mary Jackman (1994) has persuasively argued that, while oppressors may resort to coercive force, a pervasive paternalism does the day-to-day work of maintaining an ideological cocoon around the practice of authoritarianism and indeed around the entire set of social relations. Oppressors' attitudes and behavior are not pathological. They are intimately connected to cultural systems of legitimizing myths (Gaventa 1982, Sewell 1992). Such myths are held individually but aggregate socially and manifest in social relations with subordinated members of society (Sidanius and Pratto 1999).

Under normal conditions, the legitimizing myths of the dominant group are widely held and rarely challenged. While this approach holds in a wide range of social systems, it is particularly well suited to the task of explaining the prevalence of caste-based thinking. The reality of this approach becomes part of one's personal identity and part of a collective identity within a particular segment of society. A caste-based worldview is rooted in several thousand years of tradition that persists across social relations and is often adopted by higher and lower castes alike. Current manifestations of caste inequality are not as blatant in contemporary India as in the past. Caste no longer rests on the performance of ceremonial rituals; rather, it serves as the cultural underpinning of an entire unspoken system of being, relating, and knowing, irrespective of caste and class. Nowhere is this more true than in the cultural logic that has underwritten the widespread use of bonded labor in the rural Indian context (Tucker 1997, 475).

While our focus remains on perpetrators, victims and survivors of slavery are complex actors in this process as well. I was struck by a conversation with a survivor from the "untouchable" Musahar caste who had been enslaved by a particularly abusive landlord from the dominant Thakur caste, known for its strong-handed ways. I asked whether she felt she was owed an apology for the suffering she described to me, which included the murder of her father. She was unable to answer in the affirmative. She could recognize the injustice done to her, acknowledging she should receive back wages as compensation. However, she did not seem able to articulate, or perhaps even comprehend, that she was owed something simply by virtue of her membership in Indian society or the human family—a claim based in her inherent dignity. It is unclear whether this is evidence of a "culture of silence" and "fear of freedom" or is instead rooted more deeply in a fundamental lack of recognition of her rightful claim to "comparable humanity" based in human dignity, irrespective of caste (Friere [1970] 2000, Singh and Tripathi 2010). What this anecdote does make clear, however, is that perpetrators are not the only carriers of a paternalistic worldview.

These dynamics are embedded, practiced, and reproduced broadly across the status hierarchy, at a very granular level in terms of an individual's lifeworld.

Movement efforts face a particular challenge in the lack of widespread public opinion against bonded labor and other anti-Dalit rights violations.[11] Persistent casteism, widespread sexism, and entrenched poverty thwart the emergence of a broader human rights culture. When an American judge found a prominent Indian diplomat guilty of human trafficking because of the "barbaric treatment" of their domestic servant in the United States, the comments section in the *Times of India* was home to a vigorous debate between skeptics sure the lawsuit was a ploy to secure a green card and those railing against corruption among the Indian elite (Press Trust of India 2012). By my estimation, more than one-fifth of the comments questioned the merits of the case. Outrage was focused on the entitled behavior of the diplomat, not the plight of the victim. The *Times* readership represents some of the country's best-educated and most-cosmopolitan citizens as well as countless expatriate Indians living in countries in the Gulf and the West. The comments demonstrate in a microcosm the problem that antislavery efforts have more generally in the region: cosmopolitan elites are outraged over corruption and entitlement, but few had much to say about the victims of seemingly banal crimes. In this case, the most direct attention received by the victim—who had been deceived, beaten, and starved—was from those who ascribed to her motives of opportunism, jealousy, and greed.

True, there is a rich vein of solidarity flowing through contemporary India from the works of Gandhi and Ambedkar, but the tremendous weight, power, and substance of their legacy has been forced through the syringe of courageous individuals and fractious social movement actors. As suggested earlier, the transition from chattel slavery to bonded labor was facilitated by the British, whose colonial enterprises required the total control of low-cost labor but whose domestic efforts against slavery prevented them from adopting a stance other than abolition. As a solution, much of slavery's inertia passed into debt bondage, giving the Raj both political cover and free labor (Quirk 2011). This transformation precluded a radical break with the past. The British administrative shell game left basic systems of inequality largely intact while simultaneously establishing the caste system as *the* organizing principle for social, political, and economic order.

Unfortunately, independence from Britain did not affect this transformation. Rather, the postcolonial era has seen the emergence of caste identity as one of the most important points of political mobilization. The salience of caste has only increased, given the dual mechanisms of reservation and the demands of electoral politics. Identity thus becomes the terrain for new political projects and challenges. This can be seen in cases of Dalit rights and uplift, as with Mayawati's rule of the progressive BSP in Uttar Pradesh.[12] But it may also be seen in the assertion of Hindutva supremacy, as in Modi's rule of the BJP in Gujarat and subsequent national leadership.[13] Rather than erasing caste and casteism, modern political projects have had the effect of establishing Dalit identity as the foundation for collective political rights (Rao 2009, 23, 25).

For those hoping economic growth would reverse centuries of discrimination against women and lower-caste communities, there is little room for cheer. Economic transformations are unmooring laborers to pursue work in urban environs where they are vulnerable to being trafficked and forced to work under similarly exploitative conditions in a new context. This trend is not limited to bonded labor. By way of example, the western state of Gujarat is widely heralded as a breakthrough success case for its investment in infrastructure and its openness to foreign investors. But these gains correlate with development decline: Gujarat has India's highest levels of child malnutrition and is in the bottom five Indian states in the Global Hunger Index (Radhakrishna 2008, Chandhoke 2012). Nationally, an increase in household income is positively associated with *more* feticide of the unborn girl child (Times of India 2012). Improvements in income are being used to more efficiently violate rights. Bride burning, acid attacks, and rape all continue to occupy the news (Economist 2012), suggesting a new humanitarianism is needed. Economic development in India cannot be unquestioningly correlated with advances in human rights standards in Gujarat. The same holds true for Uttar Pradesh and Karnataka.

Public opinion data from the World Values Survey (2014) provide some support for this theme. The majority of Indians, regardless of class or caste, identify poverty as the country's most serious issue. However, the majority of upper-class respondents consider poverty to be the result of laziness, while nearly two-thirds of lower-class respondents attribute poverty to fundamental unfairness in society. Fifty-eight percent of upper-class respondents report that the government is doing enough, or too much, to end poverty. Those in the upper class, it may be argued, believe poverty is a serious issue whose victims are to blame and for whom enough is already being done.

Perpetrators, if we may extrapolate from the conversations with contemporary slaveholders, are often upstanding middle-class community members who take pride in their ability to care for those beneath them in the social hierarchy. That they demand subservience and nearly free labor in exchange is seen as part of a natural matter of course. It is no wonder, then, that they do not recognize themselves as criminals nor appear to have any regret for their behavior. It is additionally no wonder that an educated and wired civil society might consider the perpetrator to be a victim of unjust social movement activity rather than as a rights-violating criminal. The fact that bonded labor is a crime did not seem to bother most oppressors with whom I spoke—other than their obvious concern for being caught. It stands to reason that public-opinion data would reflect this gap between law and practice, should it be available. Indeed, this is the case with corruption in India—it is against the law, widely practiced, and the subject of broad social movements, but it is not a top social problem according to the World Values Survey.

In her work on middle-class involvement in environmental movements in India, Emma Mawdsley (2004) argues that India's middle class generally lacks concern for the public good. She draws on recent scholarship to suggest this lack of empathy is rooted in a series of socioeconomic and historical factors, including globalization, colonialism, appropriation of power, neoliberalism, and the Emergency (during which Prime Minister Indira Gandhi suspended the constitution and ruled by decree).[14] Others trace this lack of sympathy to the caste systems' dichotomization of the sacred and the profane, the home and the street, the high born and the untouchable (Gupta 2000, Douglas 2002). Whatever the source, Mawdsley (2004, 89) argues, the effect is a low value for, or understanding of, civil society.

Employer mentalities are thus fundamentally and necessarily rooted in the norms and expectations of caste's cultural logic. This has the effect of undermining more universalist conceptualizations of human rights, citizenship, and civil society—the very approaches that consider all community members to be part of the human family. When states attempt to make slavery illegal, Ethan Nadelmann argues, "slavery can only persist where *nonlegal social norms* in supporting slavery are strong, where the state is sufficiently disinterested in eradicating slavery that ignores the efforts of slave owners to retain their slaves, or where slaves acquiesce, in one way or another, to their enslavement" (Nadelmann 1990, 498, emphasis added). Each of these three factors—supportive norms, disinterested state, and relationship-based acquiescence—is at play in much of rural India.

In this way, the nonlegal social norm of caste contributes to broadly distributed public opinions about who is a part of the imagined community. Movements face a deficit in the latent cultural resources available for the creation of widespread empathy as well as a lack of other options for the oppressed (Anderson [1983] 2006). The ability to empathize is a fundamental prerequisite for any positive shift in public opinion. In the absence of supportive public opinion, movements lose a critical fulcrum in their effort to pressure targets to change their behavior, especially against their economic will. For enslaved individuals, or the untouchable Dalit recently freed from bonded labor, few cultural opportunities exist. Conversely, this broader context suggests substantial opportunities for perpetrators within the cultural sphere—they inhabit a world in which legitimizing myths of inequality permeate the life world of *all* parties, whether perpetrator, victim, lawyers, police, judges, or the general public. The net effect of these cultural forces is a significant gap between public policy and public opinion. Bluntly, public opinion, perhaps steeped in caste commitments, does not appear to be in favor of emancipation. This is exactly why resources matter in this particular case. In the absence of a social movement against bonded labor, perpetrators must yield only to their conscience and the market. Only the latter is visible to the social scientist.

Public-approval data on bonded labor simply do not exist in India. The reason for this is fairly obvious: disapproval of slavery is so high in the global North that it is not included on any measure of public opinion. My hunch is that the opposite is also true in South Asia: indifference to bonded labor is so high that it is not included in any measure of public opinion. One thing, however, is clear. The cultural opportunity is closed to Dalit claimants, especially those involved in rural labor and bonded labor. Few resources exist for the creation of an "injustice frame" that could capture the imagination of the Indian public writ large. While I have documented the experience of some employers of bonded laborers in rural India, there is no evidence that bonded labor is in general decline or at risk of becoming extinct. Changes in the political economy may undermine perpetrators' ability to maintain the status quo, but they have not led to a national movement to end bonded labor.

SUMMARY

The final lesson here is clear: emancipation is not simple. A major wave of the antislavery movement led to a botched British emancipation, which channeled slavery into the institution of bonded labor, which has subsequently been reinforced by the caste system (see Quirk 2011). The caste system bears on our story in two critical ways. The first is that it undermines humanitarian efforts to resolve social problems that lie beyond caste borders and deprives movements of the raw material for humanitarian social movements for emancipation based on appeals to individual dignity. The caste system's second effect is the sense of duty and obligation that feeds cultures of servitude and paternalistic relations between rights violators and their victims. These social realities make emancipation difficult and perpetuate everyday oppression.

Contemporary slaveholders in rural India are rights violators and criminals, but they do not fit the profile imagined by activists, policy makers, and the public. For rural landlords, feudal relations are, and always has been, a matter of fact. Bonded labor, then, is a deeply rooted social norm that defines appropriate social and economic relations. The stories told by slaveholders in the preceding chapters suggest that it is paternalism, rather than hostility or indifference, which informs their worldview.

I want to frame this case in broader terms, as a story about how so many of us face complex ethical challenges. Throughout the proceeding chapters, I have worked to clarify the Indian context without reifying it. There are two conjoined reasons for this. The first is that I do not want to essentialize and Orientalize the case. The second reason is that I believe the lessons here might be applied in other contexts. As I write these words, I am surrounded by personal analogies—my affordable trousers of dubious origins, the combustible engine of my car, my weakness for barbequed meat. I am currently living in a country plagued by intractable socioeconomic issues—the growing gap between rich and poor, a lack of universal high-quality education and health care, and incarceration policies that remove African American men from the labor market, the voting booth, and their families. Every one of these issues touches on key human rights norms and highlights those areas where we have failed to demonstrate a practical commitment to "comparable humanity." Cultural practices mask rights violations everywhere. Caste ideology facilitates bonded labor in India, and market ideologies facilitate radical inequality in the United States.

My hope is that this observation allows us to test my ideas out in other places. The sociologist Gerry Mackie has argued that socially acceptable rights violations persist for the very simple reasons that they are socially acceptable and are part of the status quo (Mackie 1996, 2000). Things may change very rapidly when practices become socially unacceptable. In effect, while there may be a real or imagined original benefit to the practice, certain contemporary behavior is the result of inertia rather than any particular set of ideological commitments. Raising the social costs of particular practices—Mackie's work focuses on campaigns to end female genital mutilation—increases the likelihood that they will be abandoned. This cost-raising process was also at play during the civil rights movement in the United States. Sit-ins and boycotts raised the price of segregation to such levels that racist storeowners abandoned racist customer policies rather than closing up their formerly profitable businesses (Luders 2006; see also Gamble 1943).

7

LONG GOODBYE
The Contemporary Antislavery Movement

Slavery is the great test question of our age and nation. It, above all others, enables us to draw the line between the precious and the vile, whether in individuals, creeds, sects, or parties.

—Frederick Douglass (1859)

I am a Southern man and a slaveholder. A kind and merciful one, I trust, and none the worse for being a slaveholder. I say, for one, I would rather meet any extremity upon earth than give up one inch of our equality, one inch of what belongs to us as members of this republic! What! Acknowledged inferiority! The surrender of life is nothing to sinking down into acknowledged inferiority!

—John C. Calhoun (1847)

Advocacy on trafficking and slavery has generated sustained popular interest over the past fifteen years.[1] Although academic types were talking about human trafficking before 2000, general attention to the topic has taken off in the intervening years. Media attention has followed the same exponential growth. The antitrafficking sector has followed suit.

While it is nearly impossible to quantify the number of small associations, campus chapters, church groups, collective-action campaigns, issue websites, and formal organizations dedicated to the issue, the number of each has increased exponentially.

States, intergovernmental agencies, and private donors in the United States and Australia have contributed more than one billion dollars to antislavery efforts (Weitzer 2014).[2] While it is always the case that more could be done, this is a relatively large amount of money. These funds are channeled through a truly global network of advocacy groups. Some organizations, such as Anti-Slavery International and Free the Slaves, are dedicated exclusively to ending slavery. Other groups, such as the International Justice Mission, have antislavery as a critical component of their broader portfolio of issues. These purpose-built groups are increasingly joined by massive organizations interested in adding slavery to their portfolios and fundraising efforts. The antislavery movement has also triggered the global spread of a relatively consistent regulatory regime. The United States pioneered legislation in both Congress (the Trafficking Victim Protection Act in 2000) and in the UN Office on Drugs and Crime (the Palermo Protocol in 2000). Political will and diplomatic pressure have resulted in the near-total diffusion of antitrafficking laws modeled off the American precedent.

The rush to make up for lost time has led to certain compromises. Early tradeoffs involved prioritizing individual rescue over broader structural reform. This has led to strategic decisions about whether to prioritize women and children or *all victims*, and whether to prioritize trafficking for sexual exploitation or *slavery in all its forms*. To be successful, emancipation must be sustainable. To rescue someone in the late afternoon and call it a day is not freedom. Sustainable emancipation requires transformations in the broader systems and structures connected to an individual's political, economic, and social life. This is no easy task. Individuals do not live in isolation but are embedded in larger sets of norms, broader social dynamics, and longstanding communities. Sustainable emancipation requires a society-centric approach. This means taking rights violators seriously. Lawsuits are critical, but they cannot be the only tool, especially when perpetrators think they are upholding an intimate moral order rather than breaking a remote secular rule. What are we to make of such a situation? I believe an answer to this question comes from a broader perspective about the historical moment in which we live. This chapter makes three distinct arguments: first, that the current antislavery movement has a history and that this history bears directly on how we think of slaveholders; second, that an exclusive focus on victims has led to general ignorance about perpetrators; and third, that a combination of faulty perspectives on and ignorance about perpetrators leads to a thin understanding of emancipation.

THE RESURGENT ANTISLAVERY MOVEMENT

Slavery is perhaps the oldest human rights violation. Antislavery is certainly the modern world's oldest form of collective action for human rights. It is only with this perspective that we may appreciate the ways in which slavery assumes different forms at different points in time and how civil society organizes itself in response. The earliest antislavery movements in England, and later in America, pioneered what are now industry-standard forms of contentious politics—petitions, banners, slogans, pamphlets, safehouses and sanctuary, economic sanctions, boycotts, buycotts legislative challenges, lawsuits, and the like.

In the United States and the United Kingdom—and indeed the Anglo-American world is the focus of this chapter[3]—there have been four discernible waves to what Joel Quirk (2011) has called the Anti-Slavery Project.[4] Together they represent not only the first global social movement but also the modern world's oldest and longest-running series of interlinked social movements.[5] The sudden explosion of activity starting in 2000 is unique, but not for the reasons many assume. After all, lots of issues gain sudden popularity. But not all issues are historically linked in this way. From the late eighteenth century onward, norm entrepreneurs have worked continuously to expand notions of human dignity, rights holders, and definitions of slavery. The links are both thematic and institutional.

The first wave of the abolitionist movement in the Anglo world emerged in eighteenth-century England. In 1787, Quakers and evangelical Anglicans formed the Society for the Abolition of the Slave Trade (Walvin 2003). Several decades later, Thomas Clarkson, an English abolitionist who helped form the society, started the Anti-Slavery Society. The Anti-Slavery Society, more recently known as Anti-Slavery International (ASI), has operated ever since. The social-movement mobilization that took place in this first wave pioneered the use of the petition and divestment from slaveholding firms (Hochschild 2005) and introduced two diplomatic devices: peacetime economic sanctions and the multinational oversight committee (Nadelmann 1990). The movement's contributions were ethical, tactical, and institutional.

The second wave of movement activity occurred in the United States in the early to mid–nineteenth century. A vast debate gripped the nation in a social movement that continued up through the Civil War, after which a botched emancipation set former slaves on a track of exploitation and marginalization that would continue unabated for another one hundred years (Bales 2004, Blackmon 2009). Together, these two movements triggered a wave of domestic and international antislavery activity that saw slavery outlawed in much of the world by the beginning of the twentieth century. The third movement wave was international and focused on ending King Leopold's rule over the Congo, which relied on slavery and forced labor.[6]

This brief overview brings us to the present outpouring of popular and legislative attention to this issue. The most recent wave of social-movement efforts to end slavery emerging in the United States and the United Kingdom bears some of the hallmarks of earlier eras, including petitions, economic boycotts, the passage of public policy, a touch of moral panic, and the like. But in other ways the current wave is happening under significantly altered circumstances. The roots of the fourth movement lie in the surge of migration that followed the collapse of the Soviet Union in 1989. As the USSR came apart, millions were on the move—not only in the former Soviet states and satellites but also in regions that had previously been frozen in Cold War rivalries. With so much migration, and with the United States and Russia each reassessing their role in the world, exploitation flourished along migratory routes the world over.[7]

Those journalists and activists who first noticed this exploitation increasingly applied the term "human trafficking" to it. As globalization accelerated both economically and culturally, new opportunities for migration emerged. People were pushed by post-1989 dislocations, and they were pulled by the opportunity to work in new places, some of which appeared considerably better than the place they were leaving. This combination of push factors—fleeing from a failing home or a collapsing economy—with pull factors—the desire for honest work and a better life elsewhere—was cemented during the 1990s and has become central to our understanding of trafficking. This understanding has some merit but is also incomplete and ahistorical.

While there have been four waves of antislavery efforts in the Anglo-Saxon world, it was ASI that remained active throughout the intermovement periods. In 1890, the organization championed the Brussels Act, which addressed the slave trade in colonies and protectorates around the world. In addition, an ASI campaign from 1904 through 1913 rallied the public against the extractive slavery practiced in the Congo Free State by King Leopold II of Belgium. In the 1920s, the agency advocated for the end of indentured labor in the British colonies, pushed for the end of slave labor in Peruvian rubber production, and lobbied the League of Nations to produce the 1926 Slavery Convention. This work continued into the 1950s (the Supplementary Convention on the Abolition of Slavery), through the 1970s and 1980s, during which ASI released a series of reports on child and bonded labor, and into the 1990s, with the organization of the 1998 Global March Against Child Labor, the push for the ILO Convention on the Worst Forms of Child Labor, and the establishment of the Special Action Programme to Combat Forced Labour in 1999.

ASI has simultaneously published the *Anti-Slavery Reporter* for a century and a half.[8] The duration of these efforts—advocating, educating, pressuring, informing, investigating, lobbying, and raising awareness—is unparalleled in the history of social movements.

The sociologist Verta Taylor (1989) has observed that the lulls between movement waves represent critical periods of abeyance—a state of disuse or suspension. Taylor's work has shown that abeyance structures—institutions or organizations that carried the flame and kept the faith, however quietly, during lulls in the women's movement—made all the difference in providing a vital spark when the moment was right. It is reasonable to argue that ASI has served as a critical abeyance structure during multiple eras of issue decline and dormancy. ASI has provided an important institutional thread for comparative-historical analysis of the movement. Likewise, a handful of scholars have emphasized the fact that the term slavery provides a similar analytical thread.

The work of scholars such as Jean Allain and Kevin Bales (2011; Allain 2012, 252) points to the persistence of slavery as "the status or condition of a person over whom any or all of the powers attaching to the right of ownership are exercised." While the world has changed and styles of exploitation have evolved, slavery's core attributes have remained relatively stable for thousands of years. Human trafficking may have picked up steam after the fall of the Berlin Wall, but the system of slavery has been a key feature of human relations throughout the twentieth century as well as the millennia preceding it. Anti-Slavery International's heritage has served as a movement structure that has allowed the antislavery movement to survive in the doldrums between the waves. This history deserves retelling. The rhetorical utility of earlier movements was on full display in 2007, when England celebrated the second centennial of abolition on its soil. Likewise, much was made—in the United States and United Kingdom—over the role of the British abolitionist William Wilberforce around the same time.

There are many lessons to learn from an assessment of these waves. One lesson involves the changing nature of the slaveholder. If an earlier era was marked by the ownership of one person by another, it made sense to speak of slave *owners*. At present, it makes more sense to speak of slave *holders*, both for reasons of legal ownership—it is no longer possible to own another person— as well as reasons of temporality. Many contemporary forms of enslavement see victims held for shorter periods of time, as lower exploitation costs mean initial investments may more easily be recouped and the period of exploitation may be reduced dramatically, when compared to earlier eras of slavery (Kara 2009, Bales 2012). While contractual relations were clear, linear, and legally enforceable in the past, relations in contemporary slavery are more fraught. The use of threats and violence to control another person takes many forms. In cases of international human trafficking, relations are often complex, as a village recruiter hands a victim off to a transporter, who deposits the victim of trafficking into the charge of an unscrupulous and abusive employer. In the end, exploitative relations are social relations, regardless of their form or duration.

DEFINING PERPETRATORS

Up to this point, exploitative landlords have been discussed as social movement targets. Yet, they are also perpetrators of contemporary slavery. By *perpetrator*, I mean *any individual directly or indirectly benefitting from the enslavement of another*. This would include recruiters, transporters, enforcers, and management, the direct net beneficiaries, and the indirect net beneficiaries. Direct net beneficiaries include, by way of example, a factory owner, a brothel owner, or a direct user, as in the case of a john using a victim of trafficking for sexual exploitation. Indirect net beneficiaries include a much larger ring of individuals and institutions that benefit from this exploitation. For example, you and I benefit from the lower prices we pay for our clothes as a result of Uzbekistan's use of forced labor to harvest cotton. In some instances, we may find a sole proprietor who has outsourced the task of finding cheap labor. In others we may find that a complex system of plausible deniability ensures that the lowest-paid workers generate the maximum revenue to corporate entities with the minimum possible legal exposure—this describes the sort of agricultural practices that are targeted by advocacy groups such as the Coalition of Immokalee Workers (Drainville 2008). For example, a village recruiter hands a victim off to a transporter, who deposits the victim of trafficking into the charge of an unscrupulous and abusive employer, as suggested earlier. This unscrupulous employer either pockets the profits (direct net economic beneficiary), shares them with investors (indirect net economic beneficiaries), or passes them along to customers (indirect net economic beneficiaries). It is safe to say that we know the most about recruiters, transporters, enforcers, and users in human trafficking but far less about these other categories of beneficiaries.[9]

FINDING PERPETRATORS

Before turning to what little we do know, I would like to take a moment to explain why we know so little. Slaveholders (and traffickers) have been generally overlooked for two important reasons. The first reason is normative; the second reason is logistical. Upon first learning that slavery still exists, most people, and a good number of institutions, want to *just do something*. The reality of the issue contradicts a longstanding and nearly global consensus on individual freedom and dignity. We are offended, we want to act, and my experience with advocacy and outreach suggests that people want to act by rescuing the victim. Since trafficking for sexual exploitation continues to be the highest-profile example of this exploitation, and since the "poster child" cases for trafficking are actual children, the response to any perpetrator, real or imagined, is fast and final. Perpetrators are "animals," "inhuman," and "criminals of the worst sort." These are understandable and appropriate human reactions to gross injustice, and they motivate triage responses for the victim and immediate incarceration for the perpetrator. Incarceration might be the best response, but it should not be the only one.

The second reason slaveholders have been overlooked is logistical. The sequencing of responses is somewhat understandable in an age of triage: rescue victims and pass new laws. This early response left little room for nuanced approaches to perpetrators. It is only recently that more work has been done on corporate accountability, labor trafficking, and other seemingly second-order issues. An additional logistical issue is related to access. Since many perpetrators are knowingly involved in lawbreaking activities, they may be unwilling to serve as research subjects. Now might be the right time for researchers to reach out and talk to perpetrators, but there probably is no ideal time for perpetrators to sit down and talk to us. I say "probably" because it is not immediately clear whether perpetrators are unwilling to talk to researchers or researchers are unwilling to talk to perpetrators. A number of new studies suggest that, under the right conditions, perpetrators are willing to tell their stories.[10]

When slaveholders do open up, a number of issues immediately present themselves. The first is the nature of the data. Scholarship covering slaveholders and traffickers comes in two varieties: data *on* perpetrators and data *from* perpetrators.[11] Data on perpetrators come from legal proceedings, arrest records, newspaper reports, and any other secondary data source. Data from perpetrators themselves come from interviews conducted in prison or in society. My sense is that, in societies where slavery practices are widely accepted, as in rural India, interviewees are willing to be relatively honest, since the likelihood of arrest is near zero. In societies with high penalties for trafficking, however, arrestees may be willing to speak more freely from jail. While I leave it to others to confirm these hypotheses, the reality is that most emerging scholarship on perpetrators comes from conversations with arrestees. Prisoners are often the only accessible sample of a generally inaccessible perpetrating population, though we should carefully consider the possibility that arrestee data tell us more about the people our societies ask the police to arrest than it does about who is actually deserving of incarceration. Social inequality patterns arrests. Many recruiters, transporters, and enforcers find themselves in jail while many direct and indirect beneficiaries are protected by police.[12]

UNDERSTANDING EMANCIPATION

Slavery is simultaneously a legal, mental, and physical category and for this reason has been the site of much debate among scholars. Abolitionist feminists, conflating prostitution and trafficking, argue that false consciousness and internalized oppression explain the "choice" to enter a lawbreaking, rights-violating, and soul-crushing social practice.[13] Both abolitionist and nonabolitionist feminists—the latter advocating a clear difference between free and forced prostitution—might find comfort in the argument advanced by Anne Gallagher (2012), that the "exploitation of the vulnerability of another" constitutes a critical leverage point for oppressors.[14] What is emancipation if vulnerability is a slippery slope to slavery? Should interventions be pursued if we do not agree on the nature of exploitation? Is the sustainable path out of sex trafficking paved by collective bargaining or laws and enforcement? Some of these debates appear intractable to me, rooted as they are in fundamentally irreconcilable philosophical differences between a camp that sees the body as a temple and another that sees it as a resource.

Changing the way we think about perpetrators should change the way we think about intervention, emancipation, and freedom. Contemporary systems of slavery, and especially international networks of human traffickers, require a host of actors operating with a range of profit motives. The nature and meaning of emancipation, then, is complicated exponentially. If the primary route out of chattel slavery was death, this appears no longer to be the case. It is safe to assume that there are more paths out of slavery than usually discussed in antitrafficking circles. These include raids and rescues, community mobilization, rebellion, voluntary manumission, self-emancipation and escape, the discharging of one's debt, being discarded, and death. It is impossible to determine the exact prevalence of these paths, since several disappear into the dark.

Public policy and organizational tactics rest on implicit assumptions about emancipation. Some organizations have opted for top-down strategies that rescue victims through raids while targeting high-visibility perpetrators with criminal prosecution. This approach rests on the assumption that high-profile cases have a demonstration effect that dissuades future abuse, whether by the defendant or others employing bonded laborers. Other organizations have instead opted for more grassroots and bottom-up approaches that challenge the balance of power between vulnerable workers and dominant employers. This approach rests on the assumption that the most important factor is the protection of individual workers and that the experience of challenging employer dominance will have a knock-on effect at the individual level. Hundreds of millions of dollars have been spent by American and European donors, both public and private.[15] These monies go toward a range of activities, including raising awareness, reducing vulnerability, prosecuting perpetrators, and, significantly for our study, bringing individuals out of exploitation through a number of activities, including rescues.

Rescues, rather obviously, are most often instances in which law enforcement officials, ideally in collaboration with victim advocates, identify a site of exploitation for a targeted intervention that removes some or all individuals from exploitative conditions.[16] The target is, therefore, the slaveholder as well as the enslaved or trafficked individuals, and the trigger for the intervention is usually a tip from activists or the community or a cry for help from victims themselves (Free the Slaves and Berkeley Human Rights Center 2004). This is the most widely recognized and recommended form of intervention, as it promises the immediate extraction of trafficked or enslaved individuals and the immediate apprehension of slaveholders.

Community mobilization is a hybrid intervention strategy used by human rights groups working with communities to address slavery and trafficking alongside other community issues. This approach to collective-action interventions emphasizes community organizing in which the formerly oppressed engaged in "blended social action." Rather than substantive and widespread social movements to end bonded labor, organizing takes the form of self-help groups, collective savings, group boycotts, and other efforts that "combine public claims making with civic forms of behavior" (Sampson et al. 2005, 673).

Using community-organizing strategies in some contexts and labor-organizing strategies in others, this approach encourages communities to bargain collectively for specific human rights, including the right to paid labor, the right to political participation, freedom of mobility, freedom of assembly, and access to economic markets and political spheres. The target and claim, therefore, vary from intervention to intervention. The trigger for this type of effort is often the conscientization of an existing group member or the efforts of a social movement or nonprofit organization. Since collective action tends to develop over longer periods of time than do rescues, there is often more time to plan for nonviolent confrontations with slaveholders. This is not always possible, as some slaveholders may respond in the short or medium term with repression or countermobilization.

In some cases, relations between enslaved individuals and slaveholders results in *rebellion*. This was an infrequent but high-profile form of resistance to slavery during the era of transatlantic trade, and it is similarly uncommon in contemporary slavery. However, it is not unheard of, as seen in the Sonbarsa uprising (Bales 2012). That case provides a clear example of an enslaved community taking up arms against their oppressors. A member of the slaveholding class was killed during community-organizing efforts, escalating the event from community mobilization to an insurrection. Rebellions tend to be short and violent confrontations that ultimately lead to either movement victory or repression. In practice, the relationship between rebellion and community organizing may become blurred, as the case of Sonbarsa demonstrates.

The first two intervention types—rescue and community mobilization—are the strategies most frequently and deliberately pursued by international and domestic human rights groups. The other paths out of slavery—rebellion, voluntary manumission, escape, discharging debt, and discarding—are all pursued by slaveholders or enslaved individuals. The same may also be said of death, if it is from something other than natural causes.

Preferences for particular interventions are patterned by differences in opinion about the precise nature of the problem and appropriate solution (Choi-Fitzpatrick 2014). For second- and third-wave feminists the primary problem is the sexual abuse of women, but the desired solution is subject to intense debate. Abolitionists advocate for an end to prostitution and "sex trafficking" and the rescue of victims; risk reductionists call for the proper regulation of sex work together with collective bargaining and unionization. For those focused on migration, the primary concern is the rights and safety of people on the move and the desired intervention involves rescuing people so they may be repatriated to their point of origin. For criminal justice enforcers, the primary concern involves the enforcement of laws, and the desired intervention is the rescue of victims. Those promoting a human rights approach focus specifically on the human rights of the trafficked person, and intervention primarily takes the form of rescues or community organizing (Choi-Fitzpatrick 2015a).

Advocates of a human rights approach have long suggested that raids and rescues undermine the self-determination and human rights of individuals who have chosen to work in prostitution while also inserting them into a legal system that is more interested in using their testimony than in letting them choose their own paths forward. Advocates of a criminal justice approach and the abolitionist wing of the prostitution debate are more likely to advocate for raids and rescues, which bring exploitation to an abrupt halt, remove victims from abusive conditions, and bring perpetrators to jail and justice (Bernstein 2010). Both are important.

I have focused on three approaches—rescue, community mobilization, and rebellion—because they are the most visible. The reason for this visibility is the presence of outside actors in each, whether they are law enforcement, advocacy groups, or the media. While each of these three approaches was used in the collective-action efforts described earlier, six additional exit routes exist.

Broad changes reported by interviewees point to the fact that rescue, countermobilization, and rebellion are not the only important paths out of slavery. Such changes in the political economy and shifts in the means of production may slowly undermine the importance and utility of slavery.[17] Ethan Nadelmann (1990, 496–497) has observed that that "the waning political and economic power of slaveholders proved crucial to the success of local abolitionist groups" in earlier abolitionist waves. This gradual erosion is important but difficult to measure because in many cases, Nadelmann argues, slavery may be replaced by forms of labor and systems of relations that closely resemble slavery (497).

Very little is known about voluntary manumission and debt repayment, but perhaps the least is known about escape, discarding, and death, largely because these tend to lack witnesses. Examples of voluntary manumission are to be found in India, as with one powerful kiln owner mentioned earlier. He released two bonded laborers, blamed their condition on a subordinate, and used the incident to demonstrate his trustworthiness in a kiln owner–NGO collaboration to draft employment policies for his industry.[18] Anecdotally, my fieldwork with bonded laborers in India suggests they are now far more likely to discharge their debt at some point in their lives than they were when I first spoke with workers fifteen years ago. This observation is supported by studies that have noted a similar transformation in the kiln sector (Gupta 2003). The same cannot be said of escape, being discarded, and death, about which almost nothing is known and for which there are rarely any witnesses, unless a survivor self-identifies to social service providers or law enforcement officials.

Just because little is known about these routes does not mean they are not heavily traversed. A simple but illustrative thought experiment suggests that a certain number of survivors exit

TABLE 7.1 ELEVEN PATHS OUT OF SLAVERY

	KEY ACTOR	TARGET*	FOCAL EVENT
More Visible			
Rescue	Police and outside groups	Focused: slaveholder and enslaved	Raid or redemption (short term)
Community mobilization	Community or outside groups	Diffused: community and/or focused: slaveholder	Nonviolent confrontation (long term)
Rebellion	Enslaved individuals	Focused: slaveholder	Violent confrontation (short term)
Less Visible			
Erosion	Varies (e.g., broach changes in political economy	Diffused	Multiple (i.e., changes in the means of production)
Voluntary manumission	Slaveholder	Focused: enslaved	Unknown
Debt repayment	Enslaved individual	N/A	Repayment of debt
Escape	Enslaved individual	Focused: slaveholder	Economic or normative push/pull
Discarded	Slaveholder	Enslaved person	Brokenness, old age, weakness
Death	Slaveholder**	Enslaved person	Abuse, old age
Antiquated			
Legal emancipation	State	Focused: Slaveholder and enslaved	Social movements; changing global norms
Passing	Enslaved individual	N/A	Desire to escape

Note: An earlier version of this table appeared in Choi-Fitzpatrick (2016b).

* "Slaveholder" should be interpreted to mean "slaveholder directly or indirectly" because slaveholders often employ intermediaries.

** Since so little is known about this category, it is difficult to explicate thoroughly. Here I have indicated slaveholder responsibility in those cases where, directly or indirectly, enslavement plays a role in the death of an enslaved person.

exploitation along routes not captured by official estimates. If five thousand people are being trafficked into the United States each year, and this random but presumably low number had been constant for the decade since the United States passed a law against trafficking, then a decade after the law's passage there would have been fifty thousand people living in slavery in the United States. If this many people lived in slavery in the United States, then advocates would have likely identified far more trafficked persons. In reality, while five thousand special visas have been set apart for survivors of trafficking each year, fewer than five thousand of these visas have been distributed in the subsequent *decade*, and this number included the visas issued to survivors' family members as well. The total number of trafficking visa applications from trafficking survivors at that point was fewer than three thousand (see U.S. Citizenship and Immigration Services 2010, Kishin and Wyler 2010, and USimmigration.com n.d.). There is a gap between the anticipated and actual size of the problem.

There are two possible explanations for this gap. The first is the very real possibility that the magnitude of the human-trafficking problem in the United States is not as large as originally thought. This explanation strikes me as very plausible.[19] The second reason is that no matter the actual number, victims eventually exit their exploitative condition and likely do so in greater numbers than captured by official estimates. The accuracy of these two hypotheses is difficult to determine, however, as these routes are nearly invisible.

TIME FOR A FRESH APPROACH

This book has taken a unique approach to an issue most commonly referred to as human trafficking. The first major difference lies in my emphasis on the lived experience of *slaveholders* rather than traffickers. Since this is the topic of the book, I will only reiterate my belief that slavery is a relationship best understood if we listen to the parties involved. While law enforcement approaches generate high-profile cases that may have a pronounced demonstration effect, the longer-term challenge remains: finding new livelihoods and transforming social relations. A human rights approach to emancipation must have alternate livelihoods for survivors *and* perpetrators, and it must posit credible alternative social structures. Some will scoff at my naiveté, and others will accuse me of indifference to *justice*, but I believe there is also a role for reconciliation.

The second major shift is in the topic at hand, which I consider to be *contemporary slavery* rather than human trafficking. Most attention in the antislavery sector is focused on a single aspect of contemporary slavery: human trafficking. This bias persists despite the fact that the majority of those held in slavery—the vast majority, if we accept the calculations provided by experts in the field[20]—are never trafficked internationally but are instead exploited in their home countries or local communities. Even more constricting is the fact that various communities deal with slavery as if it were the most recent instance of the phenomenon of greatest interest to them: advocates for women's rights tend to focus on prostitution, migration experts tend to focus on migration, law enforcement focuses on crime, international institutions focus on forced labor, and historians and sociologists are more likely to focus on slavery (Choi-Fitzpatrick 2015a). While advocates may focus on domestic trafficking and while slavery may take new forms, these must be understood as an "extension and/or reconfiguration of enduring historical themes, rather than as distinctively modern developments" (Quirk 2012, 41).[21] This historical theme is slavery. Thinking in terms of slavery significantly broadens our historical horizons, allowing us to compare and contrast the present moment with more than two hundred years of advocacy. Thinking in terms of slavery also allows us to think about slavery in all of its forms—from chattel and bonded labor to trafficking for sexual or labor exploitation.

The third major shift lies in this book's emphasis on *emancipation* rather than on slavery. Alison Brysk and I have argued that, since contemporary victims of slavery are simply the weakest link in larger systems of exploitation, protecting them requires more robust solutions for *all* women, *all* men, *all* workers, *all* migrants (Brysk and Choi-Fitzpatrick 2012b). Rights-based protection and empowerment should be the norm, regardless of citizenship, gender, type of labor, legal status, and even perpetrator status. Sustainable emancipation in places like India requires sophisticated plans for victims and perpetrators and broad development-oriented benchmarks for both. Some of the perpetrators I interviewed, for example, were net beneficiaries of development programs from well-respected nonprofit agencies.

It is clear that all emancipations are not created equal, as botched attempts make painfully clear (Bales 2007, Blackmon 2009, Quirk 2011). A human rights approach to sustainable emancipation requires access to paid work, financial savings, basic services, active integration into development projects, and the option to continue working the earth, necessitating land reform (Bales and Choi-Fitzpatrick 2012). More must be done to prepare enslaved individuals to integrate into the political and economic systems that will serve not only as bulwarks against reexploitation but also as foundations for a stronger society. To put this into the language of the U.S. Trafficking in Persons Office, the "three P's" of prevention, protection, and prosecution are important, but survivors must be trained in politics, profit, and power as well. Rescue, rehabilitation, and reintegration are critical, but so is representation in political, economic, and cultural spaces.[22] Such an approach will help ensure that slaveholders are unable to regain lost ground through repression and rejuvenated exploitation strategies.

8

BETWEEN GOOD AND EVIL

The Everyday Ethics of Resources
and Reappraisal

Daily laborers call me *Farmer*, but bonded laborers call me *My Farmer*
and *My Owner*.

—Prajapati (Interviewee 64)

We are like family.

—Goral (Interviewee 90)

This book began its life in a brothel. In the late 1990s
and early 2000s, I had turned my attention to the
issue of human trafficking. Stories of women and
children trafficked by large criminal networks and then sub-
jected to systematic degradation struck me to my core. Certainly
something—*anything*—must be done about something that is so
unequivocally wrong. I proceeded to volunteer for a new human
rights group focused exclusively on a number of justice-related
issues, trafficking chief among them. This work connected me
to the organization's outreach efforts, and later to fieldwork, in
South Asia. As an investigator in rural India, I was tasked with
two things: first, investigating cases of bonded labor in kilns,

quarries, and farms; and second, documenting instances of trafficking for sexual exploitation. Building a case against those trafficking into brothels was no mean feat. My first task was to document the presence of underage girls in private establishments. The assumption was that young and underage girls, children really, were regularly made available in brothels that catered to both domestic clientele and international tourists. The investigative team welcomed me, since they were already relatively well known to the managers and enforcers who ran the establishments. I represented a new face able to pose convincingly as a john in search of certain sexual services. This is how I found myself wearing a wire, geared up with surveillance equipment, inside a brothel.

The routine was simple. I would pose as a sex tourist and ask to see the goods. I would insist the women presented to me were not young. When their replacements got younger, I insisted they were not young enough. Feigning outrage that they had nobody young enough for my tastes, I would storm out, rejoin the investigative team, review the videotape—yes, *tape*—and then collaborate with law enforcement to develop a plan for the raid that would rescue the victims and hopefully lead to the prosecution of the perpetrators.

I grew disillusioned with this approach when it became clear to me that the substantial effort being put into prosecuting the perpetrators was not matched with a similar investment in the care and reintegration of the survivor. In telling this story I mean to highlight my empathy for the urgency over human trafficking that has gripped the international community. Certainly *something* must be done to help women and children suffering from violent exploitation. Collaboration with law enforcement, the rescue of innocents, and their protection in aftercare facilities were all laudable goals. But what often happened next in government remand homes was abuse and exploitation, thus driving survivors back into vulnerability and victimization.

The solution, I came to realize, is not at the individual level alone. Short-term interventions are necessary and important, but the longer-term work of sustainable emancipation requires social adaptation and evolution. Thinking in social terms requires taking all parties seriously. Here I have focused on human rights *violators*. They break federal and international laws, but they also abide by local norms that may seem more relevant to the issues at hand. How they respond to movement challenges tells us a lot about what happens next—whether exploitation ends decisively or mutates insidiously. While such outcomes are rarely clear-cut and are often difficult to trace, an emphasis on the process from perpetrators' perspectives tells us something about why exploitation persists as well as whether and how it might reemerge.

This study contributes an empirical case to scholarship on contemporary slavery. I hope it also has implications for social-movement theory. In this book, I have explored antislavery community mobilization using an interactive, relational, and process-oriented approach to both contentious politics and subsequent settlement. This approach draws on the political-process model advanced by Doug McAdam and his collaborators. My emphasis is on the fact that collective action emerges in response to broad change processes and is then patterned by perceptions, resources, tactics, and ongoing interactions between claimant and incumbent. This process is iterative, as actors act and react to one another over time, learning and adapting across two distinct stages of contestation, both as challenges emerge and as they are resolved. Finally, this approach is relational, as incumbents and claimants are often operating in some cultural, temporal, and spatial proximity. In this concluding chapter, I hope to draw some of these strands together, provide a broad overview of the empirical story and a brief recap of the theoretical argument, suggest some implications and outstanding questions for current and future scholarship, and end with what I think of as the broader ethical implications for how we think about periods of change.

A PROCESS-BASED APPROACH TO SOCIAL MOVEMENT EMERGENCE AND IMPACT

Contemporary slaveholders have cognitive barriers that prevent them from realizing the extent to which they had bought into their own paternalistic rationalizations. As a result, they are ill-prepared to resist movement efforts. Interview data suggest oppressors understood that they were taking advantage of laborers' dependency, sometimes passively, but often actively and deliberately. Yet slaveholding landlords had also convinced themselves that they were doing bonded laborers a favor. As long as the oppressed lacked organizational resources and political opportunities, the oppressors could continue business as usual. Over time—decades, generations, centuries—exploitative practices intertwined with cultural norms and supportive ideologies. Exploitation went unchallenged because it was a taken-for-granted seam in the social fabric. Exploitative practices were justified on the grounds that the relationship between oppressor and the oppressed was part of the natural order, and this incumbent mindset pervaded society more broadly.

Over time, however, things change. New roads are built, new laws are passed, and new ideas spread. Landholders face substantial changes in the form of rapid urbanization and migration, the collapse of commodity prices, conditions of persistent drought, the disappearance of party allies, the diminished value of caste, and an uptick in subaltern challenges. These changes give social movements a chance to perceive an opportunity for success while also shaping and affecting its ability to mobilize successfully against any subsequent countermovement. Ultimately, challengers and targets are both exposed to many of the same broader political, economic, and social-change processes. However, their social and economic positions shape their exposure to such changes. Incumbency often comes with significant advantages, especially in the form of key resources and mobilizing structures and institutions.

Individuals and groups everywhere feel compelled to make sense of how things are changing and how they should respond. For all of us this sense making is facilitated by, built upon, and drawn from an existing stock of cultural understandings and individual experiences and beliefs. These understandings, experiences, and beliefs are broadly held across distinct social strata, especially in societies punctuated by hierarchy and inequality. The powerful often possess a paternalistic ideology that is "propagated with an easy vehemence" (Jackman 1994, 8). In rural India, the divine hierarchy of the caste system continues to permeate broader social norms and doubtless serves as the implicit justification for the maintenance of the bonded-labor system. Indeed, it is unclear to upper-caste community members how landless untouchables will survive without care and attention. Or so the thinking goes. This concern for the laborer points up a second justification: the bonded-labor relationship is actually in the best interest of the bonded laborer. The landlord is willing to continue helping the bonded laborer for as long as the laborer needs it, ideally in perpetuity.

For generations, the dominant cultural ideologies of caste supported those rationalizations. When organized groups start pressing new claims in an increasingly favorable context, however, slaveholders are forced to offer justifications for their practices. These justifications themselves are not new, but movements force antagonists to speak them aloud. Such forced reflection can be problematic for the oppressor. Those vulnerable to losing power, authority, or resources are likely to view change as a threat. Their response is patterned and predicated on a combination of the resources available to them and their individual willingness to take certain sorts of action. Some oppressors respond to threats to their status with contentious or even violent attempts to reestablish the status quo and reinstate domination. Others are unwilling to do so and must make do with other responses.

Those with sufficient resources, and a lack of interest in persisting with the targeted behavior, may consider the entire affair to be an opportunity to shift out of an ailing sector or away from old behavior altogether—they may deploy their resources to quit or adapt rather than persist or repress. Those who perceive mobilization and broader change processes to be a threat will deploy their resources and select a tactic in order to engage the challenger.

What follows is an iterative process, as strategic interaction with the challenger provides the target with new information about whether they are able to afford the biases inherent in their original interpretive process. Those lacking resources and confidence may choose conciliatory tactics. Or they may choose confrontational tactics. In the end, it is the strategic interaction that provides the target with a better understanding of the real range of options available. This interactive approach is iterative and incremental, and it is fundamentally sensitive to an important explanatory factor: the gap between old opinions and new realizations.

A relational, iterative, and process-oriented model more clearly highlights the interactive nature of contestation, emphasizing the importance of incumbency's lag effect, especially as the reality of the situation settles in and new interpretations are sought. Jasper and Poulsen demonstrate that targets create problems for themselves, which they then try to solve, if they are able. There are two assessments of the situation: the original interpretation and attribution and the subsequent reinterpretation and reattribution that follow contentious interaction with the challenger.

Original actions taken by targets may be blunt reactions to offense or shock. This flinch may be contrasted with the more studied and measured response that might follow once an individual or institution has taken stock of the situation in light of the new state of affairs. Reactionary tactics may be quite different from considered strategies. We may hypothesize that the gap between the first and second response is best anticipated by the extent of the target's incumbency—in other words, the extent to which the target believed in the legitimacy of their own behavior.

Initially or ultimately, weak oppressors are left with nowhere to turn and resign themselves to the new state of affairs that movements have created through their recognition and utilization of new opportunities, the strategic use of resources, and new perspectives on old relations. Incumbent worldviews such as paternalism may be useful for sustaining inequality, but they are subject to erosion when the marginalized refuse to play by the rules of the game. As a strategy for maintaining inequality, paternalism works best when economic, cultural, and political forces favor the powerful. Former oppressors are thus left with fewer avenues of repression, since, in the final analysis, the overt use of power violates newly recognized rights and norms, albeit only at the community level. This is in clear contrast to the past, when this same behavior was mutually constitutive of dominant norms regarding the appropriate role of untouchable laborers. Appeals to paternalism ring hollow, and efforts to repress face new relational, normative, and practical challenges.

For social movement scholars, I hope this combination of familiar factors points to the relevance of *iterative, relational,* and *process-oriented* explanations of the way target-specific factors shape the emergence, evolution, and end of contestation. While considerably stylized, the following illustration connects each of the book's key arguments sequentially, perhaps providing some testable hypotheses.

Status quo tactics are rooted in earlier settlements. The longer these settlements have been in place, the greater the likelihood they have become part of broader expectations. As a result, status quo tactics such as preemption are rooted in an original

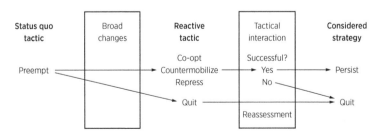

FIGURE 8.1 Three Stages: Culture/Politics/Agency

and earlier understanding of the way things should be. Whether we think of "earlier understanding" as a preexisting settlement, as false consciousness, or as the status quo, it is clear this broad set of assumptions gives rise to particular patterns of social and economic relationship and expectations for the same. In rural India, these relationships are patterned by the caste system. In other cases, the patterns will be different and follow different logics. The general point, however, is that the powerful usually know how to stay in power. Furthermore, this knowledge about how to stay in power may be recognized as a tactic, or it may be subsumed into a broader set of economic, social, and political arrangements that themselves forestall the emergence of grievances and action. These arrangements usually work so long as all other things are equal.

Sometimes all other things are not equal. In fact, broad and disruptive changes occurring in the social, political, economic, and cultural spheres undermine the very forums and processes that were used to maintain power. In other words, the consent of the governed (i.e., Lukes's third face of power) is no longer the tool it once was. Furthermore, truly broad changes are visible to many social actors—individuals may suddenly realize they are part of a larger collective, and old collectives may realize the thing that unites them is under attack. Whether these changes are opportunities or threats is up for debate both on the street and in the halls of power.

Reactive tactics are adapted by challengers and incumbents alike (and by a host of other actors as well). For incumbents, who doubtless preferred the subtle and nonconfrontational tactics of the past, more obvious and forceful tactics must fill in. It is important to note that cooptation, countermobilization, and repression are never first-order choices: they are costly and to maintain power end up requiring both additional resources and increased effort. The goal of power's third face is to make the possession of power appear effortless and a matter of fact. Through violent repression, the machinations of authority are revealed as just that: a machine rather than an ordained and divine source of authority. This is not the position the powerful would like to occupy, since it relies on direct and confrontational tactics, for example, countermobilization and repression, which emphasize crude and obvious sources of control and authority.

Direct and contentious interactions with insurgents provide incumbents with a reality check and an opportunity to reassess their situation. Tactical interactions put incumbents and insurgents in close contact. This provides targets an opportunity to go head to head with challengers but also to go head to head against reality, perhaps for the first time in a while. These are understandable reactions based on the prior status quo, and there is no way to properly predict exactly how incumbents will respond nor to predict whether they have the resources to do so, since the nature of the prior settlements varies from case to case. What we can be sure about is that decisions about the choice of tactics will be made with better and more recent data about the meaning of broader changes, the strength of incumbent resources, the support of other important elites like the state, and the desirability of alternatives. Joseph Luders (2010, 5), for example, suggests incumbents perform a cost-benefit analysis at this point and persist only if they can afford to do so.[1]

A considered strategy results from this process—tactical interaction with the challengers has allowed the incumbent to reevaluate and assess properly the exact scope of the changes. If they are minor, persistence is perhaps preferable. If they are significant, change may be inevitable. Incumbents have fewer options in the end: they generally persist in some way or quit altogether.[2]

I believe this approach takes seriously both structure (earlier settlements) and agency (the process of reassessment). Challengers and targets interact in complex ways and produce new environmental conditions. They simultaneously respond to and create reality. The case described here should go some way toward developing the more dynamic vocabulary necessary to describe target actions, as they calibrate and recalibrate and as they act and react, while also keeping an eye on the broader forces at work. Future scholarship will determine whether these factors are useful in other contexts. Future work may also take up a number of puzzles that this study has raised without resolving.

WHAT ROLE DOES THE MOVEMENT PLAY IN THE TARGET'S DECISION-MAKING PROCESS?

At the national level, Indian social movements have not been successful in framing bonded labor as an issue of mass mobilization or public outrage. Interviewees feel the ground is shifting beneath their feet, but this is the result of local challenges and national politics rather than a larger anti-bonded labor movement that has galvanized the general public. A sobering and unsurprising implication of this study is that movements may matter less than we would like to believe. The fact that interviewees in this study pointed so often to other factors and phenomena lends support to theorists like McAdam and Boudet (2012), who have called for more circumspect and rigorous assessments of when and where collective action emerges or fails to emerge.

SHOULD WE TAKE TARGETS AT THEIR WORD?

Targets also produce methodological puzzles. How might scholars best balance the lived experience of movement targets, who often perceive the deck is stacked against them, with the empirical reality of their elite status and their rights-violating behavior? Additionally, significant social movement case studies, such as the civil rights movement in the United States, benefited from a certain degree of hindsight. It is now clear that segregationists were on the wrong side of history. How do we weigh the testimony of rights violators when no such clarity is available to them or perhaps even to the scholar undertaking the study? How should we interpret incumbents' perspectives in the midst of the action? Are those more or less insightful than data sampled later?

DO TARGETS CHOOSE TACTICS IN THE SAME WAY MOVEMENTS DO?

Incumbents choose tactics drawn from a particular repertoire. Beyond this general observation, little is known about how this process works. Turning back to an anecdote briefly noted in the second chapter, in a critical moment of the civil rights movement, Martin Luther King Jr. made a deliberate move to march in Birmingham, Alabama, home to the segregationist city commissioner T. Eugene "Bull" Connor. Connor was both an avowed segregationist and a lawman. However, he allowed his personal commitments to segregation to cloud his professional judgment. At a time when a contemporaneous lawman, Laurie Pritchett, chose Ghandian tactics, Connor chose violence. King targeted Connor in the hope that he would choose to respond with repression. This is the very reason some antitrafficking groups choose to target extraordinarily violent oppressors: they make solid cases and set enduring precedents. High-profile legislation, law enforcement, and prosecution represent a particular set of movement tactics. We know that Connor consulted with Pritchett and that Pritchett emphasized his alternate approach. Connor then scrolled through a number of options and made his choice. We have history to thank for this anecdote, and it raises several provocative questions. How complex is the reasoning process in the reactive tactic stage? Do incumbents have a clear grasp on what tactics are available and preferable? If Connor consulted Pritchett, then why did he not heed the latter's advice?

WHAT MAKES MOVEMENT VICTORIES SUSTAINABLE?

I have reported how interviewees tell me they feel and how they have responded to challenges. I have not, however, attempted to explain changes in attitudes and beliefs. More sophisticated and comprehensive studies will be needed to explore the relationship between changes in attitude and changes in behavior. How is it that some victories become the new status quo while others are fundamentally hollow, especially with regard to the underlying attitudes that underpin inequality? The Emancipation Proclamation was more aspirational than actual for much of the dark century that passed between 1865 and the Civil Rights Act. Efforts to answer such questions will contribute to both social movement studies as well as human rights scholarship.

HOW MIGHT WE BEST THINK ABOUT INCUMBENCY?

I have borrowed the term incumbency from Fligstein and McAdam, and I use it to explain delays and false starts among the powerful. Systems of authority may facilitate action but may also dull judgment, especially at critical junctures where the consequences of action are amplified. This concept has competition. The Brazilian educator Paolo Friere ([1970] 2000, 58) has argued that "oppressor consciousness" transforms "everything surrounding it into an object of its domination. The earth, property, production, the creations of people, people themselves, time—everything is reduced to the status of objects at its disposal." Friere echoes an earlier philosophy advanced by Martin Buber (1970), in which the latter argues that the othering and instrumentalization of humans is fundamentally dehumanizing. Where Friere argues that a mindset pervades a distinct and entire class, Buber suggests its potential exists more broadly within every individual.[3] Mary Jackman has argued that paternalism is a kind of false consciousness that hides the true nature of expropriative relationships. The culturally embedded nature of paternalism means that both the powerful and the powerless are generally unaware of its operations (Jackman 1994, 8).

A separate line of work has attempted to tackle this same puzzle from a different direction.[4] Scholarship on right-wing authoritarianism sketches a profile of individuals who believe that the world is dangerous and that in-group norms and values should be protected (Altemeyer 1996, Adorno et al. 1950). Likewise, efforts to specify an individually held social-dominance orientation have provided a measurement attuned to individuals who feel that the world is competitive and who respond more clearly to sociocultural factors, including resource scarcity and threats coming from economic competitors (Sidanius and Pratto 1999). Those scoring high on measures of right-wing authoritarianism value coercive social control, obedience, respect for authority, and conformity to religious norms, while those scoring high on social-dominance orientation tend to value power, achievement, and the ability to dominate the weak (Duckitt and Sibley 2009, 296).

I believe incumbency is preferable to these alternatives for a number of reasons. The first is the fact that incumbency is value neutral. While each of the terms appearing above may work well to describe a particular subset of a population, rights-violating behavior falls along a spectrum of social acceptability. Abusers are as likely to be norm followers as they are lawbreakers. Incumbency points to a position vis-à-vis challengers rather than a commitment to exclusion or oppression. Incumbency is defined by the fact that one has a thing or position that others desire. Theories of loss aversion have convincingly demonstrated that people will exert more energy to protect what they have than to gain something new (Tversky and Kahneman 1991). The implication is that most anyone will resist, when faced with the likelihood of losing the thing that a movement demands.

While it may seem like a consensus position that only someone with a right-wing authoritarian personality would resist emancipation efforts, this consensus position exists only in hindsight. The view from the *right side of history* distorts as much as it illuminates. Theories of authoritarianism and dominance do a very good job at describing support for conservative parties and movements. Yet social movements target incumbents of all psychological and political stripes, and anyone faced with losing something would like to keep it. This is not the domain of conservatives; it is a human condition.

IS INCUMBENCY A USEFUL CONCEPT IN OTHER SECTORS?

Corporate managers, large and small stockholders, and small sole proprietors are all affected quite differently. The sole proprietors

I spoke with here are hardly the equivalent of the corporate decision makers captured by the business literature. But perhaps some of the lessons, especially related to the role of threats and resources, may be applied elsewhere. Groundbreaking work on social movement theory is happening in business schools, where collective-action approaches are being deployed to explain corporate behavior and to help businesses better understand both civil society and contentious politics. Future research may begin to fill the gap in knowledge between what is happening in the fields and farms of rural India and in the boardrooms and shareholder meetings of Fortune 500 companies. Are some larger principles at play, perhaps linking slaveholders' and shareholders' assessments of cost with that of politicians, whose responses to movement demands are moderated by public opinion, itself tied to anticipated voter behavior? Is incumbency a useful and portable concept that can serve comparative analysts across these sectors?[5]

WHAT DO INCUMBENTS TEACH US ABOUT THE RELATIONSHIP BETWEEN DEVELOPMENT AND HUMAN RIGHTS?

With more data, a clearer and better-balanced perspective on slaveholders is emerging. Many facilitators are small-time criminals with a stake in only one piece of the trafficking enterprise. Others are economically marginalized sole proprietors in cases of bonded labor. This is not to deny there are large amounts of money involved in some forms of exploitation—trafficking for sexual exploitation is very lucrative. But there are many kinds of slavery and many different tasks and roles for those working to support this enterprise— not everyone is making large amounts of money in their particular role. All too often, slavery and trafficking rely on poor people to exploit even poorer people. Sending perpetrators to jail may help slow the problem, but addressing social and economic inequality will help stop it altogether.

Policies focused on economic growth, educational attainment, and infrastructural modernization are directly related to emancipation.

As such, they should be considered antislavery projects. The slave-holders I spoke with were as likely to source their grievances to new roads and cheap mobile phones as they were to blame antislavery groups. I am certainly not the only one to observe that the first step to ending slavery is to address inequality head-on.[6] Yet scholars, activists, and policy makers often conceptualize inequality as something experienced by victims of slavery alone.

My observations are drawn from the Indian context, but studies in Cambodia, China, and the United States suggest poverty is a predictor for both midlevel perpetrators as well as victims.[7] Sustainable emancipation involves political, economic, and cultural power and participation for formerly enslaved individuals. It also requires addressing larger economic systems focused exclusively on profits, no matter the human cost.

CONCLUSION: THE LINE DIVIDING GOOD AND EVIL

Human rights violators are rarely monsters. Talking with current and former slaveholders helps us better understand the effects and outcomes of mobilization. This study provides a deeper understanding of how perceptions, resources, and options may galvanize action or break down resistance. Clearly, the dynamic would have been very different if these human rights groups were not mobilized, the broader circumstances were not changing, and effective counterframing to paternalistic rationales were neither voiced nor heard. The ideological justification of domination becomes a problem for oppressors when they are confronted by mobilized laborers in possession of alternative interpretations of the relationship and a broader range of options for pursuing their social, economic, and political goals. Movements matter, but so do the attributes of the incumbents they target.

To recognize that employers of bonded laborers are human beings and that the average brothel owner and trafficker is as likely to be a middle-aged woman working alone than a young man working with a syndicate is not to excuse exploitation but instead to open avenues for greater understanding of those community members responsible for exploitation and critical to sustainable emancipation (Sen and Nair 2005). Ward and Langlands's (2008) assessment of restorative justice and human rights approaches to offenders emphasizes the importance of recognizing the human rights of victims, offenders, and their communities. Slaveholders, in this light, are "purposeful moral agents who have fundamental entitlements, as well as obligations, based on their inherent dignity as human beings" (Ward and Langlands 2008, 360). They are not, in a word, moral strangers (Ward and Birgden 2007).

John Conroy (2000, 121), reflecting on his handful of interviews with torturers, confesses that "some part of me hopes that the men I have interviewed are not representative of the whole, because for several of these men, I have a certain respect" for their willingness to speak candidly. Even more complicated, it seems, is the feeling that "in a few I could see myself." I share this concern. Many of the men I interviewed had children the same age as my own, and others struck me as the classic beneficiaries of the kind of international-development programs that I tend to support the world over. But what do we make of ordinary men who are simultaneously recipients of development-aid programs as well as targets of movement-sponsored rights interventions?

In interview after interview I came away with the same sense as Conroy: "the worst part of these interviews was that they were not difficult . . . I never met the monster I anticipated" (2000, 122). Siddharth Kara (2012, 160) seems to find the same thing, as seen earlier—He was so ordinary—just a man, wearing simple village clothes. His aspect was common, his mustache trimmed, his hair neatly combed. He spoke without emotion. We were not expecting "family men . . . pillars of the local community."

What were we expecting? The villain? The monster? We are often expecting pathological evil. Yet oppression is not pathological; it is instead embedded in broader cultural systems and legitimizing myths that render the horrible somehow normal and everyday and banal (Goldhagen [1996] 2007). Individuals hold their own opinions, but these individual opinions are part of larger cultural and social commitments to inequality (Sidanius and Pratto 1999). Coercion is seldom necessary when paternalism provides a relational patina for authoritarianism (Jackman 1994).

No wonder we fail to recognize the villain. Human rights violators themselves are a far cry from John Rawls's polemical outburst: "What moves the evil man is the love of injustice: he delights in the impotence and humiliation of those subject to him and relishes being recognized by them as the author of their degradation" (Eagleton 2010, 94; Dews 2007). Perhaps rights violators in the agricultural sector, those holding bonded laborers in India, are different from those engaged in trafficking for sexual exploitation. Emerging scholarship on perpetrators of other forms of slavery suggests contemporary traffickers and slaveholders are not motivated by a love of injustice.[8] Instead, they are driven by cultural inertia, a desire for profit, or, more frequently, a need for basic sustenance. Perhaps we must "borrow the perspective of the perpetrators and view their evil not as the work of 'lunatics,' but as actions with a clear and justified purpose," considering the broader political or cultural context (Waller 2007, 271). The threat, of course, is to our own conceptualizations of ourselves as moral actors and as humans.

Scholarship on evil takes us into conversations with Nazis and *genocidaires* but rarely into the homes and lives of less illustrious or notorious perpetrators. Yet, in neither of these places—the kilns of the Nazi ovens or the hearths of slaveholders—do we find a "love of injustice." What we instead find are a thousand compromises and justifications. A thousand small steps and a few big leaps. A cultural milieu that facilitates the dehumanization of a particular group of individuals through some arbitrary trait, whether it be skin tone or touchability. What we find instead of the evil villains are husbands, fathers, mothers, and neighbors working with the cultural materials available to them, surviving as best they can with what resources they have, whether it be illiterate laborers or unwanted daughters. This is true for slavery and trafficking but also for other human rights violations more generally.

The implications are unsettling. Slovenka Drakulic, a Croatian journalist documenting Balkan war crimes trials in The Hague, writes that "as the days pass you find the criminals become increasingly human" (quoted in Smith 2011). "You watch their faces, ugly or pleasant, the way they yawn, take notes, scratch their heads or clean their nails, and you have to ask yourself: 'what if this is a man?'" If rights violators are men and women, rather than monsters, then we must ask new sets of questions about our own selves, our own involvement in systems of exploitation and discrimination. Our distorted image of the villain disappears into a more prosaic and familiar set of tensions between old habits and new ideas—tensions we may recognize in our own lives. Movements to connect popular consumer goods or commodities to slavery at the source of production or extraction of natural resources have made great strides toward linking consumers to the lives of laborers. The foregrounding of these ethical links, however strained or tenuous, are important reminders of the ways our own patterns of consumption individually and desire for profit at a national and cultural level push unprotected workers into vulnerable pockets of the global economy. We should not be surprised when we meet rights violators and find ourselves facing a funhouse mirror in which bits of our own selves may be seen.

Of course, the terms used here—slavery and slaveholder—never crossed the lips—nor perhaps even the minds—of the men I spoke with. As we broke bread, drank tea, explored plantations and silk-production houses, swam in deep wells, climbed coconut trees, and talked late into countless evenings, the term slavery never came up. What came up, time after time, was respect, honor, and dignity. The sun was setting on their way of life for a thousand different reasons, and our conversations captured a sliver of their stories, shot through with pessimism and hope. Should we believe the stories of these men, human rights violators, criminals? In their own minds they play the leading roles as victims and heroes in turn.

The book's implications are not limited to slavery, India, and emancipation. Incumbents' paternalistic worldviews may help explain how certain cultural practices shape the way the powerful think about challenges to their authority in other contexts. Although bonded-labor practices are concentrated in South Asia, legitimizing myths that support exploitation and inequality know no borders and may be found in a host of other rights-violating practices.

Taking seriously the experience of rights violators will advance our understanding of how human rights policies and interventions succeed and why they fail. In so many ways, this is a moment in which we all find ourselves. In the interregnum between generations, eras, and epochs. In the moment we realize certain practices are no longer acceptable. The racist realizes old jokes no longer get laughs. The sexist realizes old moves no longer get attention. This book focuses on that very moment of realization and asks, *what next?* The answers, it turns out, tell us quite a bit about social change, social movements, human rights, and perhaps a bit about our own lives. Surely Solzhenitsyn was right: the line dividing good and evil cuts through the heart of every human being.

NOTES

1. IN ALL ITS FORMS: SLAVERY AND ABOLITION, MOVEMENTS AND TARGETS

1. Interviewee 39. All names are pseudonyms.
2. This line of thinking leans on Kevin Bales's (2004) early and provocative essay "Slavery and the Human Right to Evil," in which he builds on Roy Baumeister's notion of the "myth of pure evil."
3. An important exception is d'Anjou (1996). For a historical perspective see Oldfield (1998, 2013), Stauffer (2001), McCarthy and Stauffer (2006), Duberman (1965), Perry and Fellman (1979), Blue (2005), Hahn (2005, part 1), Rugemer (2008), McDaniel (2013), Huzzey (2012), Harrold (1995), Delbanco (2012), and Sinha (2016).
4. The sociologist Verta Taylor (1989) has called such institutions *abeyance structures*.
5. The notion of "private wrongs," drawn from important work by Alison Brysk (2005), informs this entire study and lends a title to chapter 6.
6. Future work will doubtless build on the excellent work of political sociologists such as Kyoteru TsuTsui and political scientists such as Kathryn Sikkink, Thomas Risse, Stephen Ropp, Alison Brysk, and Emilie Hafner-Burton.
7. All interviews and focus groups were conducted through translation in either Kannada or Hindi (and occasionally in local dialects).

8. I have borrowed this leapfrog approach from Michael Lindsay's (2008) fascinating study of the American evangelical elite.
9. According to the Bellagio-Harvard Guidelines on the Legal Parameters of Slavery (2012), the following are examples of the powers attaching to the right of ownership: buying, selling, or transferring of a person; using a person; managing the use of a person; profiting from the use of a person; transferring a person to an heir or successor; disposal, mistreatment, or neglect of a person.
10. *Prosecutor v. Dragoljub Kunarac, Radomir Kovac, and Zoran Vukovic*, International Criminal Tribune for the former Yugoslavia, IT-96-23 and IT-96-23/1-A (2002).
11. This approach hews very closely to the argument developed by Kara (2012). Those skeptical of this approach to choice should be convinced that, choice aside, the inability to leave, pay down a debt, and live free of fear are certainly sufficient to determine that the individual has entered a condition of contemporary slavery. This problem has an analogy with human trafficking, where voluntary smuggling may be transformed, through threats, fraud, coercion, or the exploitation of a position of vulnerability, into human trafficking. This general argument has the support of the Indian Supreme Court, which has broadly, repeatedly, and as recently as 2010 defined "force" as "any factor which deprives a person of a choice of alternatives and compels him to adopt one particular course of action may properly be regarded as 'force' and if labour or service is compelled as a result of such 'force,' it would be 'forced labour.' Where a person is suffering from hunger or starvation, when he has no resources at all to fight disease or feed his wife and children or even to hide their nakedness, where utter grinding poverty has broken his back and reduced him to a state of helplessness and despair and where no other employment is available to alleviate the rigor of his poverty, he would have no choice but to accept any work that comes his way, even if the remuneration offered to him is less than the minimum wage. He would be in no position to bargain with the employer; he would have to accept what is offered to him. And in doing so he would be acting not as a free agent with a choice between alternatives but under the compulsion of economic circumstances and the labour or service provided by him would be clearly 'forced labour.'" See Kara (2012), UN General Assembly (2000), and Supreme Court of India, *People's Union for Democratic Rights v. Union of India and Others*, Indlaw SC88 (Asiad Workers' Case), (1982).
12. No such consensus exists in India, where slavery is often thought of as involving ownership and bonded labor as only involving control over

labor but not the whole person. This book will not bridge that gap and will be undoubtedly be received differently in the West than on the subcontinent. I thank Kiran Kamal Prasad for this observation.

13. Subsequent scholarship may find that other frameworks do similar work in other cultural contexts.

2. BEST-LAID PLANS: A PARTIAL THEORY OF SOCIAL MOVEMENT TARGETS

1. This chapter's title riffs on Robert Burns's 1785 poem "To a Mouse, on Turning Her Up in Her Nest with the Plough," which merits quoting in part: "The best-laid schemes o' mice an' men, / Gang aft agley, / An' lea'e us nought but grief an' pain, / For promis'd joy."

2. See McAdam and Boudet (2012, 4–19) for an excellent overview of these eras.

3. For one account of this era, see Doug McAdam's reflections in McAdam and Boudet (2012, 3–4).

4. My emphasis is on movement targets. Whether they are on the left or right makes little difference for my theoretical approach. It must be mentioned, however, that many studies to date have tended to focus on progressive movements for the expansion of rights and recognition for previously marginalized groups. Scholars have tended to spend less time in conversation with individuals from deeply unpopular groups, perhaps because they are dangerous or difficult to talk to. This may also be a reflection of our values, since we would often rather avoid studying groups we find objectionable (I thank Doug McAdams for this observation). There is some evidence that this narrow focus is starting to change. An important body of work has struck out in another fresh direction, focusing on conservative movements that have been traditionally overlooked by movement scholars. See Clifford (2012), McVeigh (1999, 2009), Van Dyke and Soule (2002), and Munson (2008). Movement theory is also being applied in fresh ways to corporate actors. See McDonnell and King (2013), Vasi and King (2012), Bartley and Child (2014), King and Soule (2007), and Soule (2009). In a similar vein, Kathleen Blee (2002) spent time talking to the women of the Ku Klux Klan, Kristin Luker (1984) has provided a sensitive portrait of the worldviews of pro-life and pro-choice activists, Ziad Munson (2008) took a long look at the making of pro-life activists, and Francesca Polletta (2006) edited a special issue of the journal *Mobilization* focused specifically on the puzzle presented by "Awkward Movements."

5. Gamson (1975, 14–15) helpfully defines a target of influence as "that set of individuals, groups, or social institutions that must alter their decisions or policies in order for a challenging group to correct a situation to which it objects. Such a target is the object of actual or planned influence attempts by the group, called here the group's *antagonist*." He goes on to clarify that this term applies to corporations, national regimes, and actual office holders. These antagonists, Gamson argues, must be outside of the movement's constituency (thereby excluding self-help groups and utopian communities). Gamson proceeds to introduce the "challenging groups" used to provide his seminal work on movement outcomes. No such introduction is made for the targeted groups.

Sidney Tarrow (2011, 165) defines social movements as "contentious collective challenges, based on common purposes and social solidarities, in sustained interaction with *elites, opponents, and authorities*" (emphasis added). Tarrow follows this definition with an extended discussion of the first four factors—challenges, purpose, solidarity, interaction—but remains silent on the final, and arguably most critical, factor in the interaction: the movement's target. None of these three terms—elite, opponent, authority—appear in the book's index. Subsequent discussion suggests the importance of shifting political alignments, influential allies, and divided elites in enabling movements at those moments when "institutional access opens, rifts appear within elites, allies become available, and state capacity for repression declines." The discussion of elite cleavages and allies, however, presents them as potentially enabling factors *for the movement*. The discussion is movement-centric, as if they are a simple binary variable: the broader context may or may not possess two key movement assets. It is only in the discussion of "shifting alignments" that we see elites in possession of their own verbs—political parties set out to *engage* movement actors in order to *shore up* support among a particular voting bloc.

In his entry to the comprehensive *Blackwell Companion to Social Movements*, Rucht (2004) suggests that "movements challenge external groups whom they perceive as opponents or adversaries, and vice versa." Examples "range from other social movements (i.e., countermovements) to interest groups, corporations, churches, political parties, and public administrations to distinct political leaders." This approach deserves mentioning on three accounts. To begin with, it does not actually set out to define targets as unique social actors, instead creating a movement-centric category. Second, this approach accounts for individuals and institutions but not more ideational and cultural movement targets. Finally, much to his credit, Rucht emphasizes the role perception plays in the process.

Rights violators are many, yet movements make strategic targeting decisions and engage in selective framing efforts. Movements choose their
targets. Additionally, targets also shape movements' tactical repertoires,
since the perceived defensive and offensive strength of a target provides
movement actors with important information about what approaches are
likely to work. Walker, Martin, and McCarthy (2008) refer to this as the
"target's vulnerabilities and its capacities for response." Drawing on data
from the *New York Times*, Martin, McPhail, and McCarthy (2009) divide targets into public actors, such as the state or educational institutions, and
private ones, such as businesses. This approach has the virtue of capturing
both state and nonstate targets of violence while also incorporating persons and property into the equation.

Most recently, Fligstein and McAdam (2012) have framed these sets
of relationships in terms of multiple fields of action in which incumbents
and challengers compete and coordinate in various configurations. The
focus on incumbents and challengers echoes those advanced by Gamson
(1975) yet add an important variable: change. Competition and coordina-
tion ensure there is neither a fixed range of incumbents (e.g., only elites)
nor a set band of challengers (e.g., only "the powerless") but instead a
constellation of challenges, alliances, and settlements.

Taken together, we have a sense that movements target novel configurations of individuals, groups, and institutions. The consensus definitions sketched above focus on individuals and institutions. This is good,
but such definitions miss the critical role of norms, values, and ideas. Of
course, a broad definition of "institution" includes the established range
of ideas that guides social norms and behavior. Yet here I use the term to
mean concrete social actors—perhaps the term "corporate" best differ-
entiates this complex social actor from relatively less complex individual
social actors.

Challengers set out to gain new rights and recognition at the individual and institutional level, but they also attack old or introduce new ideas.
Elizabeth Armstrong and Mary Bernstein (2008) capture this perfectly in
their assessment that movements challenge resources and rules. Symbolic
struggles and expressive strategies have material implications, and claims
for recognition or resources challenge social boundaries. Sit-ins simultaneously targeted lunch-counter proprietors, discriminatory business
practices, discriminatory laws, and the Jim Crow system. Movements have
many targets, and not all of them are individuals or institutions.

6. And where the subject is external to the challenger, thereby excluding
self-help groups.

7. *Oxford English Dictionary*, s.v. "collective."
8. Also see Taylor and Van Dyke (2004); Snow (2004); and Kriesi, Koopmans, Duyvendak, and Giugni (1995).
9. But see Luders (2006).
10. More recently, see Maher (2010).
11. Joseph Luders (2010) advances an explicit theory of threat, which he operationalizes as the costs associated with disruption and concession. Movement scholars have identified a number of specific threats, including reputational threat (McDonnell and King 2013) and risk perception by managers (Vasi and King 2012).
12. Movements target institutions (Martin, McPhail, and McCarthy 2009), create new institutions (Andrews 2002), and aim beyond institutions (Armstrong and Bernstein 2008).
13. Joseph Luders (2010) has advanced an important explanation of target behavior but did so using case studies rather than interviews.
14. See, for example, Soule and Davenport (2009) and Beyerlein, Soule, and Martin (2015).
15. Activists often choose particular targets because they are expecting certain responses from them, since the target is seen as a means to an ultimate end. Some movement actions are intended to increase public awareness of their issue, rather than to secure a particular outcome. For this reason they may target an institution that is thought to be receptive to activists' claims, rather than institutions known to be the worst offenders. Activists are often campaigning on two levels—the first focused on a particular policy or practice and the second focused more broadly on winning hearts and minds. Both targets and activists recognize that ultimately they must prevail in the battle for public opinion. Their tactical interplay—boycotts and buycotts, lobbying, and media campaigns, for example—are frequently stepping stones to greater impact on public opinion. (I thank Brayden King for this insight, which I have included here nearly verbatim from personal communication.) See King and McDonnell (2015).
16. While my theoretical take here owes much to Doug McAdam, this agent- (or player-) and process-oriented approach has emerged out of conversations with Jim Jasper. Needless to say, the hiccups, ghosts, and glitches can be claimed by myself alone.
17. In this study I have focused on individual-level incumbents rather than on incumbent institutions or ideas. This simplifies things considerably, as it is easier to track single unified actors as they respond to movement efforts and broader changes.

18. Three decades of scholarship have confirmed the importance of grievances, resources, opportunities, and cultural frames for the mobilization of individuals and our understanding of movements' impacts (see Tarrow 2011). Newer lines of thinking have emphasized the fact that these struggles take place within broader contexts—variously conceptualized as fields (Fligstein and McAdam 2012) or arenas (Jasper and Duyvendak 2014)—in which movement targets might themselves be organized in collective-action struggles targeting other centers of authority with their own claims. These approaches have the advantage of better situating any particular context or set of actors in motion and within a dynamic space. What remains to be seen is how these explanations might be best deployed by a new generation of scholars. See, for example, King and Walker (2014).

    The staying power of the political-process approach is perhaps best explained by its amenability to empirical studies. Newer explanations drawing on fields and arenas have added important nuance to our models. This nuance has not necessarily resulted in a clearer research agenda for scholars conducting the practical studies that represent the bread and butter of social movement scholarship. While general and midrange theories are considered passé in sociology, the political-process approach offers important tools for explaining movement emergence and anticipating dynamic interactions between actors. To be clear, it is not my goal to recover a static and structuralist account of state-challenger interactions. Rather, my objective is to emphasize the enduring importance of these key movement factors for both challengers and incumbents.

19. A focus on costs in this light stretch back to James Wilson's (1961) focus on "negative inducements" and Bill Gamson's (1990) emphasis on "constraints," though they are now more familiar as threats, thanks to the pioneering and enduring work of Charles Tilly. This helpful genealogy is but one of several gems in Luders's (2010, 3n3) work.

20. Whether a particular situation is "really" an opportunity or threat is not a debate I will rehash here. Those interested are advised to begin with the debate over false consciousness that followed Steven Lukes's ([1974] 2005) seminal work on power as well as with contemporary critiques of the "political opportunity" approach (see Goodwin and Jasper 1999).

21. Indeed, Gamson (1975) calls this "pre-emption."

22. Luders, for example, demonstrates that lunch-counter operators were unsure whether integration would cause white customers to shop and conduct business elsewhere. When white customers indicated they would continue frequenting integrated businesses, business owners reassessed

the threat. I thank Joseph Luders for directing my attention to this fact in personal correspondence.

23. The political-process model, as advanced by McAdam and coauthors, recognizes the fact that both parties reassess their situations (see, for example, in Fligstein and McAdam 2012, fig. 1).

24. I thank Aidan McQuade for this cogent observation.

25. This definition diverges from that provided by Gamson (1975, 29): new advantages without acceptance. The reason for this is that I use the term to describe incumbent strategies prior to the emergence of collective action. Preemption is a strategic effort to forestall the emergence of collective action in the first place, rather than a tactical attempt to halt mobilization. Much work is done to prevent the emergence of grievances and a sense that something could be done about those grievances. Of course, targets may respond to collective action with new advantages without acceptance, but I considered these responses to be a form of adaptation and persistence.

26. My use of this term generally follows the definition laid out by Gamson (1990, 29): "acceptance without new advantage," though with some clear exceptions. In some cases confrontational countermobilization efforts head off mobilization. In other cases, a strategy of co-optation attempts to reshuffle the deck by, for example, installing a low-caste proxy in an elected position.

27. Andrews (2002, 2004) observes that the tactical interaction between movement and countermovement represents more of a "loosely coupled tango" than anything else.

28. I am thankful to Joseph Luders for this observation.

29. Myra Marx Ferree (2004, 88) calls such actions "soft repression," and Jennifer Earl (2003, 50) refers to them as "observed and unobserved coercive repression by private agents."

30. Here an important alternate explanation deserves mentioning. It may be that a movement target is commitment to social dominance over the targeted population. Jim Sidanius and colleagues (Sidanius, Pratto, Laar, and Levin 2004) argue that a "social dominance orientation" is rooted in three forms of stratification—gender, age, and an arbitrary, culturally specific third distinction. Sidanius and Pratto (1999) suggest commitment to legitimizing myths aggregate socially and are held individually in the form of a "social dominance orientation"—a desire for group-based dominance. Sidanius and Pratto's theory of social dominance is strengthened by the recognition that this orientation (SDO) is unevenly distributed socially and has varying effects on members of society. While Sidanius and Pratto

offer survey-based instruments for measuring SDO, my sense is that commitments to inequality are difficult to measure, especially when the topics under consideration are in the process of being politicized through a social-movement intervention. Also see Pratto, Tatar, and Conway-Lanz (1999).

31. But emotions only carry the day if they can be sustained through critical resources like collective identity and solidarity or organizational capacity.

32. Indeed, qualitative evidence from this study suggests multiple instances in which perpetrators were both unwilling to quit and unable to persist. It is likely the segregationist Bull Connor fit into this category, as we have no indication that it was anything other than federal intervention that forced his hand and ended his anti-integration efforts. Resistance may emerge, Neil Fligstein and Doug McAdam (2012, 105) argue, when a target's "power and material advantage is fully dependent on the existing settlement, thus motivating them to fight to the bitter end to preserve their privileged position." The target's motive to resist may be clear, but the ability to persist is uneven. Some targets are able to persist but remain unwilling to do so. Why might this be?

    While I am unable to confirm my hypothesis with the data on hand, I believe the answer lies in variation in the attribution of opportunity (or of threat): Individuals may perceive new opportunities within the broader social and economic transformations that can be secured with sufficient capital. To borrow a reference from popular culture, when combined with sufficient resources, "chaos is a ladder" (Murrow 2013)—movements may provide cover for institutions and individuals to take otherwise unpopular or risky action. Likewise, perceptions of threat are just as likely to drive action, as when a stockbroker sells stock in a beleaguered company or fund. If an investment—in a company targeted by a divestment campaign or a social practice targeted by an education campaign—looks more risky than rewarding, then there is good reason to believe that a rational actor would walk away. It delights me to note a second, ultimately improvable, explanation. It may be that slaveholders in this study see the error of their ways and have a "change of heart," essentially experiencing what Doug McAdam termed cognitive liberation. Certainly there is some recourse for those who "have so internalized the self-serving account of their own advantage that they are blind to other perspectives" (Fligstein and McAdam 2012, 105). I believe some blindness can be cured, including bigotry and racism, though this tends to be an exception, and though this hypothesis is ultimately beyond empirical assessment.

33. I thank Doug McAdam for this observation, which I have included here nearly verbatim from personal communication.

34. There is a small but growing body of literature on this topic, however. See Conroy (2000), Dews (2007), Hatzfeld (2005), Meister (2011), Smith (2011), and Waller (2007).
35. I thank Joseph Luders for pushing me to recognize better the fact that these economically rooted vulnerabilities often make certain targets more vulnerable "irrespective of cultural circumstances" (personal correspondence, March 2016).

3. JUST LIKE FAMILY: SLAVEHOLDERS ON SLAVERY

1. Interviewee 126.
2. Interviewee 115.
3. Arguably, it was his brother who forced him to take the debt in the first place and later to shift out of the debt and into the promise of rehabilitation funds.
4. Founder of The Federation. As my colleague Farheen Husain has pointed out, people enter into bonded conditions to mitigate hardship, but some times also in order to gain protection against former abusing slaveholder and thereby avoid future entrapment.
5. Interviewee 90.
6. Interviewee 88.
7. Interviewee 64.
8. Ibid.
9. Interviewee 77.
10. Interviewee 64.
11. Interviewee 87.
12. Interviewee 106.
13. Interviewee 64.
14. Interviewee 112.
15. Interviewee 31.
16. Interviewee 120.
17. Interviewee 88.
18. Interviewee 79.
19. The intimacy of paternalism is perhaps the most insidious form of the third face of power advanced by Lukes ([1974] 2005) and Gaventa (1982).
20. Interviewee 64.
21. Interviewee 123.
22. An example of this can be seen in the notion of Varnas, that each caste has a sociospiritual role in the divine order. For a range of perspectives on this topic, see Bentley and Stedman Jones (2001), Cohen (2010), King (1901), and Pelczar (1993).

4. AS IF WE ARE EQUAL: SLAVEHOLDERS ON EMANCIPATION

1. All quotes in this paragraph are from interviewee 31.
2. Interviewee 68.
3. Interviewee 88.
4. Interviewee 77.
5. Colossians 3:23: "Let your hearts be in your work, as a thing done for the Lord and not for men."
6. Interviewee 103.
7. Interviewee 77.
8. Interviewee 38.
9. Ibid.
10. Interviewee 106.
11. See, for example, David Simon's *The Wire* (HBO, 2002–2008).
12. Interviewee 107 and 97, respectively. Interviewee 97 argued: "Some people don't repay their debts. People who command respect return the money. But those who don't command respect don't repay their debts."
13. Interviewee 119.
14. Helpfully, the monsoon season (Kharif crops) coincides with the work season offered by MNREGA. This allows laborers to leverage MNREGA work for higher wages.
15. Focus Group Discussion 45.
16. Interviewee 007.
17. I thank Farheen Husain for this observation.
18. Interviewee 80.
19. Interviewee 30.
20. Interviewee 007.
21. Scheduled Tribe / Scheduled Caste and Other Backward Castes, respectively.
22. Interviewee 007.
23. Focus group participant, Focus Group Discussion 45.
24. Interviewee 31.
25. Interviewee 64.
26. Interviewee 97.
27. Interviewee 120.
28. Interviewee 97.
29. Interviewee 123.
30. Interviewee 007.
31. Interviewee 123.

32. The reality is that many rural laborers cycle through urban labor markets and engage in dirty, dangerous, and difficult work, often exposed to trafficking networks and reexploitation in India's new urban economy. It stands to reason that farmers experience labor constraints because of human trafficking, which represents an exploitative subset of this outbound migration. Demand for labor is high in urban areas, and laborers are perhaps more likely to be convinced by the promises of traffickers.
33. Interviewee 112.
34. Interviewee 120.
35. Interviewee 80.
36. Interviewee 76.
37. Interviewee 142.
38. Interviewee 152.
39. Interviewee 119.

5. THE FARMER IN THE MIDDLE: TARGET RESPONSE TO THREATS

1. Interviewee 103.
2. I thank Farheen Husain for emphasizing to me the actual *and* symbolic power inherent in this position.
3. This particular formulation has been borrowed, verbatim, from personal correspondence with Joseph Luders (March 2016).
4. In the discussion that follows I address each category except "preemption," which is discussed more appropriately in chapter 3.
5. Interviewee 123.
6. Interviewee 111.
7. Movement groups often respond to consistent repression or countermobilization with a shift in tactics from community mobilization to police-coordinated raids. This has the effect of removing willful criminals from our sample by placing them in jail. Interviews with victims of these more hostile, violent, and criminal employers suggests a consistency in the findings, however.
8. Focus Group Discussion 155.
9. Such officials would include the district magistrate and the subdistrict magistrate.
10. Focus Group Discussion 148. Interviewee 155 underscores this fact with the observation that, since police are transferred so regularly, it is difficult to know whom one can trust.

11. Focus Group Discussion 153.
12. Interviewee 69, founder of Mobilizing for Change.
13. Ibid.
14. Interviewee 140.
15. Interviewee 37.
16. Though such an exploration would be difficult, as it would require securing interviews with a community that has been more seriously stigmatized than the interviewees for this project.
17. Interviewee 34.
18. Interviewee 120.
19. Interviewee 130.
20. Interviewee 79.
21. Interviewee 120.
22. Interviewee 122.
23. Interviewee 119.
24. Interviewee 122.
25. Ibid.
26. Interviewee 7.
27. Interviewee 122 and Focus Group Discussion 45. Focus Group Discussion 45: "Only those people are doing farming who are fifty or sixty years old. Those younger are not. There are some who didn't get a job anywhere. Their parents have a farm at home. They are doing it out of necessity."
28. Interviewee 122.
29. Interviewee 42, Mobilizing for Change.
30. Interviewee, leader of the Anti-Trafficking Initiative.
31. Interviewee 76, founder of Free from Bondage.
32. Interviewee 115.
33. Interviewee 126.
34. Interviewee 200.
35. Interviewee 122.
36. Interviewee 120.
37. Interviewee 123.
38. Interviewee 31.
39. Thucydides' summary of the Athenians' statements to the Melians is worth quoting in full: "We hope that you . . . will aim at what is feasible, holding in view the real sentiments of us both; since you know as well as we do that right, as the world goes, is only in question between equals in power, while the strong do what they can and the weak suffer what they must" (*History of the Peloponnesian War* 5.5.89).
40. Focus Group Discussion 45.

41. Interviewee 31.
42. Also see Ruef and Fletcher (2003).
43. Interviewee 97.
44. Interviewee 114.
45. Interviewee 64.
46. A further advantage to this arrangement is that the legal owner who obtains the sales permit from the state revenue offices may live in an urban area and outsource ongoing operations to a chain of contractors. Accountability is greatly obscured in the process. I thank Farheen Husain for pointing this out.
47. Interviewee 74.
48. Interviewee 75.
49. Interviewee 76, founder of Free from Bondage.
50. See also King and Pearce (2010) as well as King and Walker (2014).
51. Interviewee 45.

6. PRIVATE WRONGS: SLAVERY AND ANTISLAVERY IN CONTEMPORARY INDIA

1. Though Kara (2012) estimates more. Some estimates run significantly higher. The Bonded Labor Liberation Front (2013) suggests that the number is 65 million children and 300 million adults, or one-third of India's total population.
2. Hueze (2009, 168) argues that "debt appears as the point which associates the spirit of Hindu culture to capitalism and monetized social relations."
3. See Bonded Labor System (Abolition) Act, Act no. 19 of 1976, February 9, 1976, Indian Ministry of Labour and Employment.
4. According to the UN's 1956 Supplementary Convention on the Abolition of Slavery, debt bondage is "the status or condition arising from a pledge by a debtor of his personal service or those of a person under his control as a security for a debt, if the value of those services as reasonably assessed is not applied toward the liquidation of the debt or the length and nature of those services are not respectively limited and defined." The ILO (2001) defines bonded labor as a "term [that] refers to a worker who renders service under conditions of bondage arising from economic considerations, notably indebtedness through a loan or advance."
5. Data from the Planning Commission's report stops in 2007. See Government of India Planning Commission (2012).

6. Indeed, one possible reason the ILO's 2005 estimates of forced labor were so much lower (12 million) than other estimates was rumored to be the fact that India did not cooperate with the study's request for estimates.

7. Based on 2005 exchange rates from xe.com. $400/month × 12 months = $4,800. According to Forbes.com, middle class was $4,000 or more at the time of writing.

8. See Carpenter (2015), Picarelli (2015), Iacono (2014), Siegel and Blank (2010), Troshynski and Blank (2008), and Goodey (2008).

9. This finding echoes George Lakoff's (2010). I am grateful to Lars Almquist for this observation.

10. The notion of a "welfare queen," for example, is a particularly pernicious myth that legitimizes disdain for the working poor in the United States.

11. Dalit is the term I prefer to use for a group once described as "untouchable," described by Gandhi as the Harijan ("children of god"), and officially recognized by the Indian government as the "Scheduled Caste." Caste discrimination continues despite having been abolished by the Constitution and addressed by numerous laws over the intervening decades. See Macwan et al. (2010).

12. The Bahujan Samaj Party (BSP) is a national political party with center-left leanings. It draws the majority of its support from the populous state of Uttar Pradesh. The party's focus on *bahujan* (literally, the majority) takes its inspiration from B. R. Ambedkar, the author of the Indian Constitution.

13. The Bharatiya Janata Party (BJP), or "India's People's Party," is a conservative national political party that promotes Hindu nationalism.

14. Mawdsley's sentiment echoes the work of scholars such as Pavan Varma (2007, 136), who writes that "if we seek to catalogue the dominant social traits of the middle class, the first thing that comes to mind is a truly amazing imperviousness to the external milieu except in matters that impinge on its own immediate interest," as well as Andre Beteille (1991) who contends the "expanding middle class has an ugly face, and its members often appear as callous and self-serving." Also see Roy (1993), Deo and McDuie-Ra (2011), and Mawdsley (2004, 88).

7. LONG GOODBYE: THE CONTEMPORARY ANTISLAVERY MOVEMENT

1. This chapter touches on themes articulated in the *Journal of Human Rights* and in a recent edited volume. See Choi-Fitzpatrick (2015a, 2016b).

2. Weitzer (2014) writes: "From 2001 to 2011, the U.S. government alone spent a reported $1.12 billion funding international and domestic antitrafficking programs (Don't Shout Too Loud, documentary, Changing Directions Productions, 2013)."

3. Here I must make an observation about the Western-centric nature of this exercise. In what follows I trace the history and debates as they have occurred within the United States and Britain. There are two reasons for this. The first is lamentable: I am less familiar with other contexts, languages, and histories. The second reason is advantageous: the social movements described here represent the world's *first* transnational advocacy effort, antislavery is the world's *longest-running* series of loosely linked movements, and in its current form the debates occupying the Anglo-American sphere have the *most significant impact* on international law and norms, representing nearly all of the private- and public-sector funding that goes toward eradicating slavery. Hundreds of millions of dollars in spending is effected by the logics and debates detailed in this chapter. For this reason alone these predominantly Anglo-American debates matter for policies, private and public expenditure, and grassroots emancipation efforts. It is my hope that this initial effort is followed by other studies that illuminate those areas I have not.

4. The concept of "four antislavery waves" can be traced to arguments advanced by Kevin Bales. See Bales and Cornell (2008).

5. I thank Kevin Bales for this observation.

6. I would propose the addition of a third, smaller, yet salient phase in the English-speaking world. With a peak period from 1870 to 1914, both the United States and Britain experienced widespread concern over the "White Slave Trade," a panic that used the rhetoric and imagery of slavery to advocate for the protection of female chastity, peaking in the United States with the passage of the Mann Act (see Bell 1910, Day 2010). This initiative is increasingly factored into the literature as part of abolitionist history. While its inclusion is sometimes contested given its patriarchal conceptualizations of gender, it is important to emphasize because it laid the groundwork for much of the language of rescue and rehabilitation that became common in the late 1990s (see Bernstein 2010) and is still occasionally used both legally (see Mattar 2011) as well as by movement actors (see Choi-Fitzpatrick 2014, Quirk 2007).

7. See Bales (2012) for a classic overview of this story.

8. Anti-Slavery International website, http://www.antislavery.org/english/what_we_do/our_history.aspx.

9. This overview draws on ideas first advanced in Choi-Fitzpatrick (2016a).
10. See, for example, the entire special issue of the *Journal of Human Trafficking*: Feasley (2016), Denton (2016), Arhin (2016), and Gotch (2016). See also Carpenter (2015).
11. Quickly scanning the literature it is clear that recent studies have drawn from a number of sources, including socially acceptable crimes (this volume), trusted diaspora networks (Zhang 2008, 2013; Arhin 2016), data from criminal trials (Denton 2016, "Anatomy of Offending"), and data from arrestees (see Keo et al. 2014).
12. See the special issue of the *Journal of Human Trafficking* (2016), guest edited by Choi-Fitzpatrick.
13. Here I follow a division between "abolitionist abolitionists" and "risk-reduction abolitionists" articulated in Choi-Fitzpatrick (2015a).
14. In other words, vulnerability might be rooted in a lack of state protection or in systems of patriarchy, gender oppression, and the male right to sex. See Gallagher (2012).
15. See the 2014 special issue of the *Anti-Trafficking Review* on "Following the Money: Spending on Anti-Trafficking."
16. But see Appiah (2011) and Bunzl (2011) for an analysis of a recent wave of redemptions.
17. I have Aidan McQuade to thank for this observation.
18. Interviewee 140.
19. In the late 1990s the CIA estimated that as many as 50,000 individuals were trafficked into the United States every year, yet by the late 2000s the official U.S. government estimate had settled to 14,500 per year—the truth is, nobody knew. Not to be dissuaded, entrepreneurial grant recipients, committed to the cause and facing the loss of funding if funding was cut based on a lack of identified victims, rebranded prostitution as "domestic trafficking" and effectively reinflated this number. This heuristic move had the effect of bringing a much larger and more familiar community of sex workers under the trafficking umbrella and onto the agenda of local law enforcement. I believe this shift was born of a desire to maintain funding but had the effect of further cementing a perspective that prostitution is slavery. Note: the United States government is largely out of the estimation business now; for an ongoing effort to estimate slavery's global scope, see the Global Slavery Index.
20. I am thinking of Bales and Hathaway in particular here. See Hathaway (2008).
21. This broader contemporary-slavery perspective is advanced in various ways by a number of scholars generally rooted in comparative and

historical sociology. Kevin Bales's popular work (2012) was subtitled "New Slavery," and he specifically delineated the relationship between "new" and "old" slavery. The exercise, however, was intended to emphasize that while the unimportant things had changed (legal ownership, for example), the truly important things (like control) had not. While some scholars are skeptical of this dichotomy, this skepticism is rooted in a sense that significant amounts of slavery persisted between 1865 and 1989—in other words, the issue is important, but it isn't new. Important work by both Joel Quirk (2011) and Suzanne Miers (2003) has shed critical light on the persistence of slavery in postabolition contexts throughout the twentieth century.

Siddharth Kara's (2011) investigation of bonded labor in India follows the same logic. By identifying bonded labor as a form of slavery, and in emphasizing that this form of slavery is quite old, this research further undermines the notion that the problem is predominantly one of the globalization-induced trafficking of women. The slavery perspective has an older legal heritage than competing perspectives. This is true in terms of both domestic legislation (which stretches back to the Slave Trade Act of 1807 in Britain) and international law (the 1926 Slavery Convention). The Bellagio-Harvard Guidelines on the Legal Parameters of Slavery extend the 1926 Slavery Convention's determination that "slavery is the status or condition of a person over whom any or all of the powers attaching to the right of ownership are exercised" to include debt bondage in those cases where there is control over a person tantamount to possession. In sum, the argument here is that "slavery" is a category that covers the movement of people into enslavement (trafficking) quite well.

22. Over the past decade critiques of the existing human rights model (Global Alliance Against Trafficking in Women [GAATW] 2007, Gallagher 2009, Hathaway 2008) have grown in number and hopefully in sophistication, as have pieces of new thinking about what a better model might look like (Bales and Choi-Fitzpatrick 2012, Brysk and Choi-Fitzpatrick 2012a, Gallagher 2009). Groundwork for this approach has been laid in works by a number of scholars, including Bales (2012), Brysk (2005), Brysk and Choi-Fitzpatrick (2012a), Bales and Choi-Fitzpatrick (2012), and Gallagher (2009), as well as by a range of human rights groups, especially the Global Alliance Against Trafficking in Women (GAATW). See also Kempadoo (2005) as well as Kempadoo and Doezema (1998). For a critical perspective see Quirk and Bunting (forthcoming).

8. BETWEEN GOOD AND EVIL: THE EVERYDAY ETHICS OF RESOURCES AND REAPPRAISAL

1. That is to say, if concession costs are high and disruption costs are low.
2. One particular outcome that I have overlooked—ignored altogether actually—is a complete change of heart and change of mind among incumbents. While this is certainly possible, I believe that more often than not social change can be explained not by the transformation of the mind but by simple resignation and quitting. Future research may demonstrate that this is in fact an inverted U, with incumbents possessing the most and fewest options the most likely to mobilize themselves through last-ditch collective-action strategies intended to reclaim power and authority. I believe this is a probable pattern, although not one testable from the data at hand.
3. This is an important distinction. What Friere roots in personal consciousness I have located instead within culture, since the absolutely pervasive nature of oppression leads me to believe the causal mechanism is norm following rather than an individual preference for inequality. See Noelle-Neumann (1974).
4. The following discussion echoes the argument made by John Duckitt and Chris Sibley (2009) in their excellent chapter on the topic.
5. This line of thinking can be found in the work of Paul Burstein ([1985] 1998).
6. See Bales (2007) and a truncated version of this argument in Bales and Choi-Fitzpatrick (2012).
7. On Cambodia, see Keo et al. (2014); on China, see Shen (2016); and on the United States, see Carpenter (2015).
8. See, for example, Feasley (2016), Denton (2016), Shen (2016), Arhin (2016), and Gotch (2016).

REFERENCES

Adorno, Theodor W., Else Frenkel-Brunswik, Daniel Levinsonm, and Nevitt San-
ford. 1950. *The Authoritarian Personality.* New York: Harper & Row.

Aggarwal, Partap C. 2012. "Changing Religious: Their Relationship to Secular
Power in a Rajasthan Village." In *Village Society,* ed. Surinder S. Jodhka, 118–
127. Delhi: Orient Blackswan.

Allain, Jean. 2012. *Slavery in International Law: Of Human Exploitation and Trafficking.*
Leiden: Martinus Nijhoff.

Allain, Jean, and Kevin Bales. 2011. *Slavery and Its Definition.* Queen's University
Belfast Law Research Paper no. 12-06.

Altemeyer, R. A. 1996. *The Authoritarian Specter.* Cambridge, Mass.: Harvard University Press.

Anderson, Benedict. [1983] 2006. *Imagined Communities.* London: Verso.

Andrews, Kenneth T. 2002. "Movement-Countermovement Dynamics and the
Emergence of New Institutions: The Case of 'White Flight' Schools in Mississippi." *Social Forces* 80:911–936.

——. 2004. *Freedom Is a Constant Struggle: The Mississippi Civil Rights Movement and Its
Legacy.* Chicago: University of Chicago Press.

Anti-Slavery International (ASI). 2001. "The Enslavement of Dalit and Indigenous Communities in India, Nepal, and Pakistan Through Debt Bondage."
Report to the UN Subcommission on the Promotion and Protection of Human
Rights. http://www.antislavery.org/includes/documents/cm_docs/2009/g
/goonesekere.pdf.

200   REFERENCES

Appiah, Kwame Anthony, and Martin Bunzl. 2011. *Buying Freedom: The Ethics and Economics of Slave Redemption.* Princeton, N.J.: Princeton University Press.

Arhin, Antonela A. 2016. "A Diaspora Approach to Understanding Human Trafficking for Labor Exploitation." *Journal of Human Trafficking* 2 (1): 78–98.

Armstrong, Elizabeth A., and Mary Bernstein. 2008. "Culture, Power, and Institutions: A Multi-Institutional Politics Approach to Social Movements." *Sociological Theory* 26:74–99.

Bales, Kevin. 2004. "Slavery and the Human Right to Evil." *Journal of Human Rights* 3 (1): 55–65.

——. 2007. *Ending Slavery: How We Free Today's Slaves.* Berkeley: University of California Press.

——. 2012. *Disposable People: New Slavery in the Global Economy.* 3rd ed. Berkeley: University of California Press.

Bales, Kevin, and Austin Choi-Fitzpatrick. 2012. "The Beginning of the End of Slavery." In *Human Trafficking and Human Rights: Rethinking Contemporary Slavery*, ed. Alison Brysk and Austin Choi-Fitzpatrick, 195–215. Philadelphia: University of Pennsylvania Press.

Bales, Kevin, and Rebecca Cornell. 2008. *Slavery Today.* Toronto: Groundwork Guides.

Barkan, Steven E. 1984. "Legal Control of the Southern Civil Rights Movement." *American Sociological Review* 49 (4): 552–565.

Bartley, Tim, and Curtis Child. 2014. "Shaming the Corporation: The Social Production of Targets and the Anti-Sweatshop Movement." *American Sociological Review* 79 (4): 653–679.

Baumeister, Roy, and Aaron Beck. 2009. *Evil: Inside Human Violence and Cruelty.* New York: Holt.

Bell, Ernest A. 1910. *Fighting the Traffic in Young Girls; Or, War on the White Slave Trade.* Nashville, Tenn.: The Southwestern Company.

Bellagio-Harvard Guidelines on the Legal Parameters of Slavery. 2012. Research Network on the Legal Parameters of Slavery. March 3.

Belser, Patrick, Michaelle de Cock, and Farhad Mehran. 2005. "ILO Minimum Estimate of Forced Labour in the World." International Labour Organization. digitalcommons.ilr.cornell.edu/nondiscrim/7/.

Bentley, Tom, and Daniel Stedman Jones. 2001. *The Moral Universe.* London: Demos.

Bernstein, Elizabeth. 2010. "Militarized Humanitarianism Meets Carceral Feminism: The Politics of Sex, Rights, and Freedom in Contemporary Antitrafficking Campaigns." *Signs* 36 (1): 45–71.

Beteille, Andre. 1991. "The Reproduction of Inequality: Occupation, Caste and Family." *Contributions to Indian Sociology* 25 (1): 3–28.

Beyerlein, Kraig, Sarah A. Soule, and Nancy Martin. 2015. "Prayers, Protest, and Police: How Religion Influences Police Presence at Collective Action Events in the United States, 1960 to 1995." *American Sociological Review* 80 (6): 1250–1271.

Bhalla, A. S. 2005. "Recent Economic Reforms in China and India." *Asian Survey* 35 (6): 555–572.

Blackmon, Douglas. 2009. *Slavery by Another Name: The Re-Enslavement of Black Americans from the Civil War to World War II.* New York: Anchor.

Blee, Kathleen. 2002. *Inside Organized Racism: Women in the Hate Movement.* Berkeley: University of California Press.

Blue, Frederick J. 2005. *No Taint of Compromise: Crusaders in Antislavery Politics.* Baton Rouge: Louisiana State University Press.

Bob, Clifford. 2005. *The Marketing of Rebellion: Insurgents, Media, and International Activism.* Cambridge: Cambridge University Press.

——. 2012. *The Global Right Wing and the Clash of World Politics.* Cambridge: Cambridge University Press.

Bonded Labor Liberation Front. 2013. *Bandhua Mukti Morcha.* http://swamiagnivesh.com.

Breman, Jan, and Isabelle Guerin. 2009. "Introduction: On Bondage: Old and New." In *India's Unfree Workforce: Of Bondage Old and New,* ed. Jan Breman et al., 1–17. Delhi: Oxford University Press.

Breman, Jan, Isabelle Guerin, and Aseem Prakash, eds. 2009. *India's Unfree Workforce: Of Bondage Old and New.* Delhi: Oxford University Press.

Brown, Eleanor. 2007. *The Ties That Bind: Migration and Trafficking of Women and Girls for Sexual Exploitation in Cambodia.* Phnom Penh: International Organization for Migration.

Brysk, Alison. 2005. *Human Rights and Private Wrongs: Constructing Global Civil Society.* New York: Routledge.

——. 2013. *Speaking Rights to Power: Constructing Political Will.* New York: Oxford University Press.

Brysk, Alison, and Austin Choi-Fitzpatrick, eds. 2012a. *Human Trafficking and Human Rights: Rethinking Contemporary Slavery.* Philadelphia: University of Pennsylvania Press.

——. 2012b. "Rethinking Trafficking and Slavery." In *Human Trafficking and Human Rights: Rethinking Contemporary Slavery,* ed. Alison Brysk and Austin Choi-Fitzpatrick, 1–12. Philadelphia: University of Pennsylvania Press.

Buber, Martin. 1970. *I and Thou.* Trans. W. Kaufmann. New York: Scribner.

Buechler, Steven M. 2007. "Strain and Breakdown Theories." In *The Blackwell Companion to Social Movements,* ed. David A. Snow et al., 47–66. Malden, Mass.: Blackwell.

Burstein, Paul. [1985] 1998. *Discrimination, Jobs, and Politics: The Struggle for Equal Employment Opportunity in the United States since the New Deal.* 2nd ed. Chicago: University of Chicago Press.

Campbell, Gwyn. 2005. "Introduction: Slavery and Other Forms of Unfree Labour in the Indian Ocean World." In *Abolition and Its Aftermath in Indian Ocean Africa and Asia,* ed. Gwyn Campbell, 1–28. New York: Routledge.

Carpenter, Ami. 2015. "Action Logics Among Traffickers." Presentation at the 56th Annual Convention of the International Studies Association, New Orleans, Louisiana.

Central Intelligence Agency. 2013. *CIA World Factbook.* https://www.cia.gov /library/publications/the-world-factbook/geos/in.html.

Chandhoke, Neera. 2012. "Gujarat and Its Little Illusions." *Economic and Political Weekly,* December 8.

Chhibber, Pradeep K. 2001. *Democracy Without Associations: Transformation of the Party System and Social Cleavages in India.* Ann Arbor: University of Michigan Press.

Chidambaram, Shri P. 2010. "Further Discussion on the Situation Arising out of Increasing Atrocities Against the Scheduled Castes and the Scheduled Tribes in the Country Raised by Shri Gopinath Munde on the 19th August, 2010." August 19. http://164.100.47.132/LssNew/psearch/Result15.aspx?dbsl =3161&ser=&smode= t#3000*25.

Choi-Fitzpatrick, Austin. 2012. "Rethinking Trafficking: Contemporary Slavery." In *Human Trafficking and Human Rights: Rethinking Contemporary Slavery,* ed. Alison Brysk and Austin Choi-Fitzpatrick, 13–24. Philadelphia: University of Pennsylvania Press.

——. 2014. "To Seek and Save the Lost: Human Trafficking and Salvation Schemas Among American Evangelicals." *European Journal of Cultural and Political Sociology* 1 (2): 119–140.

——. 2015a. "From Rescue to Representation: A Human Rights Approach to the Contemporary Anti-Slavery Movement." *Journal of Human Rights* 14 (4).

——. 2015b. "Emancipazioni contemporanee: una tipologia delle vie d'uscita dall'asservimento [Emancipation from contemporary slavery: a typology of intervention strategies]." *Mondo Contemporaneo Rivista di Storia*—Italian Journal of Contemporary World History 21:141–161.

——. 2016a. "The Good, the Bad, the Ugly: Human Rights Violators in Comparative Perspective." *Journal of Human Trafficking* 2 (1): 1–14.

——. 2016b. "Letting Go: How Elites Manage Challenges to Contemporary Slavery." In *Contemporary Slavery and Human Rights,* ed. Joel Quirk and Annie Bunting. Vancouver: University of British Columbia Press.

Christian Aid. 2005. *The Damage Done: Aid, Death, and Dogma.* London: Christian Aid.

Cohen, Joshua. 2010. *The Arc of the Moral Universe and Other Essays*. Cambridge, Mass.: Harvard University Press.

Conroy, John. 2000. *Unspeakable Acts, Ordinary People: The Dynamics of Torture*. Berkeley: University of California Press.

d'Anjou, Leo. 1996. *Social Movements and Cultural Change*. New York: Aldine de Gruyter.

Davenport, Christian. 2007. "State Repression and Political Order." *Annual Review of Political Sociology* 10:1–23.

——. 2010. *Media Bias, Perspective, and State Repression: The Black Panther Party*. New York: Cambridge University Press.

——. 2015. *How Social Movements Die: Repression and Demobilization of the Republic of New Africa*. New York: Cambridge University Press.

Davenport, Christian, and Priyamvada Trivedi. 2013. "Activism and Awareness: Resistance, Cognitive Activation and 'Seeing' Untouchability Among 98,316 Dalits." *Journal of Peace Research* 50 (3): 369–383.

Davis, David Bryon. 1999. *The Problem of Slavery in the Age of Revolution, 1770–1823*. New York: Oxford University Press.

Day, Sophie. 2010. "The Re-emergence of 'Trafficking': Sex Work Between Slavery and Freedom." *Journal of the Royal Anthropological Institute* 16:816–834.

Delbanco, Andrew. 2012. *The Abolitionist Imagination*. Cambridge, Mass.: Harvard University Press.

Denton, Erin. 2016. "Anatomy of Offending: Human Trafficking in the United States, 2006–2011." *Journal of Human Trafficking* 2 (1): 32–62.

Deo, Nandini, and Duncan McDuie-Ra. 2011. *The Politics of Collective Advocacy in India: Tools and Traps*. Boulder, Colo.: Lynne Reinner.

Dews, Peter. 2007. *The Idea of Evil*. New York: Oxford University Press.

Douglas, Mary. 2002. *Purity and Danger: An Analysis of the Concepts of Pollution and Taboo*. New York: Routledge.

Drainville, André C. "Present in the World Economy: The Coalition of Immokalee Workers (1996–2007)." *Globalizations* 5, no. 3 (2008): 357–377.

Duberman, Martin. 1965. *The Antislavery Vanguard: New Essays on the Abolitionists*. Princeton, N.J.: Princeton University Press.

Duckitt, John, and Chris G. Sibley. 2009. "A Dual Process Motivational Model of Ideological Attitudes and System Justification." In *Social and Psychological Bases of Ideology and System Justification*, ed. John T. Jost et al., 292–313. New York: Oxford University Press.

Eagleton, Terry. 2010. *On Evil*. New Haven, Conn.: Yale University Press.

Earl, Jennifer. 2003. "Tanks, Tear Gas, and Taxes: Toward a Theory of Movement Repression." *Sociological Theory* 21 (1): 44–68.

——. 2011. "Political Repression: Iron Fists, Velvet Gloves, and Diffuse Control." *American Review of Sociology* 37:261–284.

Economist. 2012. "One Dishonorable Step Backwards." *The Economist*, May 11. http://www.economist.com/blogs/banyan/2012/05/indian-women.

Einwohner, Rachel. 2002. "Bringing the Outsiders In: Opponents' Claims and the Construction of Animal Rights Activists' Identity." *Mobilization* 7 (3): 253–268.

Etzioni, Amitai. 1969. *Demonstration Democracy*. New York: Gordon and Breach.

Feasley, Ashley. 2016. "Eliminating Corporate Exploitation: Examining Accountability Regimes as Means to Eradicate Forced Labor from Supply Chains." *Journal of Human Trafficking* 2 (1): 15–31.

Ferree, Myra Marx. 2004. "Soft Repression: Ridicule, Stigma, and Silencing in Gender-Based Movements." In *Authority in Contention, Research in Social Movements, Conflicts, and Change* 25, ed. Daniel J. Myers and Daniel M. Cress, 85–101. Bingley: Emerald Group.

Fitzgerald, Scott T. 2009. "Cooperative Collective Action: Framing Faith-Based Community Development." *Mobilization* 14 (2): 181–198.

Fligstein, Neil, and Doug McAdam. 2011. "Toward a General Theory of Strategic Action Fields." *Sociological Theory* 29 (1): 1–26.

——. 2012. *A Theory of Fields*. New York: Oxford University Press.

Foucault, Michel. 1980. *Power/Knowledge*. Trans. Colin Gordon. New York: Pantheon.

Fox-Genovese, Francis, and Eugene D. Genovese. 2005. *The Mind of the Master Class: History and Faith in the Southern Slaveholders' Worldview*. Cambridge: Cambridge University Press.

Free the Slaves and Berkeley Human Rights Center. 2004. *Hidden Slaves: Forced Labor in the United States*. Washington, D.C., and Berkeley, Calif.: Free the Slaves and Berkeley Human Rights Center.

Friedman, Monroe. 1985. *Consumer Boycotts: Effecting Change Through the Marketplace and the Media*. New York: Routledge.

Friere, Paulo. [1970] 2000. *Pedagogy of the Oppressed*. Trans. Myra Bergman Ramos. London: Bloomsbury.

Gallagher, Anne T. 2001. "Human Rights and the New UN Protocols on Trafficking and Migrant Smuggling: A Preliminary Analysis." *Human Rights Quarterly* 23 (4): 975–1004.

——. 2009. "Human Rights and Human Trafficking: Quagmire or Firm Ground? A Response to James Hathaway." *Virginia Journal of International Law* 50 (1): 789–848.

——. 2010. *The International Law of Human Trafficking*. New York: Cambridge University Press.

——. 2012. "Human Rights and Human Trafficking: A Reflection on the Influence and Evolution of the U.S. Trafficking in Persons Report." In *From Human Trafficking to Human Rights*, ed. Alison Brysk and Austin Choi-Fitzpatrick, 172–194. Philadelphia: University of Pennsylvania Press.

Gamble, Sidney. 1943. "The Disappearance of Footbinding in Tinghsien." *American Journal of Sociology* 49:181–183.

Gamson, William. 1975. *Strategies of Social Protest.* New York: Dorsey.

——. 1990. *The Strategy of Social Protest.* 2nd ed. Belmont, Calif.: Wadsworth.

Gaventa, John. 1982. *Power and Powerlessness: Quiescence and Rebellion in an Appalachian Valley.* Urbana: University of Illinois Press.

Global Alliance Against Trafficking in Women (GAATW). 2007. *Collateral Damage: The Impact of Anti-Trafficking Measures on Human Rights Around the World.* Bangkok: GAATW.

Goldhagen, Daniel Jonah. [1996] 2007. *Hitler's Willing Executioners: Ordinary Germans and the Holocaust.* New York: Vintage.

Goldstone, Jack, and Charles Tilly. 2001. "Threat (and Opportunity): Popular Action and State Response in the Dynamic of Contention Politics." In *Silence and Voice in the Study of Contentious Politics,* ed. Ronald Aminzade et al., 179–194. Cambridge: Cambridge University Press.

Goodey, Jo. 2008. "Human Trafficking: Sketchy Data and Policy Responses." *Criminology and Criminal Justice* 8 (4): 421–442.

Goodwin, Jeff, and James M. Jasper. 1999. "Caught in a Winding, Snarling Vine: The Structural Bias of Political Process Theory." *Sociological Forum* 14:27–54.

Gotch, Katherine. 2016. "Preliminary Data on a Sample of Perpetrators of Domestic Trafficking for Sexual Exploitation: Suggestions for Research and Practice." *Journal of Human Trafficking* 2 (1): 99–109.

Government of India. 2006. *Report of the Working Group to Suggest Measures to Assist Distressed Farmers.* New Delhi: Reserve Bank of India.

——. 2007. *Report of the Expert Group on Agricultural Indebtedness.* New Delhi: Ministry of Finance.

Government of India Planning Commission. 2012. "A Report on Bonded Labour Rehabilitation Scheme Under Centrally Sponsored Bonded Labour System (Abolition) Act, 1976 in the State of Madhya Pradesh, Orissa, Rajasthan, Tamil Nadu and Uttar Pradesh." Jamshedpur: Socio Economic and Educational Development Society (SEEDS).

Gozdziak, Elzbieta. 2009. "Human Trafficking in the United States: Knowledge Gaps and Research Priorities." In *Human Trafficking: New Directions for Research,* ed. International Organization for Migration (IOM). Geneva: IOM. http://www.iom.int/jahia/webdav/shared/shared/mainsite/microsites /IDM/workshops/ensuring_protection_070909/human_trafficking_new _directions_for_research.pdf.

Gupta, Devashree. 2010. "The Power of Incremental Outcomes: How Small Victories and Defeats Affect Social Movement Organizations." *Mobilization* 14 (1): 417–432.

Gupta, Dipankar. 2000. *Mistaken Modernity: India Between Worlds.* New Delhi: Harper Collins Publishers India.

Gupta, Jayoti. 2003. "Informal Labour in Brick Kilns: Need for Regulation." *Economic and Political Weekly* 38 (31): 3282–3292.

———. 2005. "Whither the Indian Village: Culture and Agriculture in 'Rural India.'" *Economic and Political Weekly* 40 (8): 751–758.

Habermas, Jürgen. 1991. *The Structural Transformation of the Public Sphere: An Inquiry Into a Category of Bourgeois Society.* Cambridge, Mass.: MIT Press.

Hahn, Steven. 2005. *A Nation Under Our Feet: Black Political Struggles in the Rural South from Slavery to the Great Migration.* Cambridge, Mass.: Belknap.

Harriss, John, J. Jeyaranjan, and K. Nagaraj. 2010. "Land, Labour, and Caste Politics in Rural Tamil Nadu in the Twentieth Century: Iruvelpattu (1916–2008)." *Economics and Political Weekly* 45 (31): 47–61.

Harrold, Stanley. 1995. *The Abolitionists and the South, 1831–1861.* Lexington: University Press of Kentucky.

Hathaway, James C. 2008. "The Human Rights Quagmire of 'Human Trafficking.'" *Virginia Journal of International Law* 49 (1): 1–60.

Hatzfeld, Jean. 2005. *A Time for Machetes: The Rwandan Genocide: The Killers Speak.* New York: Farrar, Straus and Giroux.

Hochschild, Adam. 2005. *Bury the Chains: Prophets and Rebels in the Fight to Free an Empire's Slaves.* New York: Houghton Mifflin Harcourt.

Hueze, Djallal. 2009. "Bondage in India: Representing the Past or the Present? The Case of the Dhanbad Coal Belt During the 1980s." In *India's Unfree Workforce: Of Bondage Old and New,* ed. Jan Breman et al., 147–169. Delhi: Oxford University Press.

Human Rights Watch. 2012. *Out of Control: Mining, Regulatory Failure, and Human Rights in India.* New York: Human Rights Watch.

Huzzey, Richard. 2012. *Freedom Burning: Anti-Slavery and Empire in Victorian Britain.* Ithaca, N.Y.: Cornell University Press.

Iacono, Eva Lo. 2014. "Victims, Sex Workers, and Perpetrators: Gray Areas in the Trafficking of Nigerian Women." *Trends in Organised Crime* 17:110–128.

International Labour Organization (ILO). 2001. "Stopping Forced Labour: Global Report Under the Follow-up to the ILO Declaration on Fundamental Principles and Rights at Work." Report of the Director-General. Geneva: ILO.

———. 2012. *Global Estimate of Forced Labor.* Geneva: ILO.

Jackman, Mary. 1994. *The Velvet Glove: Paternalism and Conflict in Gender, Class, and Race Relations.* Berkeley: University of California Press.

Jasper, James. 1997. *The Art of Moral Protest: Culture, Biography, and Creativity in Social Movements.* Chicago: University of Chicago Press.

Jasper, James, and Jan Willem Duyvendak, eds. 2014. *Players and Arenas: The Interactive Dynamics of Protest.* Chicago: University of Chicago Press.

Jasper, James, and Jane D. Poulsen. 1993. "Recruiting Strangers and Friends: Moral Shocks and Social Networks in Animal Rights and Anti-Nuclear Protests." *Social Problems* 42 (4): 493–512.

Jodhka, Surinder S., ed. 2012. *Village Society.* Delhi: Orient Blackswan.

Johnston, Hank. 1995. "A Methodology for Frame Analysis: From Discourse to Cognitive Schemata." In *Social Movements and Culture*, ed. Hank Johnston and Bert Klandermans, 217–246. Minneapolis: University of Minnesota Press.

Joshi, Anuradhi, and Mick Moore. 2000. "Enabling Environments: Do Anti-Poverty Programmes Mobilise the Poor?" *Journal of Development Studies* 37 (1): 25–56.

Kara, Siddharth. 2009. *Sex Trafficking: Inside the Business of Modern Slavery.* New York: Columbia University Press.

——. 2012. *Bonded Labor: Tackling the System of Slavery in South Asia.* New York: Columbia University Press.

Keck, Margaret E., and Kathryn Sikkink. 1998. *Activists Beyond Borders: Advocacy Networks in International Politics.* Ithaca, N.Y.: Cornell University Press.

Kempadoo, Kamala, ed. 2005. *Trafficking and Prostitution Reconsidered: New Perspectives on Migration, Sex Work, and Human Rights.* Boulder, Colo.: Paradigm.

Kempadoo, Kamala, and Jo Doezema, eds. 1998. *Global Sex Workers: Rights, Resistance, and Redefinition.* New York: Routledge.

Kennedy, Jonathan, and Lawrence King. n.d. "The Political Economy of Farmers' Suicides in India: Re-analyzing the *Million Death Study* Data with New Variables." Working paper, available upon request.

Keo, Chenda, Thierry Bouhours, Roderic Broadhurst, and Brigitte Bouhours. 2014. "Human Trafficking and Moral Panic in Cambodia." *The Annals of the American Academy of Political and Social Science* 653:202.

King, Brayden. 2008. "A Political Mediation Model of Corporate Response to Social Movement Activism." *Administrative Science Quarterly* 53:395–421.

King, Brayden, and Mary-Hunter McDonnell. 2015. "Good Firms, Good Targets: The Relationship Among Corporate Social Responsibility, Reputation, and Activist Targeting." In *Corporate Social Responsibility in a Globalizing World*, ed. Kiyoteru Tsutsui and Alwyn Lim, 430–454. New York: Cambridge University Press.

King, Brayden, and Nicholas Pearce. 2010. "The Contentiousness of Markets: Politics, Social Movements, and Institutional Change in Markets." *Annual Review of Sociology* 36:249–267.

King, Brayden, and Sarah Soule. 2007. "Social Movements as Extra-Institutional Entrepreneurs: The Effect of Protests on Stock Price Returns." *Administrative Science Quarterly* 52:413–442.

King, Brayden, and Edward T. Walker. 2014. "Winning Hearts and Minds: Field Theory and the Three Dimensions of Strategy." *Strategic Organization* 12 (2): 134–141.

King, George. 1901. *The Moral Universe.* New York: Eaton & Mains.

Kishin, Alison, and Liana Sun Wyler. 2010. "Trafficking in Persons: U.S. Policy and Issues for Congress." Document 7-5700, RL34317. Washington, D.C.: Congressional Research Services. http://www.scribd.com/doc/54233903/36/Table-8-T-visas-Issued-FY2002-through-FY2010.

Kriesi, Hanspeter, Ruud Koopmans, Jan Willem Duyvendak, and Marco G. Giugni. 1995. *New Social Movements in Western Europe: A Comparative Analysis.* Minneapolis: University of Minnesota Press.

Kurzman, Charles. 1996. "Structural Opportunity and Perceived Opportunity in Social-Movement Theory: The Iranian Revolution of 1979." *American Sociological Review* 61 (1): 153–170.

Laczko, Frank, and Elzbieta Gozdziak, eds. 2005. *Data and Research on Human Trafficking: A Global Survey.* Geneva: International Organization for Migration.

Lakoff, George. 2010. *Moral Politics: How Liberals and Conservatives Think.* 2nd ed. Chicago: University of Chicago Press.

Lerche, Jens. 2009. "A Global Alliance Against Forced Labour? Unfree Labour, Neo-liberal Globalization, and the International Labour Organization." In *India's Unfree Workforce: Of Bondage Old and New,* ed. Jan Breman et al., 352–385. Delhi: Oxford University Press.

Levenkron, Nomi. 2007. *"Another Delivery from Tashkent": Profile of the Israeli Trafficker.* Tel Aviv: Hotline for Migrant Workers. http://www.worldcat.org/title/another-delivery-from-tashkent-profile-of-the-israeli-trafficker/oclc/234035142.

Lichbach, Mark Irving. 1987. "Deterrence of Escalation? The Puzzle of Aggregate Studies of Repression and Dissent." *Journal of Conflict Resolution* 31:266–297.

Linden, Annette, and Bert Klandermans. 2006. "Stigmatization and Repression of Extreme-Right Activism in the Netherlands." *Mobilization* 11 (2): 213–228.

Lindsay, Michael. 2008. *Faith in the Halls of Power.* Oxford: Oxford University Press.

Linz, Juan J., and Alfred C. Stepan. 1996. *Problems of Democratic Transition and Consolidation: Southern Europe, South America, and Post-Communist Europe.* Baltimore, Md.: Johns Hopkins University Press.

Luders, Joseph. 2006. "The Economics of Movement Success: Business Response to Civil Rights Mobilization." *American Journal of Sociology* 111 (4): 963–998.

——. 2010. *The Civil Rights Movement and the Logic of Social Change.* Cambridge: Cambridge University Press.

Luker, Kristin. 1984. *Abortion and the Politics of Motherhood.* Berkeley: University of California Press.

Lukes, Steven. [1974] 2005. *Power: A Radical View.* 2nd ed. New York: Palgrave Macmillan.

Mackie, Gerry. 1996. "Ending Footbinding and Infibulation: A Convention Account." *American Sociological Review* 61:99–1017.

——. 2000. "Female Genital Cutting: The Beginning of the End." In *Female "Circumcision" in Africa: Culture, Controversy, and Change,* ed. Bettina Shell-Duncan and Ylva Hernlund, 253–282. Boulder, Colo.: Lynne Rienner.

Macwan, Martin, Christian Davenport, David Armstrong, et al. 2010. *Understanding Untouchability: A Comprehensive Study of Practices and Conditions in 1589 Villages.* New York: Navsarjan Trust and Robert F. Kennedy Center for Human Rights.

Maher, Thomas V. 2010. "Threat, Resistance, and Collective Action: The Cases of Sobibor, Treblinka, and Auschwitz." *American Sociological Review* 75:252–272.

Martin, Andrew, Clark McPhail, and John D. McCarthy. 2009. "Why Targets Matter: Toward a More Inclusive Model of Collective Violence." *American Sociological Review* 74: 821–841.

Mattar, Mohammad. 2011. "Interpreting Judicial Interpretations of the Criminal Statutes of the Trafficking Victims Protection Act: Ten Years Later." http://works.bepress.com/mohammad_mattar/1.

Mawdsley, Emma. 2004. "India's Middle Class and the Environment." *Development and Change* 35 (10): 79–103.

McAdam, Doug. 1996. "Conceptual Origins, Current Problems, Future Directions." In *Comparative Perspectives on Social Movements: Political Opportunities, Mobilizing Structures, and Cultural Framings,* ed. Doug McAdam et al., 23–40. New York: Cambridge University Press.

——. [1982] 1999. *Political Process and the Development of Black Insurgency, 1930-1970.* 2nd ed. Chicago: University of Chicago Press.

McAdam, Doug, and Hilary Boudet. 2012. *Putting Social Movements in Their Place: Explaining Opposition to Energy Projects in the United States, 2000-2005.* Cambridge: Cambridge University Press.

McAdam, Doug, and Karina Kloos. 2014. *Deeply Divided: Racial Politics and Social Movements in Postwar America.* New York: Oxford University Press.

McAdam, Doug, Sidney Tarrow, and Charles Tilly. 2001. *Dynamics of Contention.* Cambridge: Cambridge University Press.

McCarthy, John D., and Mayer N. Zald. 1977. "Resource Mobilization and Social Movements: A Partial Theory." *American Journal of Sociology* 82 (6): 1212–1241.

McCarthy, Timothy Patrick, and John Stauffer, eds. 2006. *Prophets of Protest: Reconsidering the History of American Abolitionism.* New York: The New Press.

McDaniel, W. Caleb. 2013. *The Problem of Democracy in the Age of Slavery: Garrisonian Abolitionists and Transatlantic Reform*. Baton Rouge: Louisiana State University Press.

McDonnell, Mary-Hunter, and Brayden King. 2013. "Keeping up Appearances: Reputational Threat and Impression Management After Social Movement Boycotts." *Administrative Science Quarterly* 58 (3): 387–419.

McVeigh, Rory. 1999. "Structural Incentives for Conservative Mobilization: Power Devaluation and the Rise of the Ku Klux Klan, 1915–1925." *Social Forces* 77 (4): 1461–1496.

——. 2009. *The Rise of the Ku Klux Klan: Right-Wing Movements and National Politics*. Minneapolis: University of Minnesota Press.

Meister, Robert. 2011. *After Evil: A Politics of Human Rights*. New York: Columbia University Press.

Meyer, David S., and Suzanne Staggenborg. 1996. "Movements, Countermovements, and the Structure of Political Opportunity." *American Journal of Sociology* 101:1628–1660.

Miers, Suzanne. 2003. *Slavery in the Twentieth Century: The Evolution of a Global Problem*. New York: Altamira.

Mishra, S. 2006. "Farmers Suicide in Maharashtra." *Economic and Political Weekly* 41:1538–1545.

——. 2007. "Agrarian Crisis in Post-Reform India: A Story of Distress, Despair and Death." Indira Gandhi Institute of Development Research (IGIDR) Working Paper no. 1.2. Mumbai: IGIDR.

Mouawad, Jad. 2009. "Oil Industry Braces for Trial on Rights Abuses." *New York Times*, May 21.

Munson, Ziad. 2008. *The Making of Pro-Life Activists*. Chicago: University of Chicago Press.

Murrow, R.R. 2013. *Game of Thrones*. Television program. Season 3, episode X10.

Nadelmann, Ethan A. 1990. "Global Prohibition Regimes: The Evolution of Norms in International Society." *International Organization* 44 (4): 479–526.

Nagaraj, K. 2008. *Farmers' Suicides in India: Magnitudes, Trends, and Spatial Patterns*. Madras: Madras Institute of Development Studies.

National Commission for Enterprises in the Unorganised Sector (NCEUS). 2007. "Report on Conditions of Work and Promotion of Livelihoods in the Unorganised Sector." New Delhi. http://www.prsindia.org/uploads /media/Unorganised%20Sector/bill150_20071123150_Condition_of_workers _sep_2007.pdf.

Noelle-Neumann, Elisabeth. 1974. *The Spiral of Silence: Public Opinion—Our Social Skin*. 2nd ed. Chicago: University of Chicago Press.

Nunnelley, William A. 1991. *Bull Connor*. Tuscaloosa: University of Alabama Press.

Oldfield, John R. 1998. *Popular Politics and British Anti-Slavery: The Mobilisation of Public Opinion Against the Slave Trade, 1787-1807*. London: Routledge.

——. 2013. *Transatlantic Abolitionism in the Age of Revolution: An International History of Anti-Slavery, c. 1787-1820*. New York: Cambridge University Press.

Parker, Christopher S., and Matt A. Barreto. 2013. *Change They Can't Believe In: The Tea Party and Reactionary Politics in America*. Princeton, N.J.: Princeton University Press.

Patel, Vikram, Chinthanie Ramasundarahettige, Lakshmi Vijayakumar, et al. 2012. "Suicide Mortality in India: A Nationally Representative Survey." *Lancet* 370:2343–2351.

Pelczar, Michael. 1993. *The Moral Universe*. Amherst: Amherst College.

Perry, Lewis, and Michael Fellman, eds. 1979. *Antislavery Reconsidered: New Perspectives on the Abolitionists*. Baton Rouge: Louisiana State University Press.

Picarelli, John T. 2015. "Science Versus Slavery: The National Institute of Justice and the Future Directions of Knowledge Put to the Service of the Anti-Trafficking Movement." *Journal of Human Trafficking* 1 (1): 39–55.

Polletta, Francesca. 2006. "Mobilization Forum: Awkward Movements." *Mobilization* 11 (4): 475–478.

Posani, Balamuralidhar. 2009. "Crisis in the Countryside: Farmer Suicides and the Political Economy of Agrarian Distress in India." Working Paper. Development Studies Institute, London School of Economics and Political Science.

Pouchepadass, Jacques. 2009. "After Slavery: Unfree Rural Labour in Post-1943 Eastern India." In *India's Unfree Workforce: Of Bondage Old and New*, ed. Jan Breman et al., 21–43. Delhi: Oxford University Press.

Pratto, Felicia, Deborah G. Tatar, and Sahr Conway-Lanz. 1999. "Who Gets What and Why: Determinants of Social Allocations." *Political Psychology* 20:127–150.

Press Trust of India. 2012. " 'Enslaved' Indian Maid May Get $1.5 Million as Damages." *Times of India*, March 8.

Pritchett, Laurie. 1977. "Interview with Laurie Pritchett." In *My Soul is Rested*, ed. Howell Raines, 398–404. New York: Bantam.

Quirk, Joel. 2007. "Trafficked Into Slavery." *Journal of Human Rights* 6:181–207.

——. 2011. *The Anti-Slavery Project*. Philadelphia: University of Pennsylvania Press.

——. 2012. "Uncomfortable Silences: Contemporary Slavery and the 'Lessons' of History." In *From Human Trafficking to Human Rights: Reframing Contemporary Slavery*, ed. Alison Brysk and Austin Choi-Fitzpatrick, 25–43. Philadelphia: University of Pennsylvania Press.

Quirk, Joel, and Annie Bunting. Forthcoming. *Contemporary Slavery and Human Rights*. Vancouver: University of British Columbia Press.

Radhakrishna, R., ed. 2008. *India Development Report*. Oxford: Oxford University Press.

Rai, Parshuram. 2012. "The Great MNREGA Robbery: Wretched of Bihar Robbed of Nearly Rs. 6000 Crore." New Delhi: Centre for Environment and Food Security. http://www.im4change.org/docs/668corruption-bihar-NREGA.pdf.

Raines, Howell. 1977. *My Soul Is Rested: The Story of the Civil Rights Movement in the Deep South.* New York: Penguin.

Rao, Anupama. 2009. *The Caste Question: Dalits and the Politics of Modern India.* Berkeley: University of California Press.

Rasler, Karen. 1996. "Concessions, Repression, and Political Protest in the Iranian Revolution." *American Sociological Review* 61:132–152.

Ray, Raka. 1999. *Fields of Protest: Women's Movements in India.* Minneapolis: University of Minnesota Press.

Ray, Raka, and Mary Katzenstein, eds. 2005. *Social Movements in India: Poverty, Power, and Politics.* New York: Rowman and Littlefield.

Ray, Raka, and Seemin Qayum. 2009. *Cultures of Servitude: Modernity, Domesticity, and Class in India.* Palo Alto, Calif.: Stanford University Press.

Risse, Thomas, Stephen Ropp, and Kathryn Sikkink. 2013. *The Persistent Power of Human Rights: From Commitment to Compliance.* New York: Cambridge University Press.

Roy, Ramashray. 1993. "Swadhyaya: Values and Message." In *New Social Movements in the South: Empowering People,* ed. P. Wignaraja, 183–194. London: Zed.

Royce, Edward. 1985. "The Origins of Southern Sharecropping: Explaining Social Change." *Current Perspectives in Social Theory* 6:279–299.

——. 1993. *The Origins of Southern Sharecropping.* Philadelphia: Temple University Press.

Rucht, Dieter. 2004. "Movement Allies, Adversaries, and Third Parties." In *The Blackwell Companion to Social Movements,* ed. David A. Snow et al., 197–215. Malden, Mass.: Blackwell.

Ruef, Martin, and Ben Fletcher. 2003. "Legacies of American Slavery: Status Attainment Among Southern Blacks After Emancipation." *Social Forces* 82 (2): 445–480.

Rugemer, Edward Bartlett. 2008. *The Problem of Emancipation: The Caribbean Roots of the American Civil War.* Baton Rouge: Louisiana State University Press.

Sainath, Palagummi. 2010. "17,368 Farm Suicides in 2009." *The Hindu,* December 27.

Sampson, Robert J., Doug McAdam, Heather MacIndoe, and Simón Weffer-Elizondo. 2005. "Civil Society Reconsidered: The Durable Nature of Community Structure of Collective Civic Action." *American Journal of Sociology* 111 (3): 673–714.

Sankaran, Kamala. 2009. "Bonded Labour and the Courts." In *India's Unfree Workforce: Of Bondage Old and New,* ed. Jan Breman et al., 335–351. Delhi: Oxford University Press.

Sen, Amartya. 2006. *The Argumentative Indian: Writings on Indian History, Culture, and Identity*. New York: Penguin.

Sen, Sankar, and P. M. Nair. 2005. *A Report on Trafficking in Women and Children in India: 2002-2003*. New Delhi: NHRC, UNIFEM, and ISS.

Sewell, William H. 1992. "A Theory of Structure: Duality, Agency, and Transformation." *American Journal of Sociology* 98 (1): 1-29.

Shen, Anqi. 2015. *Offending Women in Contemporary China: Gender and Pathways Into Crime*. London: Palgrave Macmillan.

——. 2016. "Female Perpetrators in Internal Child Trafficking in China: An Empirical Study." *Journal of Human Trafficking* 2 (1): 63-77.

Shlomowitz, Ralph. 1979. "The Origins of Southern Sharecropping." *Agricultural History* 53 (3): 557-575.

Shultziner, Doron. 2013. "The Social-Psychological Origins of the Montgomery Bus Boycott: Social Interaction and Humiliation in the Emergence of Social Movements." *Mobilization* 18 (2): 117-142.

Sidanius, Jim, and Felicia Pratto. 1999. *Social Dominance: An Intergroup Theory of Social Hierarchy and Oppression*. New York: Cambridge University Press.

Sidanius, Jim, Felicia Pratto, Colette van Laar, and Shana Levin. 2004. "Social Dominance Theory: Its Agenda and Method." *Political Psychology* 25 (6): 845-880.

Siegel, Dina, and Sylvia Blank. 2010. "Women Who Traffic Women: The Role of Women in Trafficking Networks—Dutch Cases." *Global Crime* 11 (4): 436-447.

Singh, Sunit, and Rama Charan Tripathi. 2010. "Why Do the Bonded Fear Freedom? Some Lessons from the Field." *Psychology and Developing Societies* 22 (2): 249-297.

Sinha, Manisha. 2016. *The Slave's Cause: A History of Abolition*. New Haven, Conn.: Yale University Press.

Smith, David Livingstone. 2011. *Less Than Human: Why We Demean, Enslave, and Exterminate Others*. New York: St. Martin's Press.

Snow, David A. 2004. "Social Movements as Challenges to Authority: Resistance to an Emerging Conceptual Hegemony." In *Authority in Contention*, Research in Social Movements, Conflicts, and Change 25, ed. Daniel J. Myers and Daniel M. Cress, 3-25. Bingley: Emerald Group.

Snow, David A., Daniel M. Cress, Liam Downey, and Andrew W. Jones. 1998. "Disrupting the 'Quotidian': Conceptualizing the Relationship Between Breakdown and the Emergence of Collective Action." *Mobilization* 3 (1): 1-22.

Snow, David A., E. Burke Rockford Jr., Steven K. Worden, and Robert D. Benford. 1986. "Frame Alignment Processes, Micromobilization, and Movement Participation." *American Sociological Review* 51: 464-481.

Snow, David A., and Sarah Anne Soule. 2000. *A Primer on Social Movements*. New York: Norton.

Soule, Sarah. 2009. *Contention and Corporate Social Responsibility.* Cambridge: Cambridge University Press.

Soule, Sarah, and Christian Davenport. 2009. "Velvet Glove, Iron Fist, or Even Hand? Protest Policing in the United States, 1960–1990." *Mobilization* 14 (1): 1–22.

Srivastava, Ravi S. 2009. "Conceptualizing Continuity and Change in Emerging Forms of Labour Bondage in India." In *India's Unfree Workforce: Of Bondage Old and New*, ed. Jan Breman et al., 129–146. Delhi: Oxford University Press.

Stauffer, John. 2001. *The Black Hearts of Men: Radical Abolitionists and the Transformation of Race.* Cambridge, Mass.: Harvard University Press.

Subramaniam, Sri, and Sairavi Subramaniam. 2009. "Does India Attain 'Self Sufficiency' in Food Production?" SSRN Working Paper Series. August.

Swidler, Ann. 1986. "Culture in Action: Symbols and Strategies." *American Sociological Review* 51 (2): 273–286.

Tarrow, Sidney. 2011. *Power in Movement: Social Movements and Contentious Politics.* 3rd ed. Cambridge: Cambridge University Press.

Taylor, Verta. 1989. "Social Movement Continuity: The Women's Movement in Abeyance." *American Sociological Review* 54 (5): 761–775.

Taylor, Verta, and Nella Van Dyke. 2004. " 'Get Up, Stand Up': Tactical Repertoires of Social Movements." In *The Blackwell Companion to Social Movements*, ed. David Snow et al., 262–293. Malden, Mass.: Blackwell.

Thompson, E. P. 1991. *The Making of the English Working Class.* Toronto: Penguin.

Tilly, Charles. 1978. *From Mobilization to Revolution.* Reading, Mass.: Addison-Wesley.

——. 1998. *Durable Inequality.* Berkeley: University of California Press.

Times of India. 2012. "End the Violence." April 19. http://articles.timesofindia .indiatimes.com/2012-04-19/edit-page/31362120_1_girl-child-dowry-baby -afreen.

Troshynski, Emily and Jennifer K. Blank. 2008. "Sex Trafficking: An Exploratory Study Interviewing Traffickers." *Trends in Organized Crime* 11: 30–41.

Tucker, Lee. 1997. "Child Slaves in Modern India: The Bonded Labor Problem." *Human Rights Quarterly* 19 (3): 572–629.

Tversky, Amos, and Daniel Kahneman.1991. "Loss Aversion in Riskless Choice: A Reference-Dependent Model." *Quarterly Journal of Economics* 106:1039–1061.

UN General Assembly. 2000. *Protocol to Prevent, Suppress and Punish Trafficking in Persons, Especially Women and Children, Supplementing the United Nations Convention Against Transnational Organized Crime.* November 15. http://www.unhcr .org/refworld/docid/ 4720706c0.html.

U.S. Citizenship and Immigration Services. 2010. USCIS National Stakeholder January Meeting. Last updated January 27. https://www.uscis.gov/outreach /notes-previous-engagements/uscis-national-stakeholder-january-meeting.

Useem, Bert. 1998. "Breakdown Theories of Collective Action." *Annual Review of Sociology* 24:215–238.

USimmigration.com. n.d. "Feds to Increase Awareness of Humanitarian Visas." http://www.usimmigration.com/awareness-of-humanitarian-visas.html.

Van Dyke, Nella, and Sarah A. Soule. 2002. "Structural Social Change and the Mobilizing Effect of Threat: Explaining Levels of Patriot and Militia Organizing in the United States." *Social Problems* 49 (4): 497–520.

Varma, Pavan. 1998. *The Great Indian Middle Class*. Delhi: Penguin.

——. 2007. *The Great Indian Middle Class*. Delhi: Penguin.

Varshney, A. 1995. *Democracy, Development, and the Countryside: Urban-Rural Struggles in India*. Cambridge: Cambridge University Press.

Vasi, Ion Bogdan, and Brayden King. 2012. "Social Movements, Risk Perceptions, and Economic Outcomes: The Effect of Primary and Secondary Stakeholder Activism on Firms' Perceived Environmental Risk and Financial Performance." *American Sociological Review* 77 (4): 573–596.

Venu Menon, S. 2006. "Globalization, State and Disempowerment: A Study of Cotton Farmers' Suicides in Warangal." Munich Personal RePEc Archive Paper no. 1633. http://mpra.ub.uni-muenchen.de/1633/1/MPRA_paper_1633.pdf.

Vidyasagar, R. 1985. "Debt Bondage in South Arcot District: A Case Study of Agricultural Labourers and Handloom Weavers." In *Chains of Servitude*, ed. U. Patnaik and M. Dingwaney, 127–161. New Delhi: Sangam.

Wahlström, Mattias. 2007. "Forestalling Violence: Police Knowledge of Interaction with Political Activists." *Mobilization* 12 (4): 389–402.

Walker, Edward T., Andrew W. Martin, and John D. McCarthy. 2008. "Confronting the State, the Corporation, and the Academy: The Influence of Institutional Targets on Social Movement Repertoires." *American Journal of Sociology* 114 (1): 35–76.

Waller, James. 2007. *Becoming Evil: How Ordinary People Commit Genocide and Mass Killings*. New York: Oxford University Press.

Walvin, James. 2003. "British Abolitionism, 1787–1838." In *The Abolitions of Slavery: From L. F. Sonthonax to Victor Schoelcher, 1793, 1794, 1848*, ed. Marcel Dorigny, 71–78. New York: Berghahn.

Ward, Tony, and Astrid Birgden. 2007. "Human Rights and Correctional Clinical Practice." *Aggression and Violent Behavior* 12:628–643.

Ward, Tony, and Robyn L. Langlands. 2008. "Restorative Justice and the Human Rights of Offenders: Convergences and Divergences." *Aggression and Violent Behavior* 13:355–372.

Weitzer, Ronald. 2014. "New Directions in Research on Human Trafficking." *Annals of the American Academy of Political and Social Science* 653:6–24.

Williams, Raymond. 1977. *Marxism and Literature*. Oxford: Oxford University Press.

Wilson, James Q. 1961. "The Strategy of Protest: Problems of Negro Civil Action." *Journal of Conflict Resolution* 3:291–303.

Woodman, Harold. 1977. "Sequel to Slavery: The New History Views the Postbellum South." *Journal of Southern History* 43 (4): 523–554.

World Bank. n.d. "Structural Adjustment in India." World Bank Independent Evaluation Group. http://lnweb90.worldbank.org/oed/oeddoclib.nsf/b5745 6d58aba40e585256ad400736404/0586cc45a28a2749852567f5005d8c89.

——. 1991. "India Adjustment Loan Is Bank's Biggest Ever." *World Bank Watch* 1 (46): 1.

World Values Survey Association. 2014. World Values Survey, Wave 5, 2005–2008. Official Aggregate v. 20140429. Aggregate File Producer: Asep/JDS. Madrid. http://www.worldvaluessurvey.org.

Zhang, Sheldon X. 2008. *Chinese Human Smuggling Organizations—Families, Social Networks, and Cultural Imperatives.* Palo Alto, Calif.: Stanford University Press.

——. 2013. "Talking to Snakeheads: Methodological Considerations for Research on Chinese Human Smuggling." In *Offenders on Offending: Learning About Crime from Criminals,* ed. W. Bernasco, 184–204. New York: Routledge.

INDEX

oppression, 197n3
Other Backward Caste group, 108
ownership, 180n9. *See also* slavery

Paratapa, 92–93, 95–96, 103; Bonded
  Labor Act violation of, 94;
  paternalism of, 94
paternalism: for bonded laborer,
  54–57; in caste system, 68, 131;
  as legitimizing myth, 55–56; of
  Paratapa, 94; power dynamics
  in, 54; rhetoric of love in, 57; of
  slaveholder, 12, 47–48, 54–57, 165;
  tactic of, 165
perpetrator: definition of, 147–48;
  finding, 148–50; of human
  trafficking, 129–31; incarceration
  of, 148; intervention resistance of,
  38; persistence of, 187n32. *See also*
  slaveholder
persistence: of Aadi, 107–9; in bonded
  labor, 110; in caste system,
  131–38; of perpetrator, 187n32;
  from profitability, 109–11; of
  slaveholder, 107–11; as targeted
  incumbent response, 36–37; trust
  and, 109–10
plantations, 5, 41
police, 21–22; repression by, 100;
  scrutiny of, 81; in trafficking,
  130
political-process theory, 185n18;
  components of, 24–29; movement
  mobilization in, 88–89;
  reattribution in, 30–31; social
  movement outcomes from, 29–30.
  See also targeted incumbents
politics: adaptation to, 117–18; Indian
  identity-based party mobilization
  in, 79–80; in Uttar Pradesh, 79–80

Posani, Balamuralidhar, 79
possession, 10
Poulsen, Jane, 22, 31, 34, 164
poverty, 4–5; antipoverty programs
  and, 77; in public opinion, 136; in
  slavery, 173
power, 33; in paternalism, 54; of
  slaveholder, 117–18; in social
  movements for human rights, 166
Prabhav, 116
Pritchett, Laurie, 31–32, 169
profitability, 109–11
prostitution, 150; as choice, 153
public opinion, 21; of bonded labor,
  134, 137; poverty in, 136; targeted
  incumbents in, 25
public policy: laborer issues with, 73;
  as slaveholder hindrance, 79–82

Qayum, Seemin, 48, 131
quarry industry, 115
Quirk, Joel, 143

Radhesh, 64, 65, 86
Rawls, John, 175
Ray, Raka, 48, 131
reappraisal, 30
rebellion, 152
repression: by police, 100; by
  slaveholder, 97–101; in slavery,
  102–3; of targeted incumbents, 35;
  threats as, 99–100
rescues, 151
resignation: as emotional state, 106;
  forms of, 105; from mobilization,
  103; of slaveholder, 103–7; as
  targeted incumbents response,
  35–36
resources, 84–88
resource scarcity, 58